CAMBRIDGE
AND ITS STORY

TRINITY COLLEGE BRIDGE

CAMBRIDGE

AND ITS STORY

BY

ARTHUR GRAY

VICE-MASTER OF JESUS COLLEGE, CAMBRIDGE

WITH SIXTEEN ILLUSTRATIONS IN COLOUR BY
MAXWELL ARMFIELD
AND SIXTEEN OTHER ILLUSTRATIONS

METHUEN & CO. LTD.
36 ESSEX STREET W.C.
LONDON

First Published in 1912

PREFACE

THIS book is a Story of Cambridge in its relation
to the national life. It has no pretension to
the title of History. Its purpose is to show
the conditions of medieval England which shaped
the University in its beginnings, and the intellectual
needs which, in successive centuries, it was the aim
of its benefactors and the founders of its colleges to
satisfy. In the chapters which deal with post-Reformation times I have made no continuous survey of
the life and studies of the University, but have aimed
at showing its character at certain epochs in its
history, and its influences on some of its most eminent
sons who have carried those influences into national
spheres of science or letters. Incidentally I have
endeavoured to present a picture of men and manners
at Cambridge at the time when it was known to each
of these great men, and of scenes in college courts and
chambers that were familiar to their eyes.

CONTENTS

LIST OF ILLUSTRATIONS

IN COLOUR

IN MONOTONE

CAMBRIDGE
AND ITS STORY

CAMBRIDGE
AND ITS STORY

CHAPTER I

THE DAWN

ὦ ταὶ λιπαραὶ καὶ ἰοστέφανοι καὶ ἀοίδιμοι,
'Ελλάδος ἔρεισμα, κλειναὶ 'Αθᾶναι,
δαιμόνιον πτολίεθρον.

PINDAR

CAMBRIDGE and Oxford have long divested themselves of a local, and within recent years of a purely national character. Formerly their students were drawn almost exclusively from England and Wales, and less than a century ago their endowments were confined in great measure to the county or the local school and to the members of a Church whose claim to be national had little basis in Ireland, none in Scotland. Now it may be said of them, as of the firmament, that their line is gone out through all the earth, and their words to the end of the world. From the Antipodes and the New World, from ancient India and modern Japan, from all sects and all nationalities they draw seekers for the knowledge of which they hold the keys. The old term, *Studium Generale*, used to designate a University in the twelfth century, has never been so realised as in recent years by the two great Universities of England. They are the schools where students of all kinds and from all parts are received.

I

And yet in their universality Cambridge and Oxford are of all Universities least cosmopolitan in character. The type of the English University is even less to-day than it was in its first beginnings the type of the continental University. It is something radically different from the Universities of Scotland or the younger foundations which have sprung up in the outgrowths of the British people beyond the seas. The old English Universities incorporate and assimilate their students. It cannot be said that, so far, their native character has been materially changed by the influx of the foreigner and the colonial.

If we say that this stability of character is due to their antiquity we shall inadequately understand its meaning. The Universities of Bologna and Paris are older than Cambridge and Oxford, but they have none of their individuality. Nor does it lie wholly in the immutability of the national character. Spain has had no Reformation, and no age-long education in the art of freedom ; the character of its people has suffered less change than ours. But the ancient Universities of Salamanca and Seville have more in common with Yale and Chicago than with Cambridge and Oxford. The type is limited to our English soil. In the sixteenth and seventeenth centuries Cambridge sent out colonies to Ireland and to Massachusetts, whose constitutions were deliberately planned on that of the mother republic. Dublin and Harvard have grown to rival the parent stock, but in another air the plants grown from English seed have developed variations which have little resemblance to their original.

To the foreigner and to the Englishman who has not come under their influences the peculiar attraction of Cambridge and Oxford may seem inexplicable—a happy ' sport ' which no genius of man can reproduce. To those who have been privileged to dwell within their reverend halls the source of it is superficially obvious. Chiefly it lies in social considerations—in the happy conjunction of the intimate ties of College with the wider communion given by the University. The great central luminary of the University is the recognised tutelary deity of Cambridge and of Oxford, but the faith of the worshipper is fortified, not diminished, by his intenser affection for the familiar godhead of the College hearth. Very largely the attraction is to material things. The spirit of man is dominated by the creations of his own hands, and our reverence and affection grow to the habitations which our fathers built to house the divinity which in speech we call Knowledge, but to our thought is something holier than Knowledge. To brick and stone our affections are grappled by tendrils that are stronger and more subtle than all the netted cords of Learning.

The stranger is struck with the family resemblance of the two English Universities : those whose intimacy with them is closer are impressed rather by their differences in feature and character. Perhaps the divergence began when either of them had reached the adult stage ; at least it is not superficially apparent before the Reformation period. We may think that a principal cause of it was the impetus of the college system which was so strongly developed about that time. Whether the change of character began then to be reflected in the discrepant types of the colleges at Cambridge and Oxford, or was itself the cause of that discrepancy, it would be hard to say. It may have been an accident, attributable to forces exterior to the University, that, while Wolsey and his

master conserved the ancient church of Saint Frides-
wide at Oxford and made their great foundation
ancillary to it, at Cambridge the same royal founder
demolished the stately churches of the Augustinian
and Franciscan Friars and planned a college which
should be independent of past ecclesiastical traditions.
If it was an accident it was one which was reflected
in the subsequent character of either foundation and
profoundly affected the Universities. Cambridge does
not lack ecclesiastical monuments worthy of its
greatness. But the chapel of Trinity belongs to the
sterile period of Queen Mary's reign and has never
dominated the College. The grand fane of King's
is a confessed exotic on Cambridge soil, and the peculiar
conditions of its birth and plan condemned the College
to centuries of ineffective isolation, from which it
only emerged in recent times when it broke the fetters
imposed upon it by the founder.

It will scarcely be disputed that this clinging to time-
consecrated forms has been, for three centuries, the
note in which Oxford has generally been contrasted
with Cambridge. But it would be a mistake to
suppose that it began with the Reformation. The
conditions of either University were, from their birth,
in great measure governed by their geographical
environment. Oxford has all the qualities of an inland
town. But the royal river on which it is situated
has always been the path of kings and of armies,
and it is the highway to London. From the stir of
court and camp Cambridge town lay remote ; in
aspect and in fact it has always been provincial. In
the Middle Ages no great highway linked it with
London, from which it was secluded by wide forest
tracts. Over broad spaces of sparsely wooded plain
Cambridge looks east and north.

If you would judge of the conditions to which Cambridge town was born, and which tempered the character of the University and the genius of the greatest of her sons, you may choose some clear day in spring or autumn to climb the modest elevation of Madingley Hill, and cast your eye over the wide prospect which it commands eastward over Cambridge and northwards over the fen flats towards Ely and St. Ives. You will see no vision of dreaming spires, bosomed in tufted trees, such as Headington Hill commands over Oxford city, and no wide-watered river to diversify the landscape. The town of Cambridge lies obscure, three miles distant, in an unrelieved plain. The unending flats are scarcely broken by the level cliff of stone upreared by King's chapel or the square mass of the tower of Saint John's. The rest of Cambridge is sunk in undistinguishable verdure. Yet, if it is not exactly beautiful, the prospect from the hill is strangely impressive. If we look northward where the even horizon stoops over Ely towers the impression is one of illimitable sea.

And the impression is no fancy. Sea it was, or what had the name of 'seas,' in the times when the University was cradled. Twelve miles from where we stand the land draws itself up in a scarcely noticeable acclivity, fringed against the sky-line with churches and windmills, and on the far horizon Ely cathedral shows like a giant ocean liner. That is 'the Isle,' which has always accounted itself a land somehow distinct from Cambridgeshire. From that land we are now parted by a narrow creek, at this distance not distinguished by the eye, which is in name the old river Ouse, though it has lost every quality of a river. From Erith Bridge, where it is deserted by the Bedford Level, to Char Fen, where it meets the

Cam, it stretches, but does not flow, for ten solitary miles—a river of forgetfulness, without a vessel on its surface or a hithe upon its brink.   In the Middle Ages, when the green plain which now encompasses this river was covered with wide waters, its solitudes were more than once invaded by fleets of the fen keels, with which English kings transported their armies to assault the Islanders when they were in revolt. The latest occasion was in 1267, when Prince Edward reduced the Disinherited, who in their fen fastness were the last upholders of the baronial cause.   That was seventeen years before the foundation of Peterhouse.

Cambridge we must conceive in the thirteenth century, and in the ages before it, as a seaport, situated at the farthest southern extremity of the inland sea which in its modern, reduced dimensions we call the Wash.   Close to the head of the bay, where the river ceased to be navigable and was crossed by a paved ford, the Romans, or some people more ancient than they, reared a mount of defence, and at its foot two great Ways intersected.   From Madingley Hill you will see the telegraph posts which line one of them traversing the plain between Cambridge and Godmanchester. Beyond Cambridge you may mark where it mounts the Gogmagog Hills, on the northern side of Wandlebury camp, in a direct course for Colchester.   That road, because it reached the western coast at Chester, we call the Via Devana.   The other road was the Akeman Street.   We cannot distinguish it from Madingley Hill, for most of it has been swallowed up in the fen, but it reached to Ely and to Brancaster on the Norfolk coast, and its southerly portion to Cirencester and the head waters of the Thames.   To these two highways and to the tidal waters which floated trading caracks almost to its quay Cambridge owed all its mercantile importance until traffic was diverted to the railway. And to the same circumstance the University owed its origin, or at least its dominance in regions beyond its immediate neighbourhood.

I do not think that it is a fancy to suppose that it was the sea-board character of the town and its vicinity to the waste Fenland which gave the University its impress of freedom of thought and individuality of character which has been its consistent note. We need not ascribe too much weight to the influence of landscape and historic association in the case of the medieval undergraduate, who was generally town-bound, and whose residence at Cambridge was limited to a few years, though those years were the most impressionable in his life. On the teacher and the permanent resident the old memories and the recent example of local warfare in the cause of liberty were a perpetual exhortation to resistance to the authority which would enslave mind or person. The first generation of scholars had witnessed the day when the last outstanders against the rule of Henry III had raided Cambridge town. The story of Hereward was still handed on in oral tale or written song. The abbot of Ely had joined in the resistance to the Conqueror, and the bishop, in a later day, to Stephen ; another bishop, Hugh of Balsham, founder of the first Cambridge college, incurred the royal displeasure for neglecting to suppress the rising of the Disinherited. If we may trust the evidence of their names many of the earliest scholars were Cambridgeshire men, full of a local patriotism. The rest of them came in many cases from Norfolk and Suffolk, counties which in the days of the Plantagenets supplied to England examples of the most vigorous municipal energy and independence.   Others were from Yorkshire and the northern counties, where the central authority was weak and individuality of character has always been strong.

Is it fancy again that sees in the scenery of Cambridge-shire something of affinity to the studies of mathematics and astronomy in which the University has conquered such wide fields ?   Certainly no part of England more closely recalls the Nile lands on which Geometry was first fostered ; and the dome of sky which the first astronomers explored from Chaldean plains was not ampler than that which vaults the flattest county in England.

From a region so destitute of any feature of romance as modern Cambridgeshire it might be supposed that Poetry was exiled.   But, though it be matter of traditional faith that the Muses dwell on the heights, in sober fact their home is generally in the plains. The Fenland, in its old unreclaimed state, did not lack poetry from the day when King Cnut ' from joy of heart,' as he was rowed by Ely, composed the song,

> Merry sang the monks in Ely
> As Cnut King rowed thereby.

The Ely chronicler tells us that the song was still popular in the fens when he wrote in the twelfth century.   How Hereward and his comrades sang three-men glees ' in the Fenmen's fashion ' we know from the *Gesta Herewardi* and Kingsley's tale.   With such ballads of local matters we may believe that Cambridge clerks, like ' hendy Nicholas ' of Oxenforde,

> made on nightes melodie
> So swetely that all the chamber rong.

Verse that claimed to be literature did not begin at

Cambridge before the days of Elizabeth, but since Spenser the sons of music there have never been brought quite low.   In any combination which you may make of the dozen greatest masters of English song it is not hazardous to say that the larger part will prove to have been Cambridge-bred.   Not a great deal of their best work has its inspiration in Cambridge life or scenes, but *Lycidas, The Prelude* and *In Memoriam* all have close links with the place where in youth the poets fed on honey-dew and drank the milk of Paradise.

CHAPTER II

THE WANDERING SCHOLARS

And let this suffice, not to enquire which of these universities is the superiour, but that neither of them have their equall, neither to aske which of them is the most auncient, but whether any be so famous.—JOHN LILY.

ON the subject of the comparative antiquity of Cambridge and Oxford a vast deal of ink was spilt by the learned of either University in the sixteenth and seventeenth centuries. Professor Maitland, addressing an Oxford audience, wittily said, " The oldest of all inter-university sports was a lying match. Oxford was founded by Mempricius in the days of Samuel the prophet, and Cambridge by the Spanish Cantaber in the days of Gurguntius Brabtruc." Dr. Rashdall generously admits that in the contest of ingenuity Cambridge had a decided advantage. It was certainly a splendid stroke of genius that ' discovered ' a Bull of Pope Honorius I—date faithfully given as 624—in which the Pope, professing to have been himself a student at Cambridge, conferred on the University exemption from episcopal authority. But, as Professor Maitland went on to say, " A match in truth-seeking is a much more thrilling contest : the rules of the game are so much more intricate." Must a Cambridge man admit that, according to the rules, Oxford has established her claim to the birthright which belongs to the elder of two sisters who are virtually twins ?   For he is constrained to acknowledge that schools of some sort did exist at Oxford about the year 1167, some forty years before they are heard of at Cambridge.

Schools there have been at Oxford, and scholars, ever since Henry II, at the time of his quarrel with Becket, recalled all English clerics from their studies beyond sea. But schools are not necessarily Universities. Schools may grow anywhere—at York, at Lincoln, at Saint Albans, or wherever a cathedral or a monastery furnishes a teaching staff. The teachers die, or they migrate, and the school disappears, unnoticed in its death as in its birth. The schools at Cambridge and Oxford never died, though sometimes they came near to it. Somehow they have got to be called Universities, and a University has privileges which secure permanence. How did they get those privileges and when ?

Almost every medieval University which came into existence after 1250 was founded by a Papal Bull. Kings and Emperors might confer local powers and immunities. But a University in its essence was not local or even national. Its scholars were drawn from all nations : their prerogative of teaching extended to all Christian lands. Therefore only the Pope could authorise the admission of a provincial school to the rank of a University. Partly, it is true, he did so because it was his business to regularise the relation of the scholastic clerk to the Bishop or Archdeacon ; but the principal reason was that his was the only recognised international authority. With the Universities as religious teachers he had no concern. It was not the business of a medieval University to instruct in Theology, except in the case of a very limited class of its students.

Cambridge and Oxford came to their birth in quite an irregular fashion, and in their younger days never troubled themselves about legitimation in the European University family. In 1318, when it had reached what may be accounted as riper years, Cambridge, having a conscientious desire to get the better of the Bishop of Ely, thought well to get baptism at papal hands, and obtained a Bull from John XXII, erecting it into a *Studium Generale*, or University. Confirmation—of its privileges—Oxford got from Innocent IV in 1254, but in name the Church never christened it as a University.

What then was the meaning of this title of University which both Cambridge and Oxford usurped, each of them a century before it was recognised by the Pope ? Of course it is no exclusively English word. The name, Universitas, is as old as the Pandects of Justinian, where it stands for much the same thing as Collegium, a corporation of any kind. Its application to scholastic corporations began with the first Italian universities, Salerno and Bologna. In the Anglo-Latin law of the twelfth century it was familiarly applied to any body of men who possessed a collective legal status and rights which could be legally enforced against individuals or other corporations. The Universitas may be a town, a county, a guild. "Noverit universitas vestra," "Know all of you," in a writ is the customary mode of addressing an organised collection of individuals. The word has no specific meaning without a defining genitive.

A teaching Universitas is a guild of scholars, Universitas Scholarium. Like a trade or craft guild it makes its own conditions of membership ; it makes by-laws for its own government ; it exacts fees of its members, and it jealously excludes outsiders from

ST. BENET'S CHURCH

meddling in its business. Like a trade guild it has its apprentices—'pupils' they were called in the University guild — and its duly qualified 'masters.' The apprentices in either case, whatever their proficiency, have to learn their trade for seven years before they can become 'masters,' whether in the 'art' of a craft or the 'liberal arts' of science and humanity. The individual 'master' or the guild may on its own authority commit the apprentice to gaol if he misconducts himself: and the same power is constantly exercised by the Chancellor and Masters of the University. Usually the apprentice lives with his master, who is bound to give him instruction. The guild usually has a hall for its general meetings, possibly a chapel and one or more chaplains. Otherwise it will assemble for secular as well as religious purposes in a parish church: so it was that the guild scholars of Cambridge successively used Saint Benet's and Saint Mary's churches as their place of assembly. The guild has a bedell or two to give notice of its meetings, to carry its mace in processions, to do various menial jobs. Out of the need for providing stipends for its officials and charitable relief for poorer members endowment is bound to come. Finally the guild has certain trade secrets which its members are strictly forbidden to reveal: and, to complete the analogy with the craft guild, the University must have its statute, binding on every master, *de secretis Universitatis non revelandis*, though it is to be doubted whether it had any secrets, or ever applied the statute.

Only in one thing the trade guild differs in its constitution from the University. The trade guild is a local affair. The guild-brother sells his wares at his shop or market-booth in the town where he lives, seek liberal arts, in Orleans authors, at Salerno gallipots, at Toledo demons, and in no place decent manners."

The English scholar was constantly on the wing. The Universities had no endowments to attach them to the soil. Hired lodgings and lecture-rooms made no abiding city for the student. It was a simple thing for him to pack up his twenty books clothed in black or red and transport them on his lean horse to fresh academic fields. Migrations on a large scale were as much the rule as the exception in the unquiet days of John and Henry III. There has always been a kind of freemasonry between Cambridge and Oxford undergraduates that shows itself in turbulence. The ' rag ' at one seat of learning has a trick of reproducing itself, with no long interval, at the other. The bond of fellowship was even stronger seven hundred years ago. It mattered little where they lived : Golyas of Oxford and Golyas of Cambridge were sworn brothers, and their hand was against all other men.

Of all things they loved a fight with the town. They are the sun, says Dr. Caius in the sixteenth century, and the townsmen are mere darkness. In malice and rusticity Erasmus thought that the common people of Cambridge surpassed even their ungracious country-men. Possibly he would have admitted the Oxford burghers *ad eundem*. Certainly the natives of either town bore the same reproach in the days of scholars long before Erasmus. A wicked old prayer of the English scholars began : " Deus qui multitudinem rusticorum ad servitium clericorum venire fecisti et inter nos et ipsos discordiam seminasti." The singer of the tribe is quite candid in his opinion of the ' lay-folk.'

> Aestimetur laicus ut brutus,
> Nam ad artem surdus est et mutus.

Simkin of Trumpington and Absalon, the parish clerk of Oxford, had unpleasant reckonings to make with ' sely clerkes.' The scholar is warned not to drink in taverns with their kind for fear of rough usage.

> O clerici dilecti,
>   Discite vitare
> Tabernam horribilem,
>   Qui cupitis regnare ;
> Nec audeant vos rustici
>   Plagis verberare !

The alehouse brawl quickly extended itself to the street. Doors burst in, houses plundered, blood flowing, dead bodies—the picture of such a call to arms is given in two lines by Matthew of Paris. The special season appointed for these battles was Lent. The Enemy of Mankind, says Matthew, is particularly active at that time of year in towns where scholars resort. In April, 1240, there was a riot at Oxford which produced a fresh influx of scholars at Cambridge. In Lent, 1249, for the like cause, the tide set backwards from Cambridge to Oxford. In Lent, 1259, there were riots both at Cambridge and Oxford. The same spark caused the explosion at either place. At one or other town—and we don't know which—the clerks had rescued a companion who, for homicide, had been committed to gaol by the townspeople, and had haled him to a church and left him there in sanctuary.

Besides the town-and-gown fights the scholars waged constant battle amongst themselves, with the like confused noise and garments rolled in blood. There was an affray at Cambridge, notable in its results, between the northern and the southern scholars in 1261, and of course the townspeople bore their part in it.

2

We may venture the surmise that in 1261 the Cambridge scholars were divided into ' Nations,' according to the practice which prevailed at Bologna, Paris and Oxford, and which still prevails in the Scottish Universities. The tendency for students of a common nationality to associate for companionship and mutual aid is apparent enough in English Universities to-day —most apparent in the case of students from the Far East. In the twelfth-century University, crowded with scholars from all parts, such groupings were the inevitable outcome of differences of speech. Alein and John, fresh from their home ' fer in the north,' must have found that their broad Northumbrian talk was all but unintelligible to their southern fellow-students, and from ridicule, or what was worse, they would find a refuge in the company of themselves and some homely companions. Natural ties developed formal combination, recognised and supported in early academic legislation. At Oxford there were two Nations, namely, *Boreales*, including Scotchmen and Englishmen from beyond the Trent, and *Australes*, including Irish, Welsh and continental students as well as southern Englishmen. The two Proctors, *procuratores*, as their name implies, were the legal representatives of the two Nations. Except incidentally, they had nothing to do with discipline or the order of the streets : such matters were altogether outside the control or concern of the University authorities.

Now the *Boreales*, no doubt because they were fewer and strangers in southern England, were in constant trouble at Oxford. They are fighting the Irish in 1252 ; in 1274 a solemn treaty of peace is sworn to by northerners and southerners. At Cambridge, in 1261, though the northerners may have had a more equal chance, the victory did not fall to them.

The result was a great secession—evidently of northerners—to Northampton. Northampton was apparently chosen because there had been a previous exodus
thither from Oxford in 1238, and it is likely that some
sort of schools had maintained themselves there since.
Two years after the settlement of the Cambridge
migrants they were reinforced by large numbers of
Oxford scholars, who had apparently been expelled
from their University by Henry III on account of
their sympathy with the barons. But the University
of Northampton, as Fuller says, " never lived to com-
mence Bachelor of Arts." It was dissolved by the
King's writ in 1265.

Soon after the occurrence of the brawl between the
northern and southern factions the King directed
the itinerant justices to inquire into the facts. Twenty-
eight southerners were found guilty and condemned
by them, but they were pardoned by the King. It
would seem that all were scholars except one, who was
a servant. The list of them given in the King's brief
is interesting. Two were Masters of Arts. Eighteen
belonged to the counties of Norfolk and Suffolk, all
the rest to Cambridgeshire. Did the southerners
from other parts take no share in the assault? Or
are we to conclude that the southerner at Cambridge
was almost without exception an East Anglian, and
that the University, in 1261, was in the main provincial ?

Though it is stated, as early as 1231, that great
numbers of scholars from beyond sea had resorted
to Cambridge for the sake of study, yet there does
seem ground for thinking that the early scholars
came mostly from the eastern counties. East Anglia,
in the thirteenth and fourteenth centuries, was probably the most densely populated region in England,

and its people the wealthiest, most enterprising and most cultivated of any outside London. Dr. Cunningham, in his *English History and Commerce*, gives a list of sixty-eight corporate towns which advanced loans to Richard II, with the sums which each furnished. At the head of it are London and Bristol. Then come three eastern towns, Norwich, Boston and Lynn. Of the whole number, twenty-two are in East Anglia and Essex. The founders of the earliest colleges were mostly men from eastern England, and the surnames of students of the fourteenth century reveal that in very many cases they came from the same parts.

But we may suspect that there was a larger infusion of north-country blood than there was at the same time at Oxford. As Fuller remarked, and as remains true to-day, " Cambridge lieth conveniently for the north and east parts ; Oxford commodiously for the south and west parts of England." The Via Devana and Ermine Street provided a much easier communication from the north with Cambridge than existed with the other University town. As term drew near those roads must have been thronged by scholars from Scotland and the north, bound for Cambridge and eager to join in study or in battle with the youths of Norfolk and Suffolk. It is not without significance that Chaucer—who knew Cambridge well—puts the tale of the two clerks from Strother town, in Northumberland, in the mouth of a Norfolk reeve.

Among the students the old distinction between northerners and southerners was perpetuated in brawls until the end of the sixteenth century at least. In a letter about Cambridge, written in 1575, William Soone says : " In standing for degrees the north-country and south-country men have warm contests with one another, as at Oxford the Welsh and English, whom the former call Saxons." The fourteenth-century statutes of the University prohibit, under pain of excommunication, the celebration of the days dedicated to the Saints Hugh, Edmund, Cuthbert or William of York in any place appointed for the meeting of scholars of any Nation. But each in his parish church may honour the saint to whom he is devoted. The four saints were patrons respectively of the men of Lincolnshire, East Anglia, the diocese of Durham, and Yorkshire. It may be remembered that Chaucer's Northumbrian clerk, John, swore by Saint Cuthbert.

But if the Nations at Cambridge ever had the formal recognition of the University they ceased to be distinguished there, as at Oxford, before the end of the reign of Henry III. Foreign students ceased to come to England in any numbers after King John lost the French provinces. Under the firm rule of Edward I the growth of a sense of national unity made provincial distinctions of less importance. Finally the scholars found in hostels and colleges the companionship and tutelage which were first provided by the looser union of the Nation. Ireland, Wales and Scotland, which had no Universities of their own, still sent their sons to Cambridge, and it is noteworthy that the earliest benefaction to the University, in 1256, was from an Irishman, William of Kilkenny, Bishop of Ely. In 1270, on the eve of the foundation of the first college, an agreement was drawn up between the burgesses and the scholars which proves that students of those three countries were present in Cambridge in sufficient numbers to necessitate special arrangements for their entertainment and good order. A council was constituted consisting of twenty-three members, who were sworn to keep the peace of the University and cause it to be kept by others   It included ten burgesses and thirteen clerks. Of the clerks five were to be taken indiscriminately from any counties of England—an indication that the division into Nations no longer existed—three from Scotland, three from Ireland and two from Wales. The number of the councillors allotted to the minor nationalities suggests either that the scholars sent by them were particularly numerous, or that the care of them demanded exceptional precautions.

This and other agreements between the town and the University were the outcome of the mediation of Prince Edward, and they were signed with the King's seal. Nothing so clearly shows the nebular condition of the University and its inability to control its own members or make terms with its neighbours in the town as its constant appeals for royal intervention. The King's writ and the sheriff's gaol are the only enforcers of order and discipline. The scholar, who may flit from Cambridge to-morrow, is not a person to be controlled by an edict which is forceless at Northampton, and the burgesses, if they cannot have their own way with the scholars, only wish heartily to be quit of them. Amid arms the laws of the University are silent. In the idle disputes of the sixteenth and seventeenth centuries about the relative antiquity of the two Universities, the Cambridge assertors, whenever they were gravelled for matter, found their readiest shift was to lay the blame on Margaret Starr, the famous old lady who confounded the learning of the clerks in 1381 by making a bonfire of the University charters in the market-place. If the college charters did not go into the flames along with those of the University it may be doubted if the pile was a big one. The University had little property, and of statutes we hear nothing at all before

1300, and very little for long afterwards. In 1278 Merton's foundation at Oxford possessed far more property in and about Cambridge than Cambridge University had. Indeed, so far as we know, the benefactions to the University up to that time were two only. The first consisted of a plot of ground given by one Nigel de Thornton, physician, on which at a much later date the University Schools were built. The other was an endowment of ten marks *per annum* given in his will, dated 1256, by Bishop Kilkenny, for maintaining two chaplains, students in Theology in the University. The bishop evidently proposed at least as much advantage to his own soul from the chaplains' prayers as to the edification of the chaplains themselves or to the University faculty. The continuance of the University was still so precarious that it was little likely to get diverted to itself much of the wealth which was being lavished about the same time on the monastic orders, and especially on the Mendicants. In fact Bishop Kilkenny makes a stipulation in his will that, " if ever it happen in process of time that the University of Cambridge is dissolved," the Bishop of Ely is to make provision for the maintenance of the chaplains out of the estate bequeathed for the purpose.

It is quite clear that the University had no buildings of its own to serve as schools for its classes or as lodgings for its members. It would have been strange if it had. Such monuments of permanence were equally unknown at Oxford. The lectures were given sometimes in hired houses, in extraordinary cases in a church. We know that the ancient church of Saint Benet was used for the purpose, and that the University paid the clerk for ringing the bell to convene the scholars.

The scholars of those primitive days lived in some

cases in lodgings with the burgesses. Nicholas, in Chaucer's Oxford story, it may be remembered, lived with a rich carpenter, and had a chamber to himself. The plan has been revived within the last century or so at either University ; but, without due restrictions, it had obvious defects, as the tale shows. Panurge was, no doubt, a delightful companion in University circles, but his ingenuity was so often employed at the expense of the citizens that they may be pardoned if they ' took it out ' in his rent and enhanced their charges for bread and ale. His Encomium of Borrowing was charming to every one but the ' gnof ' to whom he owed money, and Panurge had to pay a caution, or rent in advance, before he could find lodging. The contingencies of door-burstings, house-burnings or even a full settlement with a knife—incidents so very common in the days of the free scholar—helped to swell his rent, and domestic happiness and ' swete Alisoun ' were assessable commodities. There were also ' ribaud clerks ' who made learning a mere cloak for roaming from town to town and living at everybody's expense but their own. What boot is there in catchpolls and sheriffs' writs when benefit of clergy is pleaded ? Altogether the townsfolk were wise in regarding the University, much as a provincial lodging-keeper regards a visit of the British Association, as an occasion for making unlimited profit so long as it lasts.

Embarrassed on the one hand by the unruliness of the scholars, on the other by the greed of the townsmen, the Chancellor and Masters had all-too-frequent cause to invite the King's interference. The King always remitted the matter to the county officer, the sheriff, which amounted to a recognition of the University's independence of the jurisdiction of the town bailiffs.

In 1231 the sheriff is directed to punish the insolence of clerks and scholars by imprisonment or banishment from the University. But there is a saving proviso that he is to do so only at the command of the Bishop of Ely and at the discretion of the Chancellor and Masters of the University. Also the sheriff is to proceed to Cambridge with good and lawful men of his county, and there on the King's behalf to proclaim that no clerk who is not under the tuition of some master shall remain in the University, and that all such shall depart the town within fifteen days, after which time the sheriff is to apprehend and imprison any who remain. The Bishop of Ely, whenever requested by the Chancellor and Masters, shall require the assistance of the sheriff for the punishment of contumacious and rebellious clerks. Finally, it is ordained that, according to the custom of the University—or possibly, the King means, of *a* University—the rent of all hostels in which scholars reside shall be assessed by two masters and two good and lawful men of the town assigned for the purpose. A later enactment requires that this assessment is to be made in every fifth year.

The hostels, *hospicia*, mentioned in the King's writ no doubt included all houses occupied by students, whether ordinary dwelling-houses in which they lodged or ' hostels ' rented by a master for himself and his pupils. The hostel system began in the earliest days of the University, and it flourished for a long time in great vigour side by side with the colleges. In their fullest vogue the hostels were far more numerous than the colleges, and the largest of them probably contained as many students as a good-sized college. When colleges became the resort of paying students the hostel was looked on with jealousy as a rival trading concern, and by the middle of the sixteenth century they were all suppressed or annexed by colleges. Probably not a stone of any one of them remains to-day. The last of them—so a manuscript in Jesus College tells me—was Clement's Hostel, a hospice for lawyers, which was in Bridge Street, on the south side of Saint Clement's Church : it disappeared about the year 1562. So completely was the once familiar name of ' hosteller ' misunderstood in the middle of the sixteenth century that it was alleged by the malevolent against Archbishop Cranmer, who had once belonged to one of them, that he had been an ' ostler ' in his early days.

The hostel was at first merely a boarding-house, run as a private venture by any Master of Arts. It had no endowment and the student paid the master for his board, but it was not necessarily the master's business to give instruction. The inmates took their meals, slept and studied under one roof, or in adjoining houses, but there was nothing of a collegiate character about the buildings or the domestic arrangements. The duration of the existence of a hostel would often be limited to the tenure of the head of it ; but in process of time many of them became attached to colleges and acquired some permanence. According as the students devoted themselves to Arts or Law the house became known as a hostel, or inn, of ' artists ' or ' jurists,' and in after times every hostel was distinctively attached to one or other class.

The University also acquires the right of fixing the prices of food for the scholars—what we call the assize of bread and ale—and the King directs the sheriff to see that its ordinances are enforced. Officers called Taxors beat the market for this purpose and also attend to the question of rents. These invasions of the right of the burgess to charge what he will for his own

seem to him matter for lamentable consideration.
Nor do matters stop there. This University which
has come uninvited into our midst—it is impossible
to say how far its presumption will go. It seems as
though the liberties which we have just bought for
hard cash from King John are to count for nothing if
the King's sheriff is going to support the Chancellor
against the bailiffs. For small or no cause the Chancellor excommunicates the *major ballivus*—presently
to be known as mayor. When King Edward, in 1278,
makes an inquisition concerning the town of Cambridge,
we, the town jurors, put the matter plainly to His
Majesty. We inform him that this beggarly University, which hardly owns a rood of ground within the
borders of the borough, on its own authority is actually
requiring the town bailiffs to make corporal oath of
submission to the Chancellor and Masters. This seems
to us to concern, we will not say our personal interest
and dignity, but the prerogative of our lord the King.

' Violently astonished ' also is the Prior of Barnwell
—quite the wealthiest and most considerable individual
in the town, and the head of a corporation which is
older than the University and quite as respectable.
The Prior has a house at the corner of Bridge Street,
opposite the Round Church—a very superior house,
for it is built of stone. A Master of Arts, one Ralf of
Leicester, wants to rent the house as a hostel and offers
the Prior a ' caution,' which the Prior declines. Master
Ralf goes to the Chancellor and offers *him* the caution,
and by him is admitted as tenant against the Prior's
will. Does he pay the Prior rent for the Prior's house ?
Certainly not. He begs that the Prior will bring an
action against him in the Chancellor's court—a thing
not to be thought of. He claims that everything has
been done in accordance with the custom of the Uni-

versity and the King's ordinance about assessment of hostels. The only course open to the Prior is to bring an action of novel disseisin against Master Ralf and the Chancellor. But before it comes to trial the official of the Bishop of Ely summons the parties to a meeting in All Saints' church, and effects a compromise. The official politely tells the Chancellor that in this matter he has gone too far. " Men of religion, such as the canons of Barnwell, belong to the Bishop's jurisdiction. So, if you please, don't rob my lord of what is his."

In this matter of the Prior's house the Chancellor based his action on a very ancient statute of the University, indeed the most ancient which has descended to our knowledge. It evidently belongs to a time anterior to the foundation of our earliest college, Peterhouse. So faint and dim is all our vision of the life of the free scholar, before his liberties were reduced to the ordered limits of college respectability, that we may spend some moments in explaining the method of launching one of these hostels ' according to the University custom.'

If a ' master ' wishes to be principal of a hostel he has to go to the owner of the house which he proposes to rent and offer him a caution. Cautions can only be received between June 11 and September 8—in Long Vacation, as we should say. The first applicant is to be admitted in preference to any later comer, and, for that reason, it is recommended that applications should be made on the earliest possible day. The would-be principal offers his caution in presence of a bedell, or a notary, or any two witnesses. The caution is either the bond of two personal sureties or a book or something of the kind. If the applicant is refused by the landlord he may offer his caution and state his case to the Chancellor, and he shall admit him, if he thinks fit. But the principal may not cede his right to the hostel to any other scholar. If any one is principal of a hostel and another scholar wishes to occupy the same hostel as principal, he must go to the landlord, offer his caution and say : " Landlord, if it please thee, I wish to be admitted as principal of the hostel in such and such a parish, whensoever the principal is ready to retire or give up his right, so that I may succeed him, if thou art willing, without prejudice to his right thereto so long as he shall remain principal." If the landlord does not agree the applicant may produce his caution before the Chancellor and be admitted on the understanding that, when there shall be no principal, he shall succeed to the place in that hostel rather than any other. The Chancellor shall admit him even against the wish of the landlord and principal. If a landlord shall say to any scholar, " Dost thou desire to be principal of my hostel ? " and the scholar shall answer " Yes," but the landlord does not wish that the hostel shall be assessed, and the scholar says he does not mind, and enters into occupation as principal, and receives scholars to share the hostel with him, then those same scholars may go to the Chancellor and have their hostel assessed, contrary to the wish both of the landlord and principal. Lastly, nobody is to deprive a principal of his place or supplant him, so long as he pays his rent, unless the landlord desire himself to be the occupier, or shall sell or alienate the hostel.

Hitherto there has been a presumption that the clerks of Cambridge, like any other clerks in the diocese, are subject to the jurisdiction of the Bishop of Ely and his Archdeacon. Here, too, the University requires to have its powers extended. Fortunately the Bishop, in 1276, is the wise and generous Hugh of Balsham, himself a University man and most likely a Cambridge doctor. His decree gives the University complete independence of the Archdeacon's court. Not only the scholars but the servants who reside with them in their houses and even the illuminators, stationers and writers who make the scholars' books are to answer for themselves in the Chancellor's court and nowhere else. Two necessary exceptions are made. Scholars who are rectors, vicars or priests in the service of the Church shall be amenable, as before, to the Archdeacon. Only, if they have come to Cambridge expressly for the purpose of study, they may make election, on oath, to which jurisdiction they shall be subject. The case of the Glomerels also requires distinctive treatment. They are not in strictness scholars at all but mere grammar students, preparing for the profession of schoolmaster. For them the Master of Glomery has always been responsible, and the Master of Glomery has always been appointed by the Archdeacon. Therefore the Bishop decides that suits affecting a Glomerel shall be decided by the Master of Glomery, but shall be subject to an appeal to the Chancellor if a scholar is the plaintiff.

On the threshold of Peterhouse and in the year 1284 we part company with the infant University. Like a young Hercules it is already reaching out tentative hands and throttling some serpents that threaten it in its cradle. Presently it will astonish greater men than bailiffs and priors.

CHAPTER III

THE FIRST COLLEGES

O pulchrae sine luxu aedes, vitaeque beatae,
Splendida paupertas, ingenuusque decor!

ABRAHAM COWLEY

THERE is a belief,which I think is nowhere more prevalent than at Cambridge and Oxford, that English Universities are characteristically distinguished from those of the Continent in their possession of colleges. Undoubtedly the peculiarities which the collegiate system has developed in times comparatively recent have left it little similarity to the type which was once general in England and abroad. Undoubtedly also the medieval tradition of community of life, which has clung to the English college, has almost faded out of the Universities of the Continent. But the colleges of England sprang from the same needs and were originally constituted on much the same model as those of other lands. Colleges of some kind had existed at Paris for nearly a whole century when Walter of Merton revolutionised English University life by the rule which he prescribed to his scholars. Before the suppression of the minor colleges at Paris, in 1764, there were more colleges in the Quartier Latin than in Oxford and Cambridge combined. The last of them were swept away by the Revolution.

The Cambridge hosteller in his cramped quarters must have looked with envy on the spacious comfort of the buildings of the Augustinian canons at Barnwell. He was under no rule of asceticism, but his life was hard and bare beyond the utmost severity prescribed to monk or Mendicant, and his penury was relieved by none of the pomp and dignity with which cloister life was mitigated and adorned. His studies were broken by constant wranglings about the price of thin ale and bitter bread. In his devotions he was shouldered by the detested townsman, who grudged him the use of the parish bell. In place of library and scriptorium he had a corner in a dark room and the few volumes which the principal and the hostellers jointly furnished—treasures constantly pawned to the layman or the Jew. The canons on their side had all the benefit of proximity to the University. They attended lectures and disputations. Some had taken Cambridge degrees. For example, there is Symon of Aschele, Prior from 1265 to 1297. He is a man 'of great eloquence and eminent literary gifts,' and he is a Civil Doctor of Cambridge, as well as a Regent in Arts of Oxford. Prior Symon is likewise a warm friend of Bishop Hugh of Balsham, and his official in the diocese. Possibly the two discussed plans for the bettering of the condition of the clerks, the hardships of whom they had themselves known.

In the house of the Augustinian canons at Barnwell there was no place for the clerk who was not professed to the rule of that order. But nearer at hand there was another household of brethren of the same order, whose doors were open to the poor and sick among the townsmen. Might not the Hospital of Saint John afford an asylum to the distressed scholar as well as to the aged and the pauper ? The suggestion came naturally to Bishop Hugh, for the Bishops of Ely were patrons and visitors of the Hospital and had given it large benefactions in the past. On December 24, 1280, he obtained letters patent from the King " to introduce into the dwelling-place of the secular brethren of his Hospital of Saint John studious scholars living after the rule of the scholars in Oxford called of Merton."

Merton's foundation had been first projected in 1264, but it did not take root in Oxford until ten years later. In the scheme which he drafted for his scholars in 1264 he did not contemplate any localised residence for them. They were to pursue their studies at Oxford or at any other University. Let it be remembered that, in the year before these statutes were made, there had been the great migration from Oxford to Northampton, and that in 1264 both Universities were in virtual exile. For the benefit of his scholars Merton bought large properties at Cambridge, and it is likely enough that at one time he had conceived the idea of planting them, or some of them, in that University.

Whatever may have been his first intentions, Merton, in the statutes of 1274, assigns to his scholars a habitation to themselves at Oxford. He gives them a rule and a permanent endowment. In effect Balsham did nothing of the kind. He provided his scholars with lodgings, but no house of their own. He gave them no rule suited to their environment. He furnished no endowment. It is true that he made provision " that the accustomed alms and works of charity to the poor and sick resorting to the Hospital should not be diminished or altogether annihilated " on account of the clerks ; but we must suppose that he did so by merely temporary subventions. There is nothing in his project which looks like an elaborated plan, nothing as yet to suggest the college organism.

Though the rule which the Bishop proposed for his

3

imported scholars was professedly that which Merton had laid down, six years before, for his Oxford foundation, it is likely enough that the idea of introducing scholars into a religious hospital came from Paris. As early as 1180 a certain ' Jocius of London,' visiting Paris on his return from a pilgrimage to Jerusalem, had found there a ' Hospital of the Blessed Mary of Paris ' devoted to the same works of mercy as the Hospital of Saint John at Cambridge. In this hospital a single room was set apart for ' poor clerks,' apparently scholars. Jocius bought the room from the hospital brethren and appropriated it for ever to the support of ' eighteen scholar-clerks.' So originated the first of the Paris colleges, known as the ' Collège des Dix-huit.' The scholars were under no special rule and had no endowment : they were of the poorest class, and each received a small monthly dole out of the hospital alms. Another experiment of the same kind was made about the end of the twelfth century, when some poor scholars were placed in a hospital of regular canons which had already been established near the palace of the Louvre. The double community went by the name of ' the Religious House of the poor scholars of Saint Thomas the Martyr.' But the experiment of associating scholars and religious in one household was a failure. The fault in this case lay with some of the scholars. They attempted to break open the doors of the House of Brethren at night and violently to effect an entrance. They made no progress in their studies and molested the studies of others.

Very likely the rough colony of scholars whom Bishop Hugh had planted in the quiet hospital at Cambridge misconducted itself much as the Paris men did. On whichever side the blame lay, it stands on record in the Bishop's letters patent that " for various reasons grounds of dissension arose between the brethren of the house and the scholars, owing to which it seemed difficult or impossible for them to dwell together any longer," and both parties petitioned him to make a distribution between them of the common goods of the establishment. Which thing the Bishop did, transferring his scholars to two houses next the church of Saint Peter, outside Trumpington Gate, and assigning for their maintenance the two houses and the church, with its tithes and altar-dues ; also the appropriation of the rectory of Triplow in the county of Cambridge. Henceforth the scholars were to be known as the Scholars of the Bishops of Ely. The letters patent are dated March 31, 1284. Notice that neither the Bishop nor King Edward in his letters confirming the Bishop's action has any notion that a ' college ' is being founded. These are merely ' scholars studying in the University of Cambridge,' and following the rule of ' the Oxford scholars of Merton,' and they are to live in ' hospices.'

It had been the intention of the Bishop further to endow his scholars and to draw up ordinances for their governance, ' had not the lot of humanity opposed his design.' He died in June, 1286. The earliest statutes of his foundation, which came to be generally known as the House of Peter, were given to it by Simon Montagu, Bishop of Ely, about the year 1338. They tell us nothing of the founder's intentions : they are confessedly based on Merton's rule, and they relate to conditions which had been greatly changed in College and University alike since the day of the first of Cambridge founders.

But we can see clearly enough what, in 1284, the Bishop has done. The vision of a *college,* with its stately equipment of chapel, refectory, library, chambers and domestic offices has not entered his mind. He has combined two hospices, or hostels, in one, and has given endowment to certain scholars who are to live there. It is a step in advance of the endowment of mere studentships, such as the benefaction of Bishop Kilkenny. And there are these other differences that his scholars are secular and not under any obligation to perform priestly offices, and that their endowment is their own and not given in trust to a religious house, as Kilkenny's was to the Augustinian canons. Balsham's foundation is a direct benefaction of the University and of learning, the first of its kind at Cambridge.

The new feature about Balsham's house of scholars is that it is endowed. In other respects it is a hostel of the old pattern. Like the hostel, it consists of a ' master ' and certain ' scholars.' After the democratic plan which prevailed in hostels the scholars choose their own ' master ' ; but their choice is so far limited that the Bishop selects one of two eligible candidates presented to him by the scholars. Also, until the right was renounced by Simon Montagu, the Bishop nominated his scholars. If we take Montagu's statutes as representing herein the founder's intentions, the master, just like the principal of a hostel, has no necessary concern with education. He is not bound to attend lectures, disputations and acts, as the scholars are. There is no educational staff. The master's business is to attend to the affairs of the house, " so that the scholars may the more quietly and diligently apply themselves to their studies." The ' Head of a House ' needed no capitals to dignify his office in Balsham's day.

Endowment gives Balsham's establishment another characteristic difference from the hostel. It is purely

THE MILL AT GRANTCHESTER

eleemosynary : it has no paying students, *pensionarii*. In that respect it differs from the modern college type also. The old hostels died when the colleges departed from their original purpose by admitting ' perendinants ' to share by payment in the scholars' meals and chambers. The college of modern days combines the features of college and hostel.

The statutes which Bishop Montagu gave to Peterhouse in 1338 contain a remarkable provision, which is not repeated in the code of any later foundation and seems scarcely adapted to a college rooted, as Peterhouse then was, in Cambridge town and possessed of buildings specially created for its needs. One or two of the scholars at a time are permitted to study at Oxford, and, during their residence there, they are to receive weekly allowance for commons. They are required on oath to return to the college and give the benefit of their learning to the other scholars. The excellent historian of the Universities of Europe in the Middle Ages, commenting on this remarkable provision, looses a characteristic shaft against the University which is not his own, and sees in it " a good illustration of the relative positions of Oxford and Cambridge in the fourteenth century." I venture to say that it is nothing of the kind. We need put no gloss on the statute. The reason which it gives for affording the scholars the opportunity of study at Oxford is that good scholars are improved by study in several universities and in different sciences. There is no suggestion that the studies of Oxford are in general more advanced than those of Cambridge. If the means of the household had allowed it the scholars might have been sent to Paris or any foreign university. It is likely enough that the arrangement was part of Balsham's plan rather than a new enactment in 1338 :

the statutes of Michaelhouse, which belong to 1326, contain nothing like it.   But, whether in 1286 or 1338, nothing was more common than for a scholar to transfer himself from one university to another, as German students do to-day.   Backwards and forwards with the changing moons the tide of scholars flowed between Cambridge and Oxford.   In the statutes which he drafted for his scholars in 1264 Merton permitted them to study in any university.   They had a Hall and large estates in Cambridge.   It seems conceivable that he intended some of them to study there, even though in 1264 Cambridge was depleted by the Northampton secession.   To a plain man it looks as though the Peterhouse ordinance, whether we ascribe it to Balsham or to Montagu, is suggested by the Merton rule, which is so constantly referred to as a model in the Peterhouse statutes.   Wisely it was said by Valentine of Verona,

Home-keeping youths have ever homely wits.

It was a day of narrow interest and fettered knowledge when Cambridge and Oxford began to look on each other as jealous rivals.   A larger air invests them now.   In the spirit of Balsham their doors are open to researchers from many universities and in all sciences.   One at least, who loves and honours his mother University, on this side idolatry, as much as any, will not cease to pray that sons may never be lacking to her who will seek ' light and sacred cups ' at other Universities, and, returning, will impart them to their brethren at home.

If the humble hospices which Balsham provided for his scholars had survived to our day we should regard them with an interest and a veneration greater than is awaked by the magnificent pile of King's or the spacious quadrangle of Trinity.   Perhaps they did survive

in two ancient ' ostles ' which occupied part of the
site of the present chapel and were pulled down to
make room for it in 1628. If that is so we must
suppose them to have been mean and small structures.
For the demolition of ' the little ostle ' the college
spent no more than £1 14s. 10d. But I think that it
is more likely that they were cleared away soon after
the founder's death. By his will he left to his foundation a sum of 300 marks, with which they bought
a plot of land south of Saint Peter's church and built
thereon ' a very beautiful hall.' Very beautiful
it remains to-day, and there are portions of it which
suggested to Professor Willis that they are as old as
the thirteenth century and occupied the site even
before the Ely scholars came to it. The Norman
church of Saint Peter, which adjoined the college and
was assigned to the scholars for their devotions, fell
down about the year 1340, and, when it was recon-
structed, was dedicated to Saint Mary. But there
are portions of Norman masonry in the western wall
which are an abiding memorial of the old hostel
days.

Forty years pass over Cambridge before the work
of college-making, begun by Bishop Balsham, is taken
up by another influential Churchman, Hervey de
Stanton, Chancellor of the Exchequer to Edward II
and a canon both of Wells and York. The new
establishment consisted of six scholar-chaplains, one
of them its Master, and it was styled by the founder
the House of the Scholars of Saint Michael. They were
provisionally lodged in a house purchased by Stanton
in 1324 from a certain Roger Buttetourt and situated
in a lane called Saint Michael's Lane, now Trinity Lane.
It stood opposite the site of the Queen's Gate in the
Great Court of Trinity.

In the presence of the Prior of Barnwell, the town mayor and a large assemblage of burgesses and graduates, the six scholars were inducted into their quarters at Michaelhouse on September 27, 1324. The formality of the opening ceremony shows that Stanton was fully conscious that the occasion was one of much consequence to the University. Here were no scholars expelled, as Balsham's were, from their former lodging and hastily accommodated in any available hospice. The six members of the new household have been formally nominated. They are all priests : three are Masters of Arts, two are Bachelors of Arts of the University. The founder has not satisfied himself with a summary adoption of Merton's rule. He has drawn up statutes for the government of his society and the control of its expenditure. His college is to be something totally unlike Merton's house, or what Peterhouse became under the statutes of Montagu. It is totally unlike the somewhat later foundation of King's Hall, which, along with it, was afterwards merged in Henry VIII's great college of Trinity. Stanton's is the earliest of statute-codes laid down for Cambridge colleges. If we compare it with those of Peterhouse, King's Hall and Clare, the three foundations which stand nearest to it in date, we shall see that the college type was far from being fixed in the first half of the fourteenth century. The University and its benefactors had not yet settled in their minds what exactly were the needs which endowment should meet, or what practically was to be done to ensure its proper application.

The feature in which Michaelhouse differed from other Cambridge foundations was that it was intended only for the higher education of the secular clergy, and those clergy were to be graduates—M.A., or B.A.

at the least. After the degree of M.A. the scholar-chaplains are to apply themselves to the study of Theology. The statutes make no provision whatever for the undergraduate class. Michaelhouse, in fact, belongs to the type of the college founded by Gonville at Rushford, or that of Stoke-by-Clare, of which Matthew Parker was once dean. Another singularity in the constitution of its small society was that the Master had no special duties assigned to him in domestic or financial matters, and that each of the scholars, for a week in turn, provided the necessaries of the household, and the Master's stipend and allowances were the same as those of any other of the scholars.

In the reign of Edward II we become dimly conscious that the King is maintaining certain scholars at Cambridge. There is no permanent endowment. In a fragmentary writ, dated July 7, 1317, the King directs the sheriff of Cambridgeshire " to pay to his beloved clerks, John de Baggeshote and twelve other children of his chapel at the University of Cambridge," certain sums for their weekly commons, the rent of their hostel and other necessaries. In 1337 King Edward III by letters patent founded *de novo* a college of thirty-two scholars under a warden (*custos*). They are to dwell together in the King's house near the Hospital of Saint John, which house the King purchased of Robert de Croyland. It is to be called the Hall of the King's Scholars. The sheriff is directed to continue the payment for commons, etc., out of the issues of the county ; but in the following years large grants are made by the King for the regular endowment of the Hall, for acquiring an enlarged site and erecting new buildings, and in 1342 directions are given for ordaining a rule of conduct for the scholars.

This is a college of a totally different pattern from any which preceded or followed it. The scholars, at all events on their admission, are not graduates. They are described as ' children,' and the name, Kings Childer Lane, given to the street in which Croyland's house was situated, is a reminder of their tender age. The right of appointing the warden is reserved to the Crown. The boys are nominated in each case by a King's brief. The statutes given to the Hall by Richard II in 1380 direct that the scholars on admission must be at least fourteen years of age. They are to study logic or any other subject which the warden may approve. In everything the statutes show that they have to deal with schoolboys. But the foundation was by far the largest which Cambridge had yet seen, worthy of its royal founders and of the royal college to which, in its decease, it gave birth.

One other foundation which belonged to the generation which saw the creation of Michaelhouse and the King's Hall, losing its identity, like them, in another name, has maintained its continuity to the present time. This foundation sprang from the enterprise of the University itself. As far back as 1249 William of Durham had bequeathed a sum of 310 marks to the University of Oxford for the maintenance of ten or more masters. With a part of this sum the University purchased certain houses, in the years between 1253 and 1263, and placed in them four masters. Out of this grew ' the great University Hall,' which at a later time developed into University College. University Hall was the first establishment of the nature of a college at Oxford. The example set at Oxford was copied by the University of Cambridge in 1326, when it obtained licence to found a ' college,' and to assign to it two messuages in Milne Street, near Saint John Zachary's church. The messuages in question were part of the land given to the University about the year 1270 by Nigel de Thornton, physician, and form the present site of Clare. The college was known as the University Hall. It does not appear whether the scholars placed in it received any maintenance from the University. Probably they lived in hostels which already occupied the site.

The Chancellor to whom the King's licence was addressed was Richard de Badew. Perhaps he contributed to the purchase of the site or the endowment of the College. At all events he was called its 'founder, patron and advocate,' *i.e.* the possessor of the 'advowson,' or right of nominating the Masters. In 1338 he ceded all his rights in the College to Elizabeth de Burgo, Countess of Clare. She seems to have endowed and built the College, giving it the new title of Clare Hall, and henceforth was reckoned as its foundress. Statutes, probably based on an earlier code, were given by her to the society in 1359.

The preamble to these statutes contains expressions which are obviously borrowed from the preamble to Stanton's code, and this circumstance has led Dr. Rashdall to conclude that the Clare statutes are based on those of Michaelhouse; but, in truth, there is little resemblance between them. In some matters they employ the language of the Peterhouse code, but their main features are novel. The college is to consist of a Master and nineteen fellows (*socii*, not *scholares*). The Master is elected by the fellows; the Master and fellows choose the fellows. Six of the fellows are to be in priest's orders. The fellows are to be 'artists,' and particularly Bachelors of Arts or 'better sophists,' which probably means students who had not 'determined,' or, as we should say, taken the B.A. degree, but who had advanced beyond the elementary study of logic. Only one fellow may be a civil lawyer and one a canonist. They may be of any nation, and may have been educated elsewhere than at Cambridge. Three of the fellows must be regents. Besides the Master and fellows ten poor scholars are to be maintained on the foundation : they are to study singing, grammar and logic. In 1359 Clare has already arrived at the familiar modern distinction between fellow and scholar.

In truth, the Clare statutes are in many respects wonderfully modern. Apart from domestic details and obsolete prescriptions as to study they might pass as the statutes of any college in the unreformed days before 1856. In opening its fellowships to all nationalities and to graduates of other Universities Clare showed a liberality which was generally unknown a hundred years ago. The constitution of Peterhouse, we feel, is capable of development. Michaelhouse and King's Hall are pure medievalities which are bound to disappear, with the rest of the old *régime*, when the axe of Reformation is laid to the University tree. Clare has anticipated reform. That is because the University had some hand in shaping its statutes.

A review of the ordinances laid down for the four colleges so far established, leaves the impression that as yet the University hardly understands what it wants—at least that benefactors, as happens even nowadays, have not always a clear idea how they may best help the University. Stanton's notions are purely clerical, and his scholars are all to be clergy. At Peterhouse the scholars must have received clerical tonsure, but they are not required to take the higher orders, and there is a limited tolerance of Law and Medicine. At Clare only six of the nineteen fellows

CHOIR OF THE CHAPEL, JESUS COLLEGE

are to be in priest's orders, and Arts are preferred to any other study. There is no agreement about endowments for the 'undergraduate.' At King's Hall all the scholars are of that class : at Michaelhouse none. At Peterhouse there are only two or three ' poor scholars ' : at Clare ten. At Clare a sophister may be a fellow, but the scholar of Peterhouse must be B.A. at admission. The full scholars of Peterhouse and Michaelhouse and the fellows of Clare must be poor : there is no such condition at King's Hall. We may correct a fundamental error of modern growth about the function of a medieval college—that it was a teaching institution. The ordinary college of the Middle Ages had few 'undergraduates,' and in their relation to the other members of the society those few were menials rather than pupils. There was no teaching staff; lectures and disputations were a University affair. At the best the college only examined its members to judge of their fitness ' to respond to the question ' for the B.A. degree, or to determine the faculty to which they should devote themselves. Peterhouse had a certain number of books which were kept in one or more chests, along with the college muniments, in the custody of the dean, and they might be lent to the scholars, on oath to restore them. The three other colleges evidently had no libraries. But Bishop Bateman gave books to Trinity Hall, and his statutes, dated 1350, show that there was a college library, and that the poor scholars might have books on loan.

It follows that the conception of the college as a place of religious education, a sort of medieval theological college, is a relatively modern one. Of course all medieval life was religious in respect of ceremonies ; and religious observances are not so much insisted on in college statutes as mentioned as part of the common life, not less essential than the common meal. The student is a ' clerk ' (*clericus*), and a clerk may be a priest or an intending candidate for ordination. But he may only be in minor orders : he may not be in orders at all. The Oxford parish clerk, Absalon, however unfitly, had received the tonsure from the bishop : ' hendy Nicholas,' for the credit of the cloth, we may hope had not. The academical habit was the clerical habit, and the wearing of it no more implied ordination, or the intention of it, than the under-graduate's gown does to-day. Theological training, needless to say, was not given by the college. It was not even insisted upon as a part of the study of the scholar, even if he were in orders. The Arts course, which contained no particle of religious teaching, was all-essential for the majority of the scholars, cleric or lay. In a limited way the University was, what the bidding prayer proclaims it to be, a place of religious education, since most of its students contemplated ordination, and a limited number of them were exercised in divinity : but the jurists were probably as numerous as the theologians.

Of course religious services take up some part of the scholar's day. At Peterhouse they have to attend masses for the souls of benefactors once a week, and, unless there is reasonable cause to prevent them, they must take part in mass celebration and the canonical hours on other days. At Clare one of the chaplains of the house celebrates every day, early in the morning, before the scholars go to the schools, and, unless prevented by their studies or other just reason, they are required to attend. At Michaelhouse the founder expressly states that his intention is that attendance at celebrations shall not interfere with lectures, disputations or private study : he leaves the matter to the conscience of each individual.

But the scholar-household has no visible token that it is devoted to worship. It must from the first have its hall for common meeting and its chambers for sleep and study : but it has no chapel. Note the names which are given to the household. It is a house (*domus*) a hostel or inn (*hospicium*) or a hall (*aula*). These are names applicable to any house of the better sort. The scholars' dwelling was originally no more. The buildings of a large house were often arranged so as to enclose a yard (*curia*) and in some cases, *e.g.* Buttetourt's house, bought by Stanton, the scholar-house might be so planned. A private house of this kind might contain a private oratory, but it had no chapel. The scholar was legally the parishioner of the parish in which he happened to reside : the parson expected oblations from him while he lived, mortuary dues for him if he died. Nothing was more difficult than to obtain licence from the Bishop or the Pope to erect a chapel which should in any way interfere with the rights of the parish church. Even a religious and charitable community such as the Hospital of Saint John experienced this difficulty. When Bishop Eustace of Ely, in 1208, licensed their new chapel he required that the brethren should exclude the parishioners of All Saints' church, next which the Hospital was situated, from sacraments and oblations, and should make pecuniary compensation for tithes to the nuns of Saint Radegund, to whom the rectory of the church belonged. The first example of a chapel specially built for the uses of a college is that of Pembroke, for which the foundress obtained the Pope's licence in 1355.

The earliest colleges got their independence of the parish in another way, by appropriating the church, or, if not the parish church, some other which stood conveniently near. The appropriation was usually preliminary to the establishment of the scholars in their house. Thus Balsham and Stanton appropriated to their colleges the churches of Saint Peter and Saint Michael respectively. As All Saints', the church of the parish which contained King's Hall, was not available, Edward III assigned Saint Mary's in the Market to his college. It was usual to follow the precedent of monastic churches and to reserve a portion of the church to the parishioners. The chancel at Saint Peter's and Saint Michael's was used by the scholars : the body of the church served the parish. Clare was not able to get the appropriation of the parish church of Saint John Zachary, next to which the house stood, but the statutes direct that the college services are to be performed there. After Henry VI destroyed the church of Saint John, in order to clear the ground for his new college, the south chancel aisle of Saint Edward's church was used by Clare, and the north aisle was similarly assigned to Trinity Hall. Corpus Christi used Saint Benet's church, as the two guilds from which the college originated had done previously. The foundress of Pembroke, before she obtained licence for building a separate chapel for her college, contemplated the appropriation to it of the neighbouring church of Saint Botolph. The latest example of a college chapel shared with a parish is that of Jesus. But in this case the history is somewhat different. Part of the nave of the old conventual church of Saint Radegund's nunnery had been appropriated to the parish which took its name from the nunnery. When bishop Alcock founded the college in 1496 he reserved to the parishioners the right of using a portion of the church which he had adapted to the uses of the college. Saint Peter's Church was used as a chapel by Peterhouse until the present chapel was consecrated in 1632.

The foundation of Clare marks an epoch in the development of the collegiate system at Cambridge. Everywhere in its statutes it is plainly written that they are the work of the University itself. They are sealed with the seal of the Chancellor and University. The Chancellor and two doctors or masters are to be visitors of the society, and so they remain to the present day. It has been the peculiar good fortune of Cambridge that many of its colleges were founded by royal or noble ladies who were guided in their plans by experienced and eminent members of the University. Richard de Badew acted to the Lady Clare in the same capacity as Andrew Doket to Elizabeth Woodville and as Fisher to the Lady Margaret. The statutes of Clare expressed the academic requirements of the time and served as a model for later foundations, just as Queens', Christ's and Saint John's each in turn represented new developments in learning and furnished new ideals which have lasted to the present time. The episcopal founders of the fourteenth and fifteenth centuries were most of them possessed of a genuine enthusiasm for culture ; but not all of them had the breadth of view and singleness of purpose of a Fisher. The foundations of Merton, Wykeham and Chichele at Oxford were narrowed by preferences for the founders' kin, a restriction from which Cambridge colleges have not suffered. In other cases, as at Exeter, New College and Lincoln, the restriction was to a particular diocese or school. King's, whose statutes reveal it unmistakably as an Oxford exotic on Cambridge soil, is the only Cambridge foundation so restricted. At both Universities the clerical founder showed a partial regard for the education of the clergy and for the position and power of the Church. At Cambridge the clerical element was strongest at Michaelhouse. In the statutes which he gave to Gonville Hall and Trinity Hall Bishop Bateman gave prominence to the studies of Theology and Law, and especially of Canon Law, which in the fourteenth century was recognised as essential to the attainment of the highest places in the Church. Of the twenty fellows of Trinity Hall seventeen were to be lawyers, and at least seven of them canonists, and the canonists were required to take priest's orders. Wiser men than Bateman resented the dominance of purely professional studies in the academic curriculum—a dominance against which the 'artist' of the twentieth century still raises his protest, though with ever lessening effect. Roger Bacon regarded the undue attention paid in his time to the Civil and Canon Law as the chief hindrance to the progress of learning in philosophy and experimental science, from the pursuit of which it diverted the student to unworthy ambitions.

The six years, 1347–1352, witnessed the establishment of not less that four new colleges at Cambridge, namely, Pembroke Hall in 1347, Gonville Hall in 1348, Trinity Hall in 1350 and the House of Corpus Christi in 1352. The statutes of the first two colleges certainly, and those of the other two probably, are earlier than 1359, the date of the Clare statutes. But there is reason to think that the 1359 statutes of Clare are based on an earlier code. In any case Clare and Pembroke are most intimately associated both in the circumstances of their origin and the rule which governed each—so intimately that it is a little remarkable that no historian of Cambridge has noticed the fact. Each was founded by a noble lady in association with a University Chancellor and on a site previously occupied by a house of scholars which was either owned or controlled by the University. Pembroke was founded by the Countess of Pembroke, Marie de Valence, otherwise called Marie de Saint Pol, and she desired that it should be called the House or Hall of Valence-Marie. Part of the site which she gave to her college was occupied by a hostel, called the University Hostel, which she bought from the Chancellor, Richard Lyng, and the University. Her statutes, dated 1347, only exist in an imperfect form and probably were only a temporary draft. They show the clearest marks of affinity with those of Clare. As at Clare the foundation consists of the two classes of fellows and scholars : there are to be twenty-four of the former and six of the latter. As at Clare the studies prescribed are Arts and Theology : only two fellows are to be canonists and one a student of Medicine. As at Clare the fellows are required to be unmarried, and there is the same liberal provision that they may be chosen from students of Oxford as well as Cambridge and from all nationalities. Preference is actually given in the Pembroke statutes to students of French birth who have studied at an English University. The date of the statutes, 1347, gives the clue to this singular preference. The battle of Cressy, fought in the previous year, seemed to restore the days of English dominion in France and to encourage the drawing together of scholars from both sides of the sea. Henry III had invited the students of Paris to England in 1229, when he was embarking on schemes of conquest in France. It was the policy of

> Great Edward, with the lilies on his brow,
> From haughty Gallia torn,

to renew the invitation in like circumstances in 1347.

The college which has grown out of the household established by Edmund Gonville recognises three founders and took a different colour from each of them. Caius College has won eminence in many fields, but since the day of Doctor Caius the study in which it claims a distinction unique at either University has been that of Medicine. Edmund Gonville meant his Hall to be the special home of Arts and Theology. Bishop Bateman made his favourite study of Law, Canon and Civil, an alternative to that of Theology. Gonville had already shown his concern for the education of the secular clergy by his foundation of a college at Rushford in Norfolk consisting of a Master and four fellows, all secular priests, who were to have the spiritual charge of the parish of Rushford. Gonville Hall was established by royal licence in 1348, and the founder died about three years later, leaving it unendowed except with its small site on the eastern side of Saint Botolph's church. After his death Bateman, who was already busied with the foundation of Trinity Hall, took up Gonville's work, endowed the Hall and gave it its first statutes. He surrendered the original site to the new foundation of Corpus and transferred the Hall to a new one, which had previously belonged to the same college. He gave Gonville's Hall the new title of the College of the Annunciation of the Blessed Mary, though it still retained its old name in popular usage. The new site was that which is now occupied by the Gonville Court of Caius, the Hall,

SENATE HOUSE PASSAGE

Library and Master's lodge. Some tenements which already existed on it were made to serve the original household. They were next to Trinity Lane and nearly opposite to Michaelhouse. The entrance was in Milne Lane, now Trinity Hall Lane, and the southern boundary of the site was Henney Lane, which led from the west end of Saint Michael's church to the river, roughly bisecting the area now covered by Caius.

Enough has been said of the constitution which Bishop Bateman gave to Trinity Hall to show that that college was altogether different in design from any of its predecessors. His licence to found it is dated 1350, and his statutes belong to the same year. For the site he purchased a hostel which had been bought by John de Crawden, Prior of Ely (1321–1341), for the use of monks of Ely who availed themselves of education in the University. This hostel immediately adjoined Clare, and its site formed part of what is now the garden of the Master of Trinity Hall. Portions of its wall still remain, and, as a Norman window was visible in it so recently as 1852, it is evident that the Ely monks occupied a building which had long existed as a private house. To this small site the founder added another piece of ground, on its northern side, bounded by Henney Lane. The college was entered from Milne Lane, through a gate which was in the position of the gateway of the present New Court. Bateman's two colleges were thus in close proximity, and he drew up a curious Composition of Friendship between the two societies, binding each to live in harmony with the other and to render it assistance.

The college of Corpus Christi differs in its origin from any other college at either University. It was the outcome of the combined action of two Cambridge guilds—of Corpus Christi and of the Blessed Virgin.

These guilds were in their nature secular: their aims were partly social, partly benevolent. A guild of this kind generally maintained a chaplain: that of Saint Mary already possessed an endowment for this purpose. It argues a superior degree of enlightenment among the Cambridge townsfolk and an amicable feeling towards the University that the brethren of the two guilds started the idea of founding a college for the education of secular priests who should be charged with the duty of celebrating for the souls of deceased members. The two guilds, with the King's sanction, were united for this purpose, and several of the brethren who lived in the parishes of Saint Benet and Saint Botolph pulled down certain tenements belonging to them in Luthburne Lane—now Free School Lane—where now stands the picturesque Old Court, and on the site so cleared established a college of 'scholar-chaplains.' The licence for founding the college is dated 1352, but the Aldermen and brethren of the guilds had given it a rule as early as 1350. The first statutes (1356) are closely modelled on those of Michaelhouse. The original foundation was a modest one, consisting of a Master and two fellows only. They were required to be in priest's orders and to devote themselves to the study of Theology or the Canon Law. They were to meet for daily service in Saint Benet's church. For the first two centuries of its existence Corpus had no chapel of its own.

CHAPTER IV

LANCASTRIAN CAMBRIDGE

And kings shall be thy nursing fathers, and their queens thy nursing mothers.—ISAIAH.

THE Master or Keeper of the King's Hall at Cambridge was required to render to the Royal Exchequer an annual account of the receipts and expenditure of his household of forty scholars. In the year 1350 Thomas Powys, the Master, omitted to do so and the accounts which he delivered in the following year run from April 1, 1349, to March 1, 1351. The reason of the omission in the earlier year is not far to seek. It was the year of the Great Pestilence. Some indication of the terrible nature of the visitation in Cambridgeshire is given by the register of Bishop L'Isle of Ely which shows that, whereas there were then 145 parishes in the county, there were 92 institutions to them in the course of the year. In the immediate neighbourhood of King's Hall the pestilence was particularly deadly. Three successive Masters of the adjoining Hospital of Saint John died in the course of the summer. There is extant a letter from the Bishop to the vicar of All Saints' in the Jewry, the parish which contained both the Hospital and King's Hall. It states that "the parishioners have been so swept away by the plague in this year that the offerings of the church do not suffice for the vicar's maintenance." The accounts of the Master of King's Hall are a grim revelation of the ravages of the plague among the scholars. From day to day he reckons the 'wages' due from the Exchequer for their maintenance. He gives the name of each scholar as he is admitted or withdrawn from the list, and notes the cause of each removal. Sixteen of the forty scholars died between April 10 and August 20. In the eighteen months which followed there were no deaths.

We may well believe that the other colleges and the hostels suffered not less heavily. Clare was founded by the Lady Elizabeth in 1338; but her statutes were not given until 1359. In the preamble to them she declares that her motive in establishing the college is the desire to advance knowledge, "which, seeing that the pestilence has carried off such vast numbers, now begins lamentably to fail." The plague returned many times in the century which succeeded 1349. The memory and the menace of it were seared in men's minds. And to pestilence was added the sword. Nearly a century after 1349 King Henry VI, in the statutes which he gave to his college, like the Lady Clare, deplores "the widespread devastation of pestilence in the ranks of the clergy, who are few and grievously wasted by plague, war and the other miseries of the world." Nor were the words merely the burden of an old song. In 1447 the King was obliged to forgo his intention of being present at the ceremony of laying the foundation-stone of the college chapel by reason of "the aier and the pestilence that hath long regned in our Universite."

Cambridge and Oxford have witnessed two great epochs of college endowment. The first belongs to the reigns of the first three Edwards, the second to those of the last three Henrys. The first produced eight colleges at Cambridge and four at Oxford. Of the Cambridge foundations seven were crowded into the twenty-eight years beginning with 1324. In the second period ten colleges were created at Cambridge and six at Oxford. The blank interval of eighty years which succeeded the pestilence of 1349 saw the birth of only one college—Wykeham's foundation of New College at Oxford. War, civil and foreign, completed the ruin begun by the pestilence. Hardly any existing buildings in Cambridge colleges date from the years between 1349 and 1441.

The sterility of the time is reflected in the history of the University schools. ' The great schools in School Street' are first heard of in 1347, but the buildings which contained them were not the property of the University. In 1309 it hired from a townsman, one Nicholas the Barber, a house opposite Saint Mary's church to serve as a *domus scolarum*, for lectures in Theology, Canon and Civil Law. Another house, situated on the ground now occupied by the Old Court of Caius, was hired as the Arts School. In the old University statutes it is provided that no owner of a house usually hired by the University as a school shall let or occupy it as a dwelling-house—a curious limitation of the rights of ownership. The first permanent school was that of Theology. A legacy for its erection was left by Sir Robert Thorpe, Master of Pembroke and Lord Chancellor of England, in 1372, but for lack of funds the work of building was suspended for many years, and it was only carried to completion about the year 1400. It formed the northern side of the schools' quadrangle. The room on the upper floor—now the Catalogue Room of the Library—was the University chapel ; it was also known as the Regent House and served as the general meeting-place of the University. The other public schools were not built until a considerably later time. That of Canon Law, occupying the western side of the quadrangle, was completed in 1457; that of Civil Law not until 1470. Archbishop Rotheram, of York, completed the quadrangle with a building on its eastern side about the year 1473. The rooms on the upper floor on these three sides were occupied by the Library of the University.

A story used to be told some thirty years ago that one of a party of foreigners who were being conducted on a round of visits to the colleges embarrassed his guide, a University man, by asking, " Now that we have seen the colleges, will you be good enough to show us the University of Cambridge ? " In the seventies of last century the only monuments which to a stranger's eye betrayed the existence of the University were the Library, the Fitzwilliam Museum and Great Saint Mary's Church, the last of which had little to distinguish it from a parish church. The cicerone was relieved from a humiliating confession by the appearance, on the other side of the street, of a graduate then prominent in the councils of the University and now the occupant of the See of Bristol. " That," said he, pointing to the divine, " is the University of Cambridge."

As in 1870, so in the years before 1400, the University consisted of men, and not of things of brick and stone. The college structures of the fourteenth century were, no doubt, inconsiderable for size or architectural beauty. But they existed and were beginning to shape themselves on the now familiar plan of a quadrangle with gatehouse and hall, lodgings and offices regularly disposed about it. In the material

tokens of its corporate existence the University has
undergone more change in the years which succeeded
the statutes of 1882 than in all the centuries which
went before. There was nothing in the medieval
University which answered to the multiplied laboratories and the classrooms of professors and lecturers
of present times. The very name of Professor was
unknown in the fourteenth century, except as an
equivalent of the title of Doctor in a faculty. The
first endowed University readership was that of the
Lady Margaret in 1502. Before that time the schools
were principally used for lectures given by ' Regents '
in the various faculties, *i.e.* graduates of not more
than five years' standing from the degree of Master.
The most important business of the University was to
examine for degrees, which was done by way of exercises
or disputations. The disputations sometimes took
place in a church. Saint Benet's was so used in 1273,
and a sermon, which is the modern substitute for a
disputation in Theology, must still be preached in
Great Saint Mary's church by each candidate for the
degree of B.D. The custom of preaching in Great
Saint Mary's before the University is a very ancient
one, recognised in the earliest University statutes
of about the year 1300. After the new chapel of the
University was built congregations for the transac-
tion of University business were usually held there
But both before and after that time Saint Mary's
church or the halls of the Austin and Franciscan
friars were used for the ceremony of conferring
degrees at ' Commencement.' In 1381 the common
chest of the University was kept in Saint Mary's ;
but there was another in the house of the Carmelite
friars.

Besides the hired schools already mentioned as

existing before 1372 there was one which was called
'Gramerscole,' or 'Glomery Hall.' It had a very ancient origin and probably was the very kernel from which
the University grew. It was situated in a lane called
Glomery Lane, or Saint Mary's Lane, running west-
ward from the High Street near Saint Mary's Church,
and was near the south-east angle of the Library :
part of it extended over the easternmost bay of King's
chapel. The strange word 'Glomery' is a corruption
of *gramarye*, grammar. As exorcism was associated
in the popular mind with the Latin language, *gramarye*,
and its by-form, *glamour*, came to be applied to
anything occult or supernatural. At Cambridge the
students of grammar, *i.e.* Latin, were called 'Glomerels,'
a name which at Bury Saint Edmunds was applied to
the boys who attended the monastic grammar-school.
They had a very peculiar relation to the University,
resembling that of the 'Glomerians' of the University
of Orleans. Cambridge conferred degrees in grammar ;
but the degree itself and the status of the grammar-
scholar were held in comparative disesteem, and
college statutes are blind to the existence of the class.
The grammar-scholar aspired no higher than to be
a schoolmaster. Very singular were the proceedings
when he 'entered,' *i.e.* was admitted to the degree of
Master in Grammar. "The Bedyll in Arte shall bring
the Master of Gramer to the Vicechauncelar, delivering
him a Palmer wyth a Rodde, whych the Vicechauncelar
shall gyve to the seyde Master in Gramer, and so
create hym Master. Then shall the Bedyll purvay for
every Master in Gramer a shrewde Boy, whom the
Master in Gramer shall bete openlye in the Scolys,
and the Master in Gramer shall gyve the Boy a grote
for hys labour, and another grote to hym that provydeth
the Rodde and Palmer." At the end of the fifteenth

century the office of Master of Glomery became an antiquated curiosity and was often left unfilled : in the middle of the following century Dr. Caius could not explain the meaning of the title. Sir John Cheke was the last holder of the office, and the last degree in grammar was given in 1524.

The Master of Glomery and his Glomerels belong to the very earliest times of the University. They were a recognised class, distinct from the ordinary student, in 1276, when Bishop Balsham of Ely issued an edict defining their position in relation to the University. The Glomerels come under the jurisdiction, not of the Chancellor, but of the Archdeacon of Ely. Their Master is appointed by the Archdeacon and takes an oath of obedience to him, and he hears and decides all actions in which a Glomerel is a party, just as the masters of the University try cases in which a scholar is concerned. The Chancellor is not to interfere in suits of Glomerels among themselves or between laymen and glomerels, unless the privileges of the University are at issue. There is a bedell of Glomery, who is distinct from the University bedells, but he is not to bear his mace before the Chancellor and masters of the University, and at the funerals of regent Masters in Arts the statutes expressly forbid the official attendance of the Master and scholars in grammar.

Bishop Balsham in his edict was evidently not invading the privileges of the Chancellor and masters, but merely asserting an old prerogative of the Bishop and Archdeacon. Forty years before this King Henry III, by his writ in 1231, had made it clear that the Chancellor and masters had jurisdiction in all University matters, and that the Bishop should only intervene when requested to do so by them. But the

Glomerels are not ' clerks ' of the ordinary academic kind ; they are more akin to the boys attending monastic or cathedral schools. In the cathedral school the teaching was originally done by the chancellor of the church or the Archdeacon ; but as time went on he delegated these duties to an authorised master. At Orleans the ' Glomerians ' grew out of the episcopal school and received the licence of Masters in Grammar from a cathedral official called the Scholasticus. On the site in Glomery Lane the grammar-school had perhaps existed before the University came into being. In Cambridge deeds of the earliest years of the thirteenth century there is record of one Henry Scolemaister who, very likely, was attached to the Archdeacon's school. In the adjoining parish of Saint Michael's there was, in 1278, a house called the Archdeacon's House from the circumstance that it belonged to the Archdeacon of Ely.

We have seen that Trinity Hall grew on a plot of land which had been previously occupied by a hostel of Benedictine monks from Ely ; and after the foundation of that college some of the monks resided in it and others in Gonville Hall. But, as a rule, such monks as resorted to Cambridge for education lived in the houses of secular persons. Except the Augustinian Priory of Barnwell there was no monastic household of men in or near Cambridge, and the Augustinian canons from the first had taken up an attitude of suspicion, not to say hostility, to the University. The great and wealthy Benedictine houses of the Fen Country were slow to avail themselves of the advantage of their proximity to Cambridge. The Mendicant orders were wiser. The Franciscans had made one of their earliest English settlements at Cambridge in 1224. They were followed by the Carmelites before

1249, by the Dominicans in 1274, and by the Austin friars in 1290. In wealth and in the magnificence of their dwellings the new orders came to rival the Barnwell canons, and in their energy and popularity at their first coming they far surpassed them. They took an active, and at first not an unfriendly, part in the affairs of the University and colleges. Pembroke was especially associated by its foundress in her original statutes with the Franciscans : one of the two Rectors of the college was to be a Friar Minor. The same order executed a deed of fraternisation with Queens' College in 1452. The University allowed the religious the privilege of ' keeping terms ' by residence and study in their own cloister, in some cases even if it were not in Cambridge. From the Pope the Mendicants obtained the privilege—though not with the goodwill of the University—of taking degrees in Theology without having previously graduated in Arts, and instead of preaching before the University, as the statutes directed that inceptors in Theology should do, they were allowed to perform their exercises in their own convents.

Colleges of student-monks were established at Oxford at an early period. The first, Gloucester House, founded in 1283, was originally limited to monks of the Benedictine house of Saint Peter at Gloucester. It was followed in 1334 by Durham Hall for Benedictines from Durham. Saint Mary's College (1435) received novices of the Augustinians ; Saint Bernard's (1437) was for Cistercians. At Cambridge nothing was done by the monastic orders to provide separate housing for their students before 1426, when, at a general chapter of the Benedictine order, held at Northampton, John Sudbury, who is described as prior of the students of that order at Cambridge, obtained the sanction of the chapter to establish a house for their reception. In the result the expenses were borne by Crowland Abbey alone, and the house was reserved to students from that monastery. It had no endowment, and when it ceased to exist, after the dissolution of the monasteries, the site and the buildings on it passed to the new foundation of Magdalene. Dr. Caius says that different parts of the monks' house were built by different monasteries : " thus Ely built one chamber, Walden a second, and Ramsey a third." The chambers at Gloucester College, Oxford, were similarly built by various Benedictine monasteries. The monks' house at Cambridge was usually called Buckingham College, and took its name from Edward Stafford, Duke of Buckingham, who built the Hall about the year 1519.

Another college, founded in the same year as Buckingham College, had, like it, a short tenure of existence and left its site to be occupied by a society which has been perpetuated to the present day. God's House resembled its twin college in this also that, though it was called into being by an old need, its kind was new to Cambridge and anomalous. Elsewhere than at the Universities education had undergone a long eclipse since the reign of Edward III. In 1439 William Bingham, parson of Saint John Zachary in London, petitioned Henry VI for leave to establish a house for grammar-students. In his petition he stated that he had " found of late over the last part of the way leading from Hampton to Coventry, and so forth, no further north than Ripon, seventy schools void, or more, that were occupied within fifty years past, because that there is so great scarcity of masters of grammar." The grammar-student, as we have seen, was held in some contempt at Cambridge, and the degree was not often taken. But at Oxford William of Wykeham had set the example of connecting a school with the University and endowing it on a liberal scale. In the reign of Henry VI a new interest was being taken in school teaching and endowment. The corruption of the youth of the realm by erecting grammar-schools, which Jack Cade laid to the charge of Lord Sele, was significant of the time. Waynflete made a grammar-school a part of his foundation at Magdalen, Oxford, in 1448. At the very time when Bingham petitioned to establish his house King Henry was contemplating the foundation of Eton and King's.

God's House was a humble institution and humbly endowed. Originally it was subordinated to Clare, just as some of the hostels were attached to colleges. In its first position it stood where the west part of King's chapel now stands. When King Henry required this site for his college he gave Bingham in exchange for it a piece of land which was just outside Barnwell gate and is now occupied by part of the first and second courts of Christ's. The foundation was intended to consist of a 'Proctor' and twenty-four 'scholars'; but the ambition of the founder was never realised. The new charter, given in 1448, permitted the scholars to study in liberal faculties as well as in grammar.

The revenue of God's House was principally provided out of the estates of alien priories which had been appropriated by Henry V during his French war. The precedent for this application of the property of foreign religious houses had been set by Archbishop Chichele when he founded All Souls College at Oxford in 1438, and the example was fruitful in results at Cambridge in the century which followed.

5

With the modest exception of Saint Catherine's every college founded at Cambridge, from King's in 1441 to Trinity in 1546, was endowed with spoils taken from religious houses. The Reformation did not begin but ended the process, in which prelates were as active as kings, and it was a crowning bitterness to the sufferers that the promotion of religion was invariably alleged as the justification of the spoliation. But God's House failed to secure the large windfalls which fell to the portion of the colleges to which the New Learning gave birth after 1500. It was always a poor and struggling institution, and its society never seems to have exceeded four. An inventory of its goods, taken about the time of its dissolution in 1505, shows that it lacked even a table in its hall, and thirteen books made up its library.

Of all the colleges which so far had risen at Cambridge God's House was puniest and least promising. The scale on which Henry VI planned his noble foundation of ' the King's College of our Lady and Saint Nicholas ' placed it at once in the foremost rank of the colleges at either University, and for the first time gave to the younger University a position in which it might rival the wealth and prestige of Oxford. In the scheme of his twin foundations at Eton and Cambridge the King closely followed the plan adopted by Wykeham, seventy years earlier, for Winchester and New College. Originally, and for four hundred years after its nativity, King's was an Oxford *enclave* at Cambridge, and it is matter for some wonder that the King planted it in the less distinguished University and on soil uncongenial to its character. It is said that Henry V designed to appropriate the confiscated revenues of the alien priories to the foundation of a great college within the Castle at Oxford. Henry VI altered the destination of the endowment to Cambridge and Eton. Eton and Oxford were both in Lincoln diocese. Locally and ecclesiastically Eton should be associated with Oxford, and there is a suspicion that Henry's first intention was so to associate it. In the statutes which he gave to King's he gave it as much independence of Cambridge as the University could be induced to admit. He exempted it from the jurisdiction of the Bishop and Archdeacon of Ely, and made the Bishop of Lincoln its visitor ; and, what was of more serious consequence to it in the process of centuries, he exempted it from the interference of the Chancellor and Masters of Cambridge. The college unfortunately encroached on the privileges of the University even further than its statutes sanctioned, by claiming that its members should be admitted to University degrees without the test of a University examination. The affiliation of the college to a school was an Oxford tradition, more natural in the case of New College, but hardly less prejudicial there than at King's, and the limitations made Henry's college a parasite in the University where it should have been a worthy bidden guest. For four centuries it stood as a splendid ' cenotaph of learning.'

Suspicion is written all over the elaborate statutes which the boy-King prepared for his college. If ' the aier ' that reigned in the University of Cambridge on its opening day seemed to him tainted and dangerous, even more suspect, metaphorically, was that of Oxford. Deeply though they had drunk of the temporalities of the Church the house of Lancaster had ever professed a rigid and sombre orthodoxy. Oxford, since the days of Wycliffe, was ' the University of heresies '—so it was proclaimed by Archbishop

Courtenay. By the virus of Lollardy Cambridge had hitherto been uninfected.

Of heresie Cambridge had never blame.

So at least it seemed to Lydgate, writing in the early days of Henry VII ; and in 1457 Bishop Gray of Ely, when required by the Archbishop of Canterbury to make inquisition in his diocese for heretical books, made return that none such were to be found. The speculative unrest of Oxford was illustrated afresh in the generation which witnessed the foundation of King's by the polemical writings of Reginald Pecock, a doctor of Oxford and Bishop of Chichester. The King's spiritual advisers doubtless suggested to him the selection of Cambridge as the site of his new Castle of the Faith. In the closing words of the immense code which he gave to his college the King requires that every scholar on his admission to it shall swear that he will not countenance the damnable errors and heresies of John Wycliffe and Reginald Pecock. In language of surpassing solemnity he invokes upon the executors of his will, according as they promote or hinder its purposes, the blessings or the curses of Gerizim and Ebal. It was a special tragedy that another Lancastrian Henry, who claimed to share with him the founder-ship of King's, retained his sterilising restrictions, but frustrated the royal saint's religious aims, and that scant rain of spiritual grace descended, until centuries were past, on the college of his planting.

The will of King Henry, in which he made provision for his two colleges, bears date March 12, 1448. It was a melancholy time in the national history, full of forebodings of trouble. The final downfall of

SOUTH DOOR, KING'S COLLEGE CHAPEL

the English arms in France followed in the next year, Jack Cade's rising in 1450, the imbecility of the King in 1454, the first pitched field in the Civil War in 1455. For the building of his college on the magnificent scale prescribed in the will the King provided an annual sum of £1000 out of the revenues of the Duchy of Lancaster. Fitfully and in part this contribution was paid until 1451. Feebly and at intervals, with the aid of subscriptions and small subventions from the royal treasury, the work on the chapel was continued in the reigns of Edward IV and Richard III. Then for twenty-four years operations were totally suspended. Henry VII, in the last year of his reign, and Henry VIII after him applied themselves with energy to the consummation of the great monument of the Lancastrian dynasty. The fabric of the chapel was apparently completed in 1515, the glazing of the windows in 1531, the stall-work in 1536. The arms and initials of Anne Boleyn placed on the rood-loft mark the date at which the work was brought to an end, and gave emphatic warning that the medieval spirit which inspired it was dead, and that in the dawning light of intellectualism, as clear as it was hard, there was no place for the visions of the royal saint.

The long period of sixty-nine years during which the chapel was in building witnessed less change in architectural development than any which had preceded it since the Conquest, and, though alterations in detail were introduced as the work progressed, the chapel remains virtually the embodiment of its founder's designs. It was far otherwise with the King's plan for the domestic buildings of his college. Their plan was as grand as that of the chapel, and it interests us because King's was the first college at

Cambridge whose courts were modelled on a fixed design. The earlier colleges had grown almost fortuitously out of ordinary dwelling-houses. The Tudor colleges had for their model Queens', not King's. There is no college at Cambridge which at all resembles the college planned by Henry. It so far resembled New College, Oxford, and Eton College that a cloister cemetery, detached from the buildings, entered into the plan of each, and, as at New College, the cloister of King's was to be dominated by a lofty tower. It so far resembled the Tudor colleges that it included the feature of a gate-tower, which was copied at Queens' and in the colleges of the first half of the sixteenth century, but is foreign to the Oxford plan. In its other arrangements the design of King's had no exemplar and no successor at Cambridge.

In this design the Great Court occupied the site of the present principal quadrangle, and on its eastern and southern sides was contained by ranges of chambers. In the south-west angle was the Provost's lodge. Next to it in the western range was the hall, and between the hall and the chapel was placed the library. The position of these buildings was quite different from that which was traditional in Cambridge colleges from the fourteenth to the middle of the sixteenth century. A conduit in the middle of the court gave the suggestion for that in the Great Court of Trinity, and a bridge across the river was the first of the many which are now a picturesque feature of the backs of the colleges. The garden grounds of King's were to be vastly more extensive than any that the older colleges possessed, and stretched along both banks of the river. A lofty wall, fourteen feet high, ' crested and embattled and fortified with towers,' was to encompass the whole of the grounds on the hither side of the Cam and to demonstrate to the town and the University the proud isolation of the royal college.

What was the intention and significance of these arrangements, so unlike those of the colleges that then were or were afterwards to be? King's was to be a curious hybrid—half college, half monastery. The encircling wall recalls the fortified ramparts which gave privacy and security to the town convents of the Middle Ages. Even the river-bank was guarded by the wall, and the bridge was commanded by a tower which, isolated as it was from other buildings, would have borne, had it been completed, a decided resemblance to the fortalice which barred many a medieval bridge. Another tower commanded the entrance from the High Street. An entrance gate tower had been built a few years previously (1428–1435) at King's Hall; it was the first of the many gate-towers which are a characteristic of Cambridge colleges. Though their purpose was ornamental their appearance is suggestive of defence, and at King's College defences were not unneeded. The exceptional privileges and immunities arrogated by the college moved the deepest resentment in town and University. In 1454 a riotous assault with guns and habiliments of war was made on the college by Masters of Arts and others of the University, and at the same time statutes were passed in Congregation to prevent members of the college from taking degrees until they renounced their privileges. The dominating church, the central conduit, the cloister garth, the kitchen court, even the great library were features as constant in monastic arrangement as they were strange to the colleges before 1450. The position of the Provost's lodge, remote from the chapel, has no counterpart in the medieval college plan but resembles that of the abbot's quarters in a monastery. The hall, built above a vaulted cellar, was a repetition of the design of a refectory, the only example of which at Cambridge is the monastic hall of Jesus.

The prodigious plans of the King involved a clearance of the site which practically took the heart out of the town and caused profound indignation in the civic breast. Between river and market-place was the busiest part of medieval Cambridge. From north to south, from the ground now occupied by Trinity Great Court to the mills beyond Queens', it was traversed by Milne Street, one of the most frequented thoroughfares of the town. On its western side stood the church of Saint John Zachary, and in or near the street were five University hostels, an inn called the Boar's Head, and a large number of tenements in the occupation of townsmen. On the river-bank was a hithe called Salthithe. All these were sacrificed to the King's will. The church of Saint John, *pietatis causa*, was rebuilt on another site, but, as the parish was destroyed, it served no useful purpose and disappeared in a few years. Milne Street ceased to be a thoroughfare ; the lanes connecting the High Street with the waterside were enclosed ; and the process, continued in the next century, of severing the trade of the town from the river-bank was begun. Henceforward the town of Cambridge begins to be entirely subordinated to the colleges.

The pity of it was that this widespread devastation did very little to advance the King's aims. For nearly three centuries afterwards sheep grazed in the middle of the town on the empty site where men had once dwelt and trafficked, and where the fenmen's keels

OLD GATE TOWER OF KING'S COLLEGE

had discharged their wares. No portion of the domestic buildings planned in the King's will was even begun, and on another site, northwards of the chapel, rose the unpretentious court, humble amongst the humblest of college structures, which for three centuries was destined to house the society of King's. The Old Court, as it came to be known after the erection of Gibbs' building in 1724, represented the college of Henry's first design—abandoned when he embarked on the plan laid down in his will. Hastily finished with rough materials and without an ordered arrangement, it lasted until 1835, when the site was purchased by the University for the extension of its Library, and the buildings on it were destroyed. The noble gate-tower is the sole remaining fragment of the domestic portion of the founder's college. For more than four centuries it stood uncompleted beyond the first storey—a witness to the majesty and beauty of the King's conceptions and to their melancholy disappointment. By the skilful hands of the late Mr. Pearson it has been incorporated in the University Library, and, with its surroundings, forms one of the most charming 'bits' of revived antiquity in Cambridge. There is a parable in college gates, as Dr. Caius saw. Henry's gateway still leads nowhere.

In the circumstances of its foundation Queens' College repeats the history of Clare and gives a suggestion which was taken up at a later time when endowment was needed for the establishment of Saint John's and Trinity. Andrew Doket, like Richard de Badew, was a resident in the University, active in its interests and liberal in advancing them. In 1446 he obtained a licence from Henry VI to incorporate a College of Saint Bernard for a President and four

fellows. Like de Badew, he found the enterprise
beyond his means, and in 1448 he enlisted the influence
of Queen Margaret in support of his foundation. A
new charter, issued in the same year, licensed the Queen
to establish a college, named the Queen's College of
Saint Margaret and Saint Bernard, "beside the most
noble and glorious college royal of Our Lady and Saint
Nicholas founded by the King's highness." Queen's
was in most respects a sister college to King's and
shared its family fortunes ; but its lowlier status
saved it from the collapse which befell its royal brother,
and it was spared from the tyrannous limitations
which maimed the activities of its grander neighbour.
As in the case of King's, the House of York showed
some not very effective interest in the legacy of the
dynasty which it had supplanted, and Edward IV's
Queen, Elizabeth Woodville, was induced to lend her
name to the society as its patroness and co-foundress ;
and, since the apostrophe has taken a place in English
typography, it has become the fashion to mark the
possessive dual by spelling the name of the college
' Queens'.' But it does not appear that either royal lady
contributed to its endowment. Poor and straitened
it was for the first half-century of its existence. But
it was not hampered by the architectural encumbrances
of King's. The colossal shadow of Henry's endowment
did not stifle the spontaneous liberality of humbler
men, and Queens' made none of the arrogant pretensions
which alienated from the larger college the goodwill
of town and University. In a special way Queens'
owed its comparative prosperity to the joint activity
of burgesses and clerks. Its real founder, Doket,
was at once Principal of the Hostel of Saint Bernard
and Vicar of Saint Botolph's. The donor of the original
site of the college was a townsman, and townsmen

QUEENS' COLLEGE FROM THE RIVER BANK

figured among its early benefactors. Doket, the first President, fortunately lived to direct the fortunes of the college for nearly forty years, during which he actively fanned the small spark of his kindling into a brilliance surpassing that of King's or any of the older colleges. His merits are dimmed by the greater lustre of the men who entered into his labours at Queens'. Fisher and Erasmus made his college the centre of intellectual life at Cambridge and in England. But it was Doket who led his followers within sight of the Promised Land.

Fortunately the statutes of Queens' were not moulded under the same influences as those of King's. The earliest edition of them—of uncertain date—seems to have been given to the college by Elizabeth Woodville. They provide for a President and twelve fellows, all of whom were to be in priest's orders. But though the statutes allowed the society more latitude to develop in its own way than was permitted to King's they contain some resemblances which seem to be a survival from the times of Henry VI. The title of President given to the Head is as clearly a borrowing from Oxford as that of Provost is at King's. As at King's the fellow on admission was required to abjure the heresies of Pecock and Wycliffe. A special favour is shown to Lincoln diocese, in that three fellows might be elected from it, not more than two from any other.

The site which Doket procured for his college included all the area between the Carmelite Friary, N., Silver Street (formerly Small Bridges Street), S., Milne Street, E., and the river, W., as well as the land on the opposite bank. At the Dissolution the society obtained the ground occupied by the Carmelites, and thereby extended its borders to the site which had been cleared for the erection of the Great Court designed by Henry for King's. On the site first procured Doket began and completed in twelve months a court which at the time was not only the most complete and substantial but architecturally the most well-designed of any then existing. The growth of the society necessitated the addition of a range of chambers on the river-bank only twelve years after the foundation. Some of the new features introduced in Henry's plan for King's were reproduced at Queens'—notably the cloister and the entrance gateway—and it is likely, says Mr. J. W. Clark, that the same architects were employed in both colleges. But the plan of Queens' is not like that which Henry laid down for the Great Court of King's. It is something new, and it was to serve as a pattern for all the colleges which were built in the century which followed.

The little Hall of Saint Catherine, founded in 1475, was a sucker thrown up from the parent stem of King's. Robert Wodelark, its founder, was Provost of King's from 1452 until 1479, and had twice been chosen Chancellor of the University. He was not a wealthy man and held no rich preferment. As Master of the Works at King's he had advanced large sums which were never repaid to him. In personal energy he was no Doket. Beyond purchasing the site of his college in Milne Street he provided no permanent endowment at first, and he defrayed its annual expenses out of his income. The original society consisted of a Master and three fellows. The small court which contained it has utterly disappeared, but we know that it included a chapel, cloisters, hall and library.

With the foundation of Jesus College the series of colleges modelled on the medieval pattern may be considered to end. Nine years only separated the creation of Jesus from that of Christ's, fifteen from that of Saint John's. But the energising spirit which entered into the University in the short interval made it a wider gulf than the half-century which divided King's from Jesus. Like Saint John's, Jesus had a long retrospect when it started its career as a college. But the unwisdom of putting new wine into old bottles was more clearly seen by Fisher in 1511 than by Alcock in 1496. In the early years of King Stephen, long before the scholars had made their home in Cambridge, the Benedictine nunnery of Saint Mary and Saint Radegund had come into being at much the same time as the Hospital of Saint John. In the unrest of a world of ever-changing ideas the two religious houses—neither of them very rich, nor very poor—had lived on, quietly unchanging, or changed only by the deterioration which comes of the unconsciousness of change. Stories are told of the prodigality and immorality of either household; but it was of anæmia that they died. The veracity of the stories has been questioned; but they are true. The piety of the two bishops, and especially of Alcock, was grappled by the cords of a tender affection to old tradition. We have no reason to suppose that Alcock was a man of particularly advanced ideas in education or religion. He had dealt wisely and mercifully with the shortcomings of other religious houses which had been brought to his knowledge as diocesan. At Saint Radegund's he tried his hand at reform, but the ruin was past remedy, and the nuns showed, by their desertion of the house, that they were conscious of the fact. Something had to be done, and to be done at once, to save the revenues of the house from the dissipation which had long been going on, and its noble buildings from desolation and ruin. Wisely con-

servative, Alcock forestalled such disaster as befell
Cambridge when the axes and hammers of the lay
spoiler broke down the house of the Grey Friars,
though Ascham and the University petitioned that it
might be preserved for the uses of the scholars.

Alcock was perhaps hardly prepared to deal with
the emergency in 1496, when he obtained the licence
of Henry VII to dissolve the nunnery and to found in
its place a college dedicated to the Virgin, Saint John
the Evangelist and Saint Radegund, and consisting
of a Master, six fellows and six boys. He died in 1500,
and it does not appear that he endowed the college
or gave it any statutes. Benefactions procured from
personal friends, with what was saved from the wreck
of the nunnery property, sufficed to launch the college
on its modest career. Alcock's part in its foundation
was perhaps limited to the rebuilding of the nunnery
premises. He was comptroller of the royal works
and buildings to Henry VII, and his architectural
skill and taste are evidenced by his work at Ely,
Malvern and elsewhere. His adaptation of the nuns'
buildings to the uses of the scholars shows at once
his practical ability and artistic feeling. The great
church of Saint Radegund was in a ruinous condition.
With the evidence of the stranded leviathan of King's
then before his eyes Alcock was too wise to lay on his
society the burden of an ecclesiastical monument far
beyond its needs and means. What was dilapidated
he rebuilt; what was unnecessary he converted to
other uses; whatever combined beauty with utility
he reverently conserved. With a prospect of new life
and energy Jesus looked back on centuries of hallowed
tradition. It was Fisher's wish that Saint John's
should do so too; but the natural piety which had
linked his foundation with an immemorial past was

FELLOWS GARDEN – JESUS.
M.A. '07

JESUS COLLEGE FROM THE FELLOWS' GARDEN

rudely disregarded when its society destroyed the ancient chapel and infirmary of the Hospital.

The cloister was a feature newly introduced at King's, Queens' and Saint Catherine's, and Alcock did well to retain it at Jesus. He built a new gate-tower : it was not of the pattern of King's and Queens', but something original. The gate-tower of King's Hall (1428) and the later examples at Queens', Christ's, Saint John's and Trinity by their square massiveness, projecting angles and corner turrets suggest defence. Alcock's tower is all elegance and spirituality.

The earliest existing statutes of the college were given to it by Alcock's successor at Ely, bishop Stanley. They make provision for a Master and eight fellows, as well as for four ' youths ' and four ' boys.' The ' youths ' studied Arts ; the ' boys ' were schoolboys who were taught grammar and served as choristers and acolytes. There was a schoolhouse in the outer court in which other boys besides those on the foundation were taught. The schoolmaster and usher had rooms in the college and statutable stipends ; indeed, they were better endowed than the fellows. In these provisions we see fresh evidence of reviving interest in the education of boys : also that grammar, once food for grown ' Glomerels,' is now being relegated to children. One of the fellows is to study Civil and Canon Law ; the others are mainly to devote themselves to Theology, and one is to be in priest's orders. It is a remarkable feature of the statutes—the more so that they were made by a Bishop—that none of the other fellows, nor even the Master, are specifically required to take orders. The statutes are further remarkable in that they make provision for teaching within the walls of the college. There is a reader in Theology, and all the society, except doctors, are required once a week to attend exercises superintended by the dean. But the date of the statutes shows that they are dictated by the spirit not of Alcock but Erasmus.

CHAPTER V

TRANSITION

> As we often see, against some storm,
> A silence in the heavens, the rack stand still,
> The bold winds speechless, and the orb below
> As hush as death, anon the dreadful thunder
> Doth rend the region.
>
> SHAKESPEARE

ON October 1, 1500, died John Alcock, Bishop of Ely and founder of Jesus College. Five months before him died his friend and once associate in the Lord Chancellorship of England, Thomas Rotheram, Archbishop of York. Wise, good and patriotic men both, they lived to see the establishment of national peace, for which they had laboured in a generation which would have no peace, and they had hoped continually for the University in days of heaviest discouragement. Rotheram, Chancellor of the University and once Master of Pembroke, had been a liberal benefactor of King's when the royal bounty had been withdrawn from it, and he had built the east part of the University schools, with a library above, which he furnished with valuable books. Sensible of its indebtedness to its Chancellor, the University, in his lifetime, decreed that his name should be for ever enrolled among its principal benefactors : and so he is commemorated to the present day.

6

On what present outlook for the University did the dying eyes of these good men rest ? Visions of the changed order that was soon to come were denied them, for they were men whose good was done for the age in which they lived, and they had no far-seen ideals. Perkin Warbeck went to the gallows twelve months before they laid themselves down to die, and the Tudors were evidently come to stay. So far that is good. Successively the University in this past half-century has prayed for the good estate of many kings : whether they were called Henry or Edward or Richard made no matter. Given the chance, kings may be counted on to stand by the University : in will, if not in deed, Crookback was as good a friend as the royal saint. Kings are never quite blind to national responsibilities, and a rich, quiet sovereign, such as Henry VII, is likely to do much.

It is otherwise with the baronage. To their bloody graves they have gone unregretted and promptly forgotten. To the wealthy and titled aristocracy of the Middle Ages the University owes nothing : and it will owe nothing to the hungry placemen who shall succeed them about the courts of Tudor and Stuart. Essex, the two Buckinghams and Monmouth will cloak their naked deformities in the Chancellor's robes, and give nothing in return to the University. An Audley will masquerade as founder of Magdalene, poorest of Cambridge colleges, and will give it a beggarly dole out of the vast spoils which he has netted from the monasteries. Not until the noble family of Cavendish recognises that the most exalted post in academic Cambridge brings responsibilities as well as dignity will any ' high potentate ' deserve to walk in the stately procession of ' dames of royal birth and mitred fathers ' whom a Cambridge poet complimented by ranking them in the train of a Duke of Grafton.

To royal ladies and to the sage and sober Churchmen who were their almoners and counsellors Alcock and Rotheram might turn their eyes with better hope. ' Furnished with ability and dwelling peaceably ' after storm and stress, the good Margaret Beaufort, mother of Henry VII, seemed not unlikely to succeed to the part successively played by the foundresses of Clare, Pembroke and Queens' ; and John Fisher, Master of Michaelhouse since 1495, and appointed by the great lady, in 1497, to be her confessor, by his wise suggestion may outdo Badew and Doket in benefits procured for the University. In the same year in which she made him her confessor the Countess Margaret established at either University a readership in divinity—which we now call the Lady Margaret Professorship—the first of endowed professorships.

For the rest, there is hope and there is discouragement in the immediate position. There is sore discouragement in the failure—total and final it might seem in 1500—of the magnificent plans of Henry VI. For fifteen years past the half-hewn stones, brought for the building of King's chapel, have lain untouched, and of the Great Court no beginning has been made. For twenty-two years the building of Saint Mary's church has alternately stagnated or loitered tediously to its completion. The University sends out begging letters, but funds are slow in coming in, and the church will not be ready for service until 1519. Everywhere is penury. Fisher, looking back on those days in a more prosperous time, said of them that, for some cause, whether it were the quarrels with the townsmen, the ever-recurring pestilence or the lack of patrons, a weariness of learning had come upon the University, and the best of its sons were meditating how they might depart from it with advantage.

As loyal and prudent pastors of the Church and its trustees in the University, Alcock and Rotheram might end their days in content. Heresy—never the reproach of Cambridge—had burnt itself out, never, it might seem, to be rekindled while the fortunes of the Church were guided by the orthodox House of Tudor. Wealth and stability were the assured prerogative of the Church while it stood by the King. Nevertheless, in the same year, and, it may be, in the same month in which Alcock died, there comes to Clare a freshman, named Hugh Latimer, who will live to see and do much that is undreamt of in 1500. Abuses in the religious orders were, alas! too notorious to escape the notice of watchful and conscientious prelates; but the very abuses to which Alcock applied the knife at Saint Radegund's nunnery opened a new way of usefulness to the Church and the University.

Education and learning, it might confidently be anticipated, would continue on the lines approved by the Church : other lines there were none. The business of the reformer was, what is nowadays called ' University extension,' to widen the circle of recipients of academic teaching, not to reform the teaching itself. It was the fashion of the University in those days to require a ' caution ' of its members, as a guarantee that in due course they would perform the exercises which would qualify them for a degree. The cautions were deposited with the proctors and registered in a book. Sometimes they consisted of money, plate or articles of dress ; more often of books useful to the student and marketable by the University pawnbrokers. Of these books, many hundreds in number, lists have been compiled from the Grace Books, covering the years from 1454 to 1511. They are all in Latin. Most common are service books. Among authors the schoolmen, Aquinas and Scotus, easily lead the way. Latin translations of Aristotle are fairly common, and in the last years there is a single translation of Plato. Theology and Canon Law are amply represented, Civil Law not quite so well, Medicine hardly at all. Greek is unheard of, and English books have no place in the scholar's library. A stray student deposits a copy of Virgil or Seneca. Otherwise poetry, history and oratory, even in a Latin dress, are subjects unexplored by the students of the late fifteenth and early sixteenth centuries.

John Fisher, a native of Beverley, the same town which gave birth to Alcock, was Master of Michaelhouse from 1495 to 1505, when he passed to the new and more vigorous house of Queens'. To the practical north-country sense of Alcock he added a burning desire to equip the University, in which he was a resident, for spheres of conquest which had not entered into the visions of Alcock in 1496. About him he saw little but stranded wreckage. His own college, Michaelhouse, was still harboured in the cradle provided for its infant days in the fourteenth century. It had no court, no chapel, few chambers and no endowment for the poor scholar who was not a fellow. God's House, destitute of so much as a table in its hall, existed but hardly lived. The ancient Hospital of Saint John, which comparatively recently had obtained recognition as a college of the University, was gradually settling down into a quagmire of insolvency, and most of its brethren about this time deserted it.

If tradition says truly that Fisher was originally a student of God's House it was natural piety which claimed his attention first for that poor establishment.

When he enlisted the help of the Lady Margaret to convert it into Christ's College the old society were continued as Master and fellows in the new. That new society was to be far larger than any which had so far been constituted at Cambridge, excepting only King's. It consisted of a Master, twelve fellows and the remarkable number of forty-seven scholars.

It may be conjectured that the statutes, in most respects closely followed in those of Saint John's, were entirely the work of Fisher. But both in the somewhat narrow intensity of her religious feeling and in the breadth of her mental culture, phenomenal in a woman in that age, the Lady Margaret was wholly in sympathy with her confessor. " Right studious she was in books, which she had in great number, both in French and English." The codes of both colleges contain a provision, copied from that of God's House, that half of the society, including the scholars, must be drawn from the northern parts of England. As northerners were probably a minority of the students at Cambridge this limitation amounted to a preference for them. Partly this may have been attributable to Fisher's affection for the north country to which he belonged, but it may have had another meaning which would be consistent with his somewhat narrow orthodoxy. The northern counties, then and afterwards, were the stronghold of religious conservatism.

The statutes of Christ's contain some notable innovations. Large as its endowed society was they provided for a class of ' pensioners ' who were not maintained on the foundation. The recognition of this class betokens a new conception of the function of a college. Henceforth it will take under its dis-

cipline and tuition students who are able to pay for
their maintenance and education. During the half-
century which follows, the hosteller and the unattached
student gradually fade out of existence. As had been
already done at Queens', the College assumes direct
responsibility for the education of its younger students.
A college lecturer is appointed, and attendance at
his lectures is compulsory. It is significant that one
of the subjects in which he is required to give instruction
is the ' works of the poets and orators.' Possibly the
rule has a retrospective aspect. The grammar-scholars
of God's House were exercised in ' Priscian, Virgil
and other poets.' Possibly it is a conscious innovation.
Greek was unknown to Cambridge before 1511, when
Erasmus began his lectures there ; but the recognition
in the study of Arts of Latin *belles lettres* is premonitory
of the new spirit which was invading the hard, professional routine of medieval study.

For so large a community correspondingly extensive
buildings were required, and the court of Christ's,
substantially identical with the present first court,
was by far the largest then existing in the University.
The distribution of the buildings was exactly copied
from that of Queens', but additional chamber space
was obtained by making the chapel extend eastward
beyond the court. The whole of the buildings were
completed before the death of the Lady Margaret,
in 1509. Christ's, like Queens', which had been
erected in an even shorter time, was not the outcome
of centuries of evolution. It was planned by one
mind and executed at one time.

The two generations which came after the foundation
of King's had witnessed the establishment at Cambridge
of the four colleges of Queens', Saint Catherine's,
Jesus and Christ's. Within the same limit of time

and awkwardly near to one another, on the northern side of the Hospital area. Of these the northernmost was a building of the twelfth or early thirteenth century, originally divided by a screen into two parts, of which the eastern one was evidently a chapel. It is generally supposed, perhaps on insufficient evidence, that this building was the original infirmary of the Hospital. The other range was somewhat longer and a century later in date. It was similarly divided into two portions, of which the eastern was likewise a chapel. It would seem as though it was substituted for the earlier and ruder building, and served the same purposes in the Hospital. When the College court was built this chapel was re-edified and became the College chapel : the western end of the building was converted into a lodge for the Master, and the whole range occupied the northern side of the court. The so-called infirmary was utilised as a range of chambers, external to the court and approached from it by a circuitous passage at the east end of the chapel. ' The Labyrinth,' as it was known in college days, was no doubt the veritable home of Balsham's clerks and the scene of their wrangles with the Hospital brethren. In an unfortunate frenzy of megalomania, inspired by an occupant of the Lady Margaret's chair, who was also a canon in Balsham's cathedral, the College, in the year 1869, destroyed this venerable monument which linked the Lady Margaret's college with the Bishop's scholars, and at the same time it effaced its ancient chapel. Attached to the chapel was Fisher's chantry, in which he had intended that his body should be laid. Long previous desecration seemed to justify and invite its removal, and it shared the general demolition. " Glorious beyond all former time will be the fabric of our ancient House " was the curiously inapposite

GATE OF ENTRANCE, ST. JOHN'S COLLEGE

utterance of the eloquent divine who prompted the household of Saint John to obliterate the only material evidence of its primordial antiquity. " Ancient men who had seen the former house " may well have " wept with a loud voice " when the foundation of the new was laid.

The rest of the court was completed by 1520. It was somewhat larger than that of Christ's, on which it was closely modelled ; but brick, as at Queens', was the material employed, not clunch, as at Christ's. At the end of the century the growth of the college necessitated the building of a second court, the beautiful work of Ralf Symons. With its noble gallery, occupying the whole of the first floor on the north side, its gate-tower in the western range and the Master's tower in the north-west angle, it recalls the House of Pride, of which Spenser sang a few years before the court was built—

> A stately pallace built of squared bricke . . .
> High lifted up were many loftie towres,
> And goodly galeries far over laid,
> Full of faire windows and delightful bowres,
> And on the top a diall told the timely howres.

Trinity Hall and Queens' already had second courts, but that of Saint John's was the earliest which had four complete sides.

Here, in the year 1511, we stand on the confines of two worlds. The appointment of Erasmus to the Lady Margaret's readership in divinity, in that year, is the first streak of light revealing new and untrodden regions : but the daylight will not be yet. The old world has been invested with a setting splendour by the recent endowments of Margaret Beaufort. It is well and wisely governed by its Chancellor, Fisher, who is Bishop of Rochester and may be trusted to guide it in the safe walks of religious tradition. The monastic houses stand perpetual, as it might seem. They are a recognised element of the University, but yet are hardly in it. Monk and friar graduate in divinity according to ancient form ; but their studies and disputations are carried on in their own cloisters and halls. Cambridge teaches what it has always taught. The misty paths of *trivium* and *quadrivium* are un-illuminated by any acquaintance with literature, Latin, Greek or English. Cambridge has indeed discovered an English poet in John Skelton, and crowns him with laurel ; but not until the same honour has been paid to him at Oxford and in parts beyond sea. Also, because its own Latinity is noto-riously faulty, the University hires another ' poet,' an Italian named Caius Auberinus, to write its letters, at twenty pence a letter. The same official delivers lectures on Terence in long vacation, and receives 26s. 8d. from the University for each course. A lecturer on mathematics gets the same stipend : but mathematics are a ' post-graduate ' subject.

The hostels are as numerous and as full as ever ; but the discipline of the hostels is bad, and they are always fighting one another or somebody else. The Vice-Chancellor and doctors have a ' potacion ' over the settlement of a quarrel between Ovyng's Inn and Saint Hugh's Hostel in 1482. The proctors have to keep the peace between Saint Clement's and the other hostels in 1497. There is a fray between the men of Christ's College and Saint Nicholas' Hostel in 1508. In 1521 a violent assault is made on Gonville Hall by ' certain men of the northern faction,' belonging to Gerard's Hostel and Ovyng's Inn, both of which stood in Saint Michael's Lane, opposite to Gonville Hall. They burnt the postern gate, broke into the court, invaded the buttery, emptied all the beer-barrels, and would have carried off the silver plate had not the butler hidden it, some in a cask, some in the well. For which damage the raiders had to pay compensation. Such abuses are corrected by the colleges when they open their doors to ' pensioners,' not to the advantage of the poor scholars. The turbulence of the hostellers is bred of superior wealth. In 1550 it is complained that the hostellers " are fain to creep into colleges, and put poor men from bare livings."

So far, in 1511, fifteen colleges have come into being. The relative importance of these fifteen and of the hostels is shown by the scheme, devised in 1514, for the nomination of proctors. The colleges and hostels in rotation nominate two in each year, and a cycle of forty-four years is arranged. The electors are the Head and fellows in the colleges and the principals of the hostels. In the cycle the hostels have eleven turns : Pembroke, King's, Queens' and Saint John's each have eight : next come Peterhouse, Michaelhouse, Clare and Christ's, each with six : King's Hall, Gonville Hall, Corpus, Saint Catherine's and Jesus each have four turns, Buckingham College only one, and Trinity Hall is not represented.

A whole generation was to pass away after the foundation of Saint John's before another college was added to the fifteen already in existence. The flood which swept away the monasteries and at one time threatened to absorb the colleges also had begun to ebb in 1542, and in the rise of Magdalene we see the first tokens of an emerging world from which many old landmarks have disappeared. The Augustinian Priory at Barnwell and the four houses of the mendicant friars had gone down in the general dissolution, and

so utterly had their buildings vanished when Richard
Lyne made his plan of Cambridge, in 1574, that hardly
a vestige of any of them remained to mark their sites.
How Croyland first, and other Benedictine monasteries
afterwards, established students of their order in
Buckingham College the last chapter has told.   There
is much that is obscure in the later history of the
College, and, unless secular students, as well as monks,
were admitted to it, it is not easy to see how Sir Robert
Rede, Chief Justice of the Common Pleas in 1506, should
have been a student there.   In any case it was a
genuine college, not merely affiliated to the University,
as the friars' houses were.   The buildings were of
the collegiate pattern, and the thrifty founder of
Magdalene must have remarked with satisfaction
that he was not called upon to expend a penny in
alterations or additions.   There was neither cloister
nor common dormitory.   Hall, chapel, offices and
chambers stood in their usual places.   The only
difference from the typical plan, seen at Queens', is
that the chambers which were formerly the Prior's
and became the Master's lodge were not, as usual,
between hall and chapel but at the western end of
the hall.   The monks presumably went out in 1539,
and, as there is no evidence that their affairs were
mismanaged, the buildings were probably in decent
repair in 1542, when the scholars came in.

According to the charter of foundation the society
was to consist of a Master and eight fellows : but so
mean was the provision left for it by Audley in his
will (1544) that the number of the fellows was successively reduced to six and to four.   The dead hand
of the founder was heavy on the small community.
The mastership was to be for ever in the gift of the
possessor of the estate at Audley End, into the owner-

FISHERS' LANE, NEXT THE GREAT BRIDGE

ship of which Audley had crept after the dissolution
of Walden Abbey. Powers altogether tyrannical
were given to the Master, and he was not even called
upon to reside. Though the statutes were not drawn
up until many years after Audley's death, in these
particulars they seem to give effect to his wishes.
He died in 1544 and was buried at Walden in an altar-
tomb of black marble. " The stone is not harder,"
says Fuller, " nor the marble blacker than the heart
of him who lies beneath." By the University he
was remembered, not as its benefactor, but as the
corrupt and servile judge who did to death the noble
Fisher.

In 1545 an act was passed for the dissolution of
colleges and vesting their property in the King and
his successors. The courtiers, who had been fleshed
in the spoils of the monasteries, like ' wolves agape,'
as Archbishop Parker wrote, were baying for the possessions of the scholars. It was a time of sore discouragement in the University. In moving terms they
petitioned Queen Katherine Parr to stand their friend
with the King. Gently she replied to their urgency
that she had " attempted the King's majesty for
the stablishment of their livelihood and possessions " ;
and her prayers were listened to. In 1546 Henry lay
dying. Some solicitude for the future of his soul,
perhaps some compunction for Fisher's blood, may
have wrought with the dying King : certainly his
heart was stirred with pity for the poverty of the
University, which had served his turn so well in the
matter of the divorce, and with disgust at the rapacity
of his courtiers. A commission which had been
appointed in 1545 to inquire into the revenues of the
colleges revealed the fact that, with hardly an exception,
they were unequal to the necessary outgoings. Henry

exceeded those of any college, except King's and Saint John's, their buildings were confined, irregular and ill-adapted to the enlarged social requirements of the sixteenth century.

The present Great Court of Trinity has the appearance of having been designed at one time and by a single mind, as was the case at Queens'. As a matter of fact it is the outcome of sixty years of evolution, and the buildings which it contains range in date from the reign of Edward III to that of James I. Some portions of Michaelhouse probably exist in the chambers in the south-west angle of the court, next Trinity Lane ; and the walls of its hall are retained in the present butteries and combination-room. The new hall was not built until 1605, and until that time the old hall, kitchen and butteries of Michaelhouse served the college. The Michaelhouse range, containing the hall, was prolonged northwards in 1554, so as to complete the western side of the court ; but originally it was only carried as far as the present door of the Master's lodge. There it joined a range built at right angles to it, in 1554, which was carried eastwards as far as the gate-tower of Edward III. This tower had served as the entrance to the court of King's Hall, and was built about 1432 : it stood where the sundial now stands, between the Great Gate and the Master's lodge. The chapel was finished, as the date above the east window shows, in 1564, and occupied its present site. The eastern range and the southern range, extending as far as the chambers retained from Michaelhouse, were finished before 1599. Queen Elizabeth's gate-tower, in the southern range, bears on it the date 1597. The Great Gate, which is now the principal entrance to the College, had belonged to King's Hall, and was completed in 1535. Another

THE FOUNTAIN AND KING EDWARD III'S TOWER IN THE FIRST COURT,
TRINITY COLLEGE

portion of King's Hall survives in the range which
faces the bowling-green and extends northwards from
King Edward's gate-tower. After ages of degradation
this charming relic of the fourteenth century has
been recently rediscovered and restored to something
of its original form and beauty by the skill of Mr.
Caröe.

The lines of the ranges so far erected were dictated
by those of the buildings which were retained from
Michaelhouse, King's Hall and some of the incorporated hostels. The result, as shown in Lyne's plan
of 1574, was a very irregular court. The portion of
the northern range which stood between the lodge
and King Edward's gate was advanced much further
south than the chapel. Dr. Nevile, who was Master
from 1593 to 1615 and directed all the works, including the new hall, in those years conceived a bold
plan for correcting the irregularity and bringing the
court into harmony with the usual collegiate plan.
He took down King Edward's gate-tower and the
building between it and the lodge. He re-erected
the tower in its present position, at the west end of
the chapel, and built anew the north-western part of
the court, prolonging the western and northern ranges
so as to make the court quadrangular. This work,
which greatly enlarged the lodge, was done in 1600.
He added the conduit in the centre of the court in
1602. The water was and is supplied by an aqueduct
made in 1325 by the Franciscan friars for the
supply of their house, which then stood on the site
of Sidney College. King's Hall had obtained leave
to utilise it about the year 1434. Nevile's next
work was the erection of the northern and southern
ranges of the cloister court, which still goes by
his name. The western side, containing the library,

was added by Wren between 1675 and 1690. The stone used in the building of the Great Court came principally from the desolated house of the Franciscans.

The charter of Henry VIII (1546) specifies that the College is to consist of a Master and sixty fellows *and* scholars. The original statutes were drawn up in 1552; a revised code was issued in 1560. In the latter the society is said to consist of a Master, sixty fellows, sixty-nine scholars, sixteen sizars, six chaplains, six lay-clerks and ten boy choristers. Among officials of the College the statutes prescribe that there shall be nine lecturers or examiners.

It is evidence of the broad, national lines on which the Elizabethan reforms are drawn that, whereas the statutes of 1552 require that not more than three of the fellows shall be of the same county, in the revised code there is no such restriction as to locality either in the case of fellows or scholars. The only limitations of the power of free choice were the provisos that an undefined number of the scholars should be supplied by Westminster School, *if they were fit*— and the College did its best to restrict the number as much as possible—and that, other things being equal, preference should be given to candidates from places from which the College derived its revenues. This liberty of choice is quite a new feature in Cambridge statutes and marks a characteristic difference between Trinity and Saint John's. The rules which were general in the statutes of the smaller colleges, that not more than one fellow may be elected from any single county, and that the number of 'northerners' should equal that of 'southerners,' was, no doubt, originally intended to extend the range of selection

by precluding county and local cliques ; but in
process of time it had a directly contrary effect. Men
of ability either went unrewarded or were obliged to
migrate to other colleges if it happened that at their
own they were barred by the county limitation ;
and the smaller, less progressive counties and remoter
parts of England secured an unintentional preference.
Scotchmen, Irishmen and foreigners were altogether
excluded, unless a royal mandate was obtained for
their admission. County and school preferences were
always more marked at Oxford than at Cambridge,
and, from the circumstance that at Oriel there were no
such limitations, an Oriel fellowship came to be regarded as the blue ribbon of University distinction
at Oxford. More than to its numbers, wealth and
royal patronage the society of Trinity owed its
intellectual eminence and freedom from prejudice
to the absence of restriction in the selection of its
members.

The first statutes of Trinity (1552) have certain
other features which distinguish them from those of
the earlier foundations, and are symptomatic of a
changed conception of the function of a college in
relation to its junior members. Trinity is remarkable
for the large number of scholars maintained on its
foundation : they are more in number than the fellows.
This was the case at Christ's, but at no other college.
Elaborate provision is made for a teaching staff within
the College, and a schedule of the subjects of education
is drawn up which conforms to the new curriculum
of study which in the reign of Edward VI was substituted for the old routine prescribed for *trivium* and
quadrivium.

Pensioners, as well as scholars, are required to
submit themselves to the College rules of study, and

the same conditions are exacted for their admission
as for scholars. At Michaelmas there is an examination of candidates for admission, lasting two
days, in which they are required to show the extent
of their knowledge in Greek, Latin and other subjects.
All ' disciples '—the term is much more convenient
than its modern equivalent, ' persons *in statu pupillari* '
—must have a tutor, who is to supervise their education and morals, and to be responsible to the College
for their dues. This is the first recognition in college
statutes of the now familiar relationship of tutor
and pupil, though it had unquestionably existed earlier.
The total number of pensioners is restricted by the
regulation that no fellow is to have more than one
pensioner-pupil, except the President, who may have
four. Lectures take place in the morning. Those for
bachelors are given in the parlour, for undergraduates
in the hall. A ' master of the hall ' is to note the
attendance, diligence and proficiency of the disciples,
and to report thereon to the ' seniority.' If a disciple
does not attend regularly he ' loses his term.' There
are certain *quaesitores aulae*, called in the 1560 statutes
lectores, who are to see that their classes make progress
in the special subjects of Plato, Demosthenes and
Cicero.

The order of study is minutely prescribed. In
his first year the disciple reads dialectic and the
elements of Euclid : this is considered to be the best
introduction to Greek philosophy, for, as Plato writes,
μηδεὶς ἀγεωμέτρητος εἰσίτω. In his second year he
is engaged on logic ; in his third on ethics, politics
and rhetoric ; in his fourth on physical science. In
all these subjects Aristotle is the textbook. Afterwards
he joins the bachelor in the parlour, and in subsequent
years, until M.A., he revises and amplifies his know-

ledge of Aristotle. If he does not take the B.A. degree in due course he is 'sent down.' Besides lectures there are 'repetitions.' In the student's first year he translates Demosthenes into Latin and the orations of Cicero into Greek ; in the next year he similarly renders Plato and the philosophical works of Cicero. The third and fourth years are devoted to revision. The disciple must provide himself, within two years, with copies of Aristotle, Plato, Demosthenes, Cicero, a Greek Testament and a Bible in Latin. If he fails to do so he is removed from the College.

On Mondays, Wednesdays and Fridays there are declamations in the hall in English, Latin and Greek : the subjects to be discussed are posted in the hall at dinner-time. After admission to the M.A. degree in June, and until the following Michaelmas, the student is learning the elements of Hebrew. The sixteenth-century disciple possessed, or was expected to possess, an amazing gift of tongues. Except on occasions recognised by the statutes he is never to speak in any language but Greek, Latin or Hebrew : a fellow offending in this article is to be fined a half-penny ; a disciple is let off with a farthing. A Greek and a Latin play are to be acted each year at the College charges, and the master of the hall and the *quaesitores* are to superintend its production. On appointed feast-days every one has to write one copy of Greek verses and another of Latin, and post them up in the hall. Mercifully he is not required to write more than six lines of either.

An encyclopædic education truly ! Outside the specialised subjects of the faculties no study that was within the compass of sixteenth-century know-

CHAPTER VI

THE REFORMED COLLEGES

And they said, Let us rise up and build. So they strengthened their hands for this good work.—NEHEMIAH.

IN the autumn of the year 1558 an elderly man, small and bearded, might have been noticed wandering in the streets of Cambridge, looking in at new college gateways and penetrating to halls, chapels and parlours. His garb sufficiently distinguished him as a physician, and from his bearing one might conclude that he was of eminence in his profession—a man, perhaps, who had travelled and knew the minds and manners of many men, including kings ; evidently, one would say, no stranger to the University and town, though his wistful, puzzled looks show that they have become somehow strange to him. He is looking for old haunts and old faces that have long passed away. With Wordsworth he might have said—

It is not now as it has been of yore—
Turn wheresoe'er I may,
By night or day,
The things which I have seen I now can see no more.

He turns out of the High Street and passes down Saint Michael's Lane, where the workmen are pulling down Physwick Hostel to make room for the court of Trinity. At the gate of Gonville Hall he stops, and his eyes rest with a sense of familiarity on the ancient building that confronts him. It is just as it was in his freshman days, some thirty years ago. There, to his right, is the building of blackened and weather-worn clunch where Gonville quartered his scholars two centuries ago, a structure that was old even in that far-gone time—more ancient than Peterhouse itself. He turns into the court and looks around him. Chapel, lodge, hall, library—they are all unchanged, but they are extraordinarily dilapidated, in painful contrast with the bran-new buildings that are being put up at the college over the way, Trinity. The courts are ' a stable of Augeas ' for filth. Their pavement is broken and uneven ; cattle wander in at the gate, which has no bar to fasten it. He looks inside the chapel, and there he finds unwelcome change. He can remember how in his undergraduate days the Butley monks from Suffolk sat in the stalls above him. ' Altar-pillows ' and frontlets ' with the salutation of Our Lady wrought in gold '—these, too, he remembers well. Now the chapel utensils have been turned to private uses, and vestments serve to cover beds. Slatternly neglect under Mary has completed the ruin begun by Puritanism under Edward. Possibly there are old faces still about the College that were young when the stranger was a college ' lad.' Possibly the janitor recognises him as a former fellow, and, if we ask him, will tell us that it is master doctor Caius, the renowned London physician.

Caius left Cambridge in 1539, studied at Padua for four years, and then travelled in various foreign lands, ransacking libraries in search of ancient MSS. Then he returned to England, set up in practice in London, was chosen President of the College of Physicians and professionally attended Edward VI, Mary and

Of course he remembers the Augustinian Priory at Barnwell and the four Houses of the friars, which, he says, were regarded in some sense as hostels, and he exactly describes the garb of each order. He recalls how in his time the graduation ceremonies, in summer and winter, since transferred to Saint Mary's Church, took place in the Franciscans' hall. He describes the scene presented on such an occasion in the days of his youth. A great wooden ' theatre ' was put up. On one side visitors looked on ; on the other the doctors disputed ; in the middle sat the rest of the University, as in an arena or valley. In winter the newly made bachelors wore laurel wreaths, as a mark that they had conquered the difficulties of their profession, and he fancifully derives the title of baccalaureus from the garland then worn. In summer the wreaths were of roses or other flowers. " In my youth," he says, " no one, whatever his rank, presumed, even in salutation, to bare his head or remove his cap, which was esteemed the mark of approved merit. Now, alas ! roses and flowers are scorned and we parade our wealth by a display of chains and ornaments of gold."

Nothing is more deplored by the good doctor than the change in dress and the marks of luxury which he sees all about him. But one thing he confesses that he can hardly credit, were it not that he has it on the testimony of John Mayor of Scotland, who was a student at God's House in the last years of the preceding century. Then it was the fashion of the students, on account of their perpetual frays with the townsmen, to carry bows and swords in the streets. Since Caius' own student days manners have lamentably decayed. Then every graduate walked abroad wearing a hood and a large, long and flowing gown, and a square cap on his head. When the masters were to dispute in the schools they went thither preceded by the bedells and each attended by all the members of his college—whom he had first entertained at a frugal breakfast—every man decently clad in the habit of his academic rank. Nobody went about wasting money in wine-shops and taverns; indeed, wine was unknown, except at the greater feasts. Games were only permitted as a relaxation from study: the Christmas play-acting was amusement enough. Now the old simplicity is gone. College fare is extravagant, chambers are luxuriously furnished. One sees students with frilled shirts, baggy trunk-hose and tight nether-stocks. They actually wear round caps or, worse still, hats, even at disputations. They dice, and go about the streets ' jetting ' at night, though the practice is strictly forbidden by the University statutes. These are things sadly ominous to Dr. Caius, preparing to take his leave of Cambridge and the world in 1573. The philosophy of clothes meant much to the sixteenth century—always means much to a University. The black morning coat, universal half a century ago, lives on in the ceremony of degree-taking, though the ' scholar ' of to-day has no such raiment in his wardrobe and borrows or hires it for the occasion. It seems only yesterday that the reverend Master of a college was vigilant in hunting down in his courts the wearers of brown boots, and that, at another college, the wearing of a boating ' blazer ' was strictly forbidden in its precincts.

The college which Caius reconstituted in 1557 at the present day somewhat insistently claims to be known by the full designation given to it by him, Gonville and Caius College. It is right that it should do so; for, unlike Henry VIII in his work at Trinity,

Caius did not destroy in order to recreate. The negligent master and fellows of Gonville Hall were retained in their places in the new foundation, and though the ancient buildings that enclosed Gonville's court were in a sordid state of decay, the natural piety, or the lack of means, of the founder forbade their demolition. They were simply repaired without structural alteration. On their southern side he built a new court or 'college,' as he called it, the present Caius Court, closed on the north by the lodge and chapel of Gonville Hall, and flanked on the east and west by new ranges of chambers. In his statutes Dr. Caius decreed, with a regard for sanitation in advance of his age, that no building should ever be placed on the southern side of his court, 'lest the air, from being confined within a narrow space, should become foul and dangerous.' Though Caius is more town-bound and its population has grown more intensely, perhaps, than that of other colleges, the founder's direction is piously and wisely observed to this day. The example of a three-sided court, in design, at least, foreign to the earlier colleges, was copied at Sidney and Emmanuel, and in Neville's Court at Trinity.

On the east of the college, towards Trinity Street, Dr. Caius purchased from Trinity a large site which at first was left vacant, but in the next century was used for the erection of Tree Court. The ancient gate of Gonville Hall, in Saint Michael's Lane, remained until the eighteenth century, but Caius made entrances to the new part of his college on its eastern and southern sides. In the High Street stood the Gate of Humility, which did not then open on a court. An avenue of trees conducted from it to the interior college portal, variously styled the Gate of Virtue or the Gate of Wisdom. A third gate, of an enriched and charming

GATE OF HONOUR AND TOWER OF GATE OF VIRTUE, CAIUS COLLEGE

design, the Gate of Honour, served as exit in the direction of the University Schools, which stood on the opposite side of the street, then called Caius Street, now Senate House Passage—a blind lane, blocked by houses at the High Street end.   We have seen that Queen Elizabeth's Gate at Trinity, occupying a similar relative position to that of the Gate of Honour at Caius, but built some twenty years later, was called Porta Honoris.   The allegory was a graft of medieval fancy, characteristic of the English side of Caius, but the architecture was of the newest Renaissance, which he had admired in Italy.   The gate and its even more satisfying fellow of Virtue have an interest beyond their beauty as showing the first conscious adoption of a foreign model in Cambridge architecture.

It was not Italian art only which Caius revealed to Cambridge.   From Padua, he imported the new science of Anatomy, which he had studied under the eminent Vesalius.   Gonville had intended that his fellows should principally study Theology; Bateman made his favourite subjects of the Canon and Civil Law alternative to Theology.   Caius in his statutes ordained that two of the three fellowships which he added to the old foundation should be attached to the study of Medicine.   From such an apparently small acorn grew the tree of science which, after centuries of maturing, might now seem to overshadow the University and grapple its foundations with its roots.   If small, the endowment was nevertheless notable for its novelty in 1557, and for its results in the half-century which followed.   William Harvey, greatest of England's anatomists, passed out to the Schools through the Gate of Honour in 1597.

Before the days of Caius Medicine had hardly been recognised among Cambridge studies : Anatomy not

8

at all. Law, Canon and Civil, was a permitted branch of learning for the fellows at most of the colleges, and was compulsory on nearly all at Trinity Hall. As a subject of practical concern to the State it was deliberately fostered by the Government. So lately as 1549 it had been proposed by a royal commission to unite Trinity Hall and Clare in a single college of Civil Law. Medicine was almost ignored in college statutes. Trinity was the first foundation in which any fellowships—they were two in number—were actually reserved to it. At Saint John's a lectureship of Physic had been endowed in some sort by Linacre in 1524; and the Regius Professorship of Physic was established in 1540. Until the last days of Henry VIII students ambitious to profit in Medicine almost necessarily crossed the sea for their training. The original members of the College of Physicians, incorporated in 1518, were all, like Linacre and Caius, graduates of foreign universities—Padua, Montpellier or Leyden. In the first forty-two years of the sixteenth century only one M.D. degree was taken at Cambridge. In the following forty-seven years no less than sixty-three proceeded to that degree. From the days of Caius there has never been ' any lack of persons duly qualified' in physic and surgery at Cambridge. Medicine brought natural science in its train. Francis Bacon matriculated at Trinity in the same year in which Caius died.

With kindly, rugged Caius, most human of college-founders, Cambridge parted in circumstances sad and dishonouring to itself. There is a passage in his History which he must have written just before his death with conscious reference to the disgraceful usage which he had experienced at the hands of colleagues whom he had richly benefited.

Nicholas Metcalfe, master of Saint John's, enriched the annual revenues of his college to the extent of four hundred marks, through the pious liberality of good men, which by his diligence he procured : a man not unlearned, a marvellous lover of learned men and the students' friend. Hot coals and hatred were his reward. In his old age his colleagues drove him out. Breed puppies and you will raise wolves.

Take that passage in connection with the old man's story of his own treatment by the fellows who lived on his bounty. The words are bitter ; but how much of bitterness do they leave unsaid !

On the 13th of December, 1572, all the ornaments of the College were torn and cut to shreds by the private authority of Thomas Bynge, Vice-Chancellor, as he said himself. [An erasure after this line suggests that an anathema on the offender was deleted by the doctor's dying hand.] To him nothing was so detestable as the name and image of Christ crucified, the Blessed Mary and the Holy Trinity. Outrageously he treated them, cutting them in pieces, casting them in the fire, and assailing them with horrible names and epithets. It was done at the instigation of some ill-disposed fellows of the College. Some of them held an entertainment to screen the affair ; others watched all night to prevent their preservation or removal in the darkness. Some of them God has removed by death ; others in various ways He has taken away and disgraced. They took great pains to dissemble their offence, and laid all the blame on one Dinsdall, a pensioner of the College, though they were themselves the movers of the wickedness. Present at the fire from midnight until three o'clock were the same Thomas Bynge, John Whitegifte, Master of Trinity, and William Gode, Provost of King's. Finally, what they could not burn they broke and defaced with hammers. Such was their heat against religion that neither personal benefit nor gratitude for the University could persuade them to spare books or building.

So six months later Caius lays down the ungrateful burden of the mastership. A month later he orders the preparation of his tomb in the chapel. In the same month of July, ' burdened with years and infirmity, waiting God's will,' he lays himself down to die. Under the tabernacle of the Annunciation of the Blessed Mary, as he had given direction, his bones were laid ;

and an immense concourse of the University attended him to the grave. *Vivit post funera Virtus*. The genius of the good man lives on in the college, which to-day aptly perpetuates the combined humanism and scientific learning of its founder.

The reconstitution of Gonville's college (1557) is separated from the foundation of Emmanuel (1584) by just over a quarter of a century. What a flood of change swept over Cambridge and England in the interval! John Caius, the Catholic, and Walter Mildmay, the Puritan, stand out as sea-marks on either side of it. On that side are the green fields of humanist culture, the broadening lights of science, the warm colours of religion with the overcasting shadows of ancient prejudice ; on this side we see dull Genevan flats, the quickset hedges and narrow plots of religious particularists, a seminary for their sun. The Protestant Reformation, we say, was the emancipation of thought ; and such, in its beginning, it unquestionably was, though we are apt to forget that the new birth of secular learning had its share in the work. But it may be questioned whether the emancipation was not more than completed at Cambridge when Elizabeth became queen. Afterwards religious thought became anarchic, and had to be put in a very strait waistcoat by Chancellor Burleigh. It wandered in dry places of dogmatism with very little profit to religion, the nation or the University. Always it was in scarcely concealed revolt against the Elizabethan settlement and the authority which enforced it. Only the external pressure of Mary of Scotland and Philip of Spain forced the University into any kind of cohesion. National feeling and government constraint held it together; but for them, it would have dropped into dust.

That the period between 1557 and 1584 was one of extraordinary growth at the universities is indisputable. The number of B.A. degrees taken at Cambridge in any year prior to 1560 was never more than fifty ; in 1584 they exceeded two hundred. New wealth, new studies, new national fervour and the reaction from Marian repression all helped to raise the University to a greatness in numbers and in fame which it had never known before ; and unquestionably, so long as the nation was of one mind in its protest against foreign domination in religion, the Protestant university stood high in its favour. But it is note-worthy that, though Emmanuel itself was crowded with students from the time when it opened its doors, yet the annual total of degrees in the University per-ceptibly declined after 1584. It rose again and reached a point unsurpassed for two hundred years afterwards, when Anglicanism, under Laud, offered itself as a religious type which, for all its narrowness, had some claim to be national. It fell disastrously after 1662, when Anglican subscription barred the doors of the University to Nonconformity. It rose with leaps and bounds after all disqualifications of creed were removed in 1871.

What is the conclusion ? The nation has always looked to its universities that they shall be in the widest sense national. With a university limiting itself to class or creed it has very faint sympathy. Certainly it asks for the influences of religion and the training of its ministers ; certainly also it does not want the preferential treatment of any sect. And what is true of the University is not less true of its constituent members, the colleges. Sectarian ardour founds colleges to promote its limited aims : it wastes its pains. The ardour which comes from without the academic body makes no heat within. At Cambridge the same blood must circulate in all the arteries of the University ; the transfused element will perish of attenuation, or it will be assimilated.

The ardour of the promoters of Emmanuel carried the college far in the first two generations of its existence. In 1644 eighty-one admissions were recorded at the college ; there were but nine in the same year at Saint John's. And in the narrow walks of Calvinistic theology its members showed a zeal and learning which should have been exemplary to other colleges. It is no small glory to the ' pure house ' that among its fellows the Parliament, in 1644, was able to discover not less than seven men of sufficient capacity to fill the places of ejected masters at other colleges. But the effort of parturition was fatal to the parent. Prosperity and pietism equally disappeared before the Restoration, and the first endeavour of Sancroft, appointed to the mastership in 1662, was to divest the society ' of that former singularity which rendered it so unhappily remarkable.'

Emmanuel has proved itself worthier than its founder's intentions. Divested of ' singularity ' it takes its rank among the foremost of the free colleges of Cambridge. But its foundation was a mistake. It was a mistake because Mildmay intended his college solely for ordination candidates—a limitation foreign to the conception of a college or university. It was a mistake because it exploited the University to promote sectional interests, and it gave an ill precedent for the reprisals of 1662. Also the establishment of a separatist college in 1584 had no reasonable justification. Many of the existing colleges—and notably Mildmay's own college, Christ's—were advanced posts of Puritan theology, and offered guarantees that

Calvinistic views would be respected in education.
It is difficult to see in his design anything but a timid
suspicion of the breadth of academic culture.   Equally
he is suspicious of the morals of the young ' sons of
the prophets.'   A system of espionage is fostered by
the statutes.   One or two of the fellows, at least
twice a week and at night, are to visit the scholars'
chambers and ' carefully examine what they are
doing.'   Playing, feasting, talking is to be stopped ;
the ' idle gossip of youths ' is ' waste of time ' and
' a bad habit for young minds.'   Offenders are to be
whipped by the Dean-catechist.   Besides chapel attendance and ' frequent hearing of sermons ' every
undergraduate and bachelor must attend his tutor's
prayers each night at 8 p.m.   At 3 p.m. on each
Sabbath day the Dean is to lecture on some article
of the Christian faith, and to catechise all the inmates
of the College.

Of the original buildings of Emmanuel little has to
be said.   The site acquired was that lately occupied
by the house and grounds of the Dominican or Preacher
Friars; but it does not appear that, beyond foundations,
any pre-existing structures were incorporated in the
College buildings.   There were two original quad-
rangles.   The smaller one, on the northern side,
contained the gate of entrance, which was in Emmanuel
Lane : two passages gave communication between
this and the larger court.   The south side of the
entrance court was occupied by the hall and lodge ;
the western range contained the kitchen and chambers ;
the chapel, now the library, was in the eastern range,
and was perversely set north and south ; the northern
side, next Emmanuel Lane, was left open.   The
larger court also had only three ranges.   The new
chapel, on the eastern side of this court, with its

picturesque cloister supporting the Master's gallery, was the work of Christopher Wren (1668-1672). Its central position in the eastern side of the quadrangle, independent of the ranges of the court and projecting eastwards from it, as well as its colonnade, was obviously copied from Peterhouse chapel, built just forty years earlier by Wren's uncle, Dr. Matthew Wren. Matthew Wren also employed his nephew as the architect of the new chapel which he erected at Pembroke in 1663-1665. The chapel of Pembroke closely resembles that of Emmanuel. Bishop Wren had been Master successively of Peterhouse and Pembroke, and for eighteen years (1642-1660) was imprisoned in the Tower by Parliament. His length of days—he lived to eighty-two—enabled him to take part in the last effort of decaying Gothic and the erection of the first chapel at Cambridge designed after the new Italian pattern. The change in architectural taste was indicative of a profounder change of ideas which penetrated the University after 1660. From indigenous English sentiment and the continuous tradition of centuries it broke away. Henceforth the freemason builder disappears from Cambridge, and his place is taken by the travelled architect who borrows his designs from the palaces of Italian nobles. The squire's or parson's son, familiar with the darkness and inconvenience of his Gothic home, had little comfort in the cold refinement of his new college chamber, and the superior elegance of the foreign architecture did not reconcile his father to the loss of old, homely associations. So the spirit of the University, like its architecture, ceased to be national ; and, when the life that informed the foreign art ebbed out in the course of the eighteenth century, the pulse of Cambridge beat very faintly indeed.

ENTRANCE COURT, EMMANUEL COLLEGE

The foundation of Sidney Sussex (1596) followed hard upon that of Emmanuel. As in the case of Emmanuel, the site chosen for it had been previously occupied by a house of Mendicants. The only remaining relic of the once stately abode of the Grey Friars at the time when the site was procured for Sidney was an old building used as a malthouse. The property, consisting of about six acres of land, had been granted to Trinity in 1546, eight years after the Dissolution, and by that college it was, and remains, leased to Sidney for ever for an annual rent of £13, 6s. 8d.

Sidney was the latest example of a Cambridge college founded by a noble lady. It does not appear that her beneficence had been solicited by any member of the University. Frances Sidney was married to Leicester's rival, the Earl of Sussex ; she was the aunt of the famous Sir Philip Sidney. She died in 1589, and by her will left a sum of £5000, together with all her unbequeathed estate, for the purpose of founding a college, to be called ' the Lady Frances Sidney Sussex College,' and for maintaining in it a Master, ten fellows and twenty scholars. Henry Gray, Earl of Kent, and Sir John Harrington were the executors appointed to supervise the work of founding the College. They gave statutes to it in 1598. The Sidney statutes are closely copied from those of Emmanuel, which they follow in most things to the letter. The same expressions as in the Emmanuel code are used to designate the purpose which the College is to serve. It is to be a ' seminary ' for the education of candidates for ordination. Mildmay's scriptural comparison of his college with the schools of the sons of the prophets at Naioth, Bethel, etc., is exchanged for the more rhetorical similes of a nursery-garden, a hive, a peach tree perennially putting forth fruit and flower. Again we meet with the catechising Dean, the sempiternal sermons, the patrolling of the students' chambers and all the sanctimonious tyranny of Mildmay's statutes. The scholars must purpose ordination; the Master on election must declare his whole-hearted abhorrence and detestation of Popery—an expression which was to become memorable in the days of James II, when a Popish Master was thrust upon the College.

In its buildings also Sidney imitated the model of Emmanuel. The builder employed at both colleges was Ralf Symons; but Symons' work at both colleges was of less durable kind than his masterpiece at Saint John's, and much of it had presently to be removed or rebuilt. As at Emmanuel, one side, that next Sidney Street, was merely fenced by a wall, which contained the gate of entrance, and there was no tower. As was the case at Emmanuel four turrets occupied the angles of the quadrangle. With the same perversity as at Emmanuel the chapel was turned north and south. It was constructed out of the old malthouse, which possibly had originally been the refectory of the Franciscans, and stood outside the court, projecting from its S.E. angle. Over the chapel was the library. The funds at the disposal of the executors of the Lady Sidney's will were so scanty that some contrivance was necessary to obtain all the constituent parts of a college. The Master's lodge, in the eastern wing, was placed on an upper floor above the buttery and kitchen. But the hall in the same wing extended to the full height of the range. It will be observed that Emmanuel and Sidney are the only colleges of the older foundation which completely disregard the traditional college plan. The practical common sense of that plan is shown by the fact that both colleges in process of time had to re-adapt their arrangements.

In this chapter I shall complete the story of college-founding at Cambridge, though, to do so, I must take flights over large tracts of time and make descent at widely-spaced intervals.   The seventeenth and eighteenth centuries saw the rise of no new college at Cambridge.   At Oxford four colleges, Wadham, Pembroke, Worcester and Hertford, came into being in those centuries.   The long interval of time between the foundation of Sidney and that of Downing points to a change in the class of the benefactor rather than to a stoppage in the flow of benefactions to the University.   Not even the Reformation period was more actively interested in the Universities than the first two-thirds of the seventeenth century, nor was the area wider from which new endowment was supplied.   But the old sources were completely dried up.

Protestantism supplied none of the compelling motives for meritorious works that were an engine in the hands of men like Fisher.   The monastic spoils were dissipated.   The vast wealth of the dignitaries of the medieval Church was unknown to their married successors after the Reformation.   The Stuart kings had neither wealth nor will to endow learning.   For the well-being of the Universities the new courtiers showed as complete a disregard as the old nobility had done.   The Countess of Sussex was the last of the line of noble women who gave their wealth to found colleges; and the tenuity of her endowment of Sidney was an indication that that vein too was well-nigh exhausted.

Endowment on the grand scale was a thing of the

past. But endowment of a smaller kind and by humbler persons was commoner in the seventeenth century than at any previous time, and the cumulative result of the benefactions was hardly less than that of the ambitious work of great founders. From the Reformation onwards education and learning are the concern of the untitled gentry or the professional and merchant classes—such men as Caius and Mildmay at Cambridge and all the post-Reformation founders of colleges at Oxford. At Cambridge their work was to enrich the existing colleges—in most cases from gratitude for personal benefit derived from them ; to make provision for a teaching staff in the University or, more often, in the colleges ; especially to help poor men with scholarships. This last business had generally occupied a very subordinate place in the medieval scheme. The poor scholar in early days obtained the means of education by begging in vacations, by menial service at Cambridge or by the assistance of a rich patron. In the seventeenth century it is the class which itself has benefited by Cambridge training and the men who, as students, have known poverty themselves or seen it in their college ' chums ' who lend the helping hand. It was natural and, in those days, not unwise to give a personal character to such benefits and to confine them to a particular class, locality or school. To the University the stimulus of such endowment and the intimate relations which it fostered with those sections of the community which were most concerned in what concerned the University outweighed in value the gifts of princes. The springs of it were perennial so long as the University remained in close touch with the thriving middle class. The dignity and independence of the learner were guaranteed. Even the local distribution of the benefits had this advantage that, while no great monopoly was created, such as that of Eton at King's, the University cast its nets over the whole area of the kingdom.

Sir George Downing, of Gamlingay, in the county of Cambridge, by his will, dated in 1717, directed that, in the event of the failure of certain trusts created in the will, his estate should be applied to the foundation of a college at Cambridge, to be called Downing's College. He died in 1749, and the devisees named in the trusts were all dead, without issue, in 1764 ; but litigation delayed the foundation of the college until 1800. The statutes were given in 1805. Certain trustees appointed in the charter of foundation purchased from the town a site consisting of thirty acres in the common ground then known as Saint Thomas' Leys, and buildings on a grandiose scale ' in the Grecian style ' were begun ; but the college was not open for residence until 1821. It was to consist of a Master, two professors—one of Medicine, the other of the Laws of England—sixteen fellows—of whom the statutes absurdly required that fourteen should necessarily be laymen, the other two necessarily in orders—and only six scholars. The endowments of the college were preposterously over-estimated by the trustees, and fabulous sums were expended in the erection of the buildings. The most extravagant expectations were excited by the new foundation. In architectural splendour it was to surpass all its predecessors, and in size its quadrangle was to exceed the Great Court of Trinity. ' Grand ' is the epithet which at the time was constantly bestowed in anticipation on the work of Wilkins, the architect, and the college was to form ' a principal feature in the view of Cambridge from the London Road ' Maria Edgeworth, when she visited Cambridge in 1813, went to view it as one of the 'lions'; but she confesses that she 'was sadly disappointed; it will never bear comparison with King's College chapel.' The quadrangle, pictured and described in books such as Le Keux's *Memorials of Cambridge*, was never half completed. The library and chapel, the Propylæum—no less a name would serve the gate of entrance—the stately colonnades that should have lined the court remain to this day an unrealised dream, and the material attraction of Downing lies in sylvan charm. The endowment proved utterly inadequate for the maintenance of a society reduced much below the numbers contemplated in the charter.

So Downing remains an unfortunate torso, as King's once did. But, in spite of its diminished opportunities, it has taken a place in the family of colleges which is honourable and unique. By the two professorships attached to it, Downing has got an impress distinct from any other college, and in law and medicine it may reasonably boast of many distinguished names. The Regius Professorships which Henry VIII linked with Trinity, no doubt, gave the suggestion for the similar connection at Downing. Recent legislation has extended the principle, while admitting some latitude of choice, to all the colleges of the University; and at this day nobody will question that the advantage given to the colleges by their association with the professoriate is even greater than the gain to the University by the employment of fellowships as a subvention to its teaching funds.

With Downing ends the series of Cambridge colleges. It is likely that the future development of the University will be mainly on the lines of college organisation

DOWNING COLLEGE

as first laid down by Balsham. But the last fifty years
have witnessed departures which, though new to our
times, are in reality a reversion to the practice of
an age earlier than Balsham's. The non-collegiate
system, established in 1869, presents some, but not all,
of the features of university life in its primitive stage.
The hostels, public and private, which have established
themselves from time to time since the statutes of
1858 in their loose attachment to the University
recall the *hospicia* of the thirteenth century, of which
the colleges were a development, but they adapt
themselves to students of another type than the
' hosteller ' of the Middle Ages. In the theological
colleges of various denominations which tend to gather
about the University nucleus it is not fanciful to see
a resemblance to the houses of monk and friar which
derived advantage from the proximity of the University
while they asserted their independence of it. The
superior equipment and prestige of the colleges condemned these medieval experiments in free study
first to comparative sterility, finally to extinction.
The same fate has attended some of the modern
experiments in the same line, and ages of experience,
or, it may be, prejudice make their establishment
more difficult and their existence more precarious
than in days when colleges were themselves experimental. The private hostel system was directed to
securing either economy in living or more direct
tuition in subjects, such as medicine, which at the
time were neglected in the college routine. So far
as they aimed at the latter purpose, they resembled
the Hospicia Juristarum of antiquity ; but the
hosteller of old was a man of ampler means than his
fellow-student in college. The private hostels failed
to perpetuate themselves because the colleges presently

recognised their duty of combining economy and efficiency, and a like fate overtook the later experiment, on similar lines, of the first public hostel, Cavendish College. Another public hostel, Selwyn, established in 1882, recommends itself on the double ground of economy and exclusive attachment to the Church of England. It has no endowment, but it has grown and thriven and supplies a need which is perhaps more recognised outside the limits of the University than within it. It is the merit of the College that its attachment to a denomination has not entailed restriction to a section of it. Wisdom is to be gathered from the history of Emmanuel. In the twentieth century, more than in the seventeenth, the freest interchange of views is most healthful. The University has nothing to do with party segregations, and asks only for a frank acceptance of its gifts. Over each college gate might be inscribed the motto which met Britomart on the portals of Busyrane, ' Be bold,' though the interior court may bear the qualifying admonition, ' Be not too bold.'

The non-collegiate system will live and grow. It supplies, without condition or restriction, the best that the University can give on terms which as yet are not open to the unendowed student of a college. It is of the essence of University life, of which life the colleges are accidents. At present its usefulness is hampered by lack of endowment. When this is supplied its sphere will not be less splendid than that of the colleges.

So the wheel is come full circle, and Cambridge ends to-day with the same conditions and problems with which it began in Plantagenet times. But one problem is new, and asks a solution. Cambridge was the first residential University to open its teaching and examinations to women-students. Girton College, originally started in a private house at Hitchin, in 1869, was transferred to its present site in 1872. Courses of lectures for women were begun at Cambridge in 1870, and a house for resident students was opened in the town in the following year. In connection with the latter movement an Association for Promoting the Higher Education of Women at Cambridge was formed in 1873, and in 1875 a Hall of residence at Newnham was completed and occupied. Both of the women's colleges have vastly expanded since then, and their success has far more than justified the expectations of their promoters. Each has received gifts, either in buildings or in endowment, which testify to the enthusiasm of their supporters and the splendid service rendered by the colleges ; and each is now fairly equipped with rewards for the learner and stipends for the teacher. Some impatience is expressed—mainly in circles which are not acquainted with the circumstances—that the original concessions of the University have not been followed up by the grant of degrees. It should fairly be borne in mind that the education of women-students at Cambridge is in many cases rendered possible by its cheapness, and that the greater cheapness of the women's colleges is largely due to the circumstance that they are exempted from the University taxation which falls upon the men's colleges and the men-students individually. If the more or less shadowy grievance of the degree were removed the imposition of that burden on the women's colleges, though logic, justice and the needs of the University would demand it, would constitute a ground of complaint more serious and injurious to the cause of women's education. Girton and Newnham have the reality, and they are strong enough to

9

dispense with the unsubstantial and costly tinsel of the degree.

Vastly the colleges have grown in their numbers, their buildings, their educational equipment since the reform of their statutes in 1858. But they would ill have adapted themselves to the needs of the day had reform been limited to the narrow circuit of the instruction which they could separately supply. The reforms of 1858, like those of Elizabeth, removed the worst abuses and limitations which hampered them in their individual spheres. The new statutes of 1882 recreated the University and emancipated the parent from thraldom to its children. Thirty years ago it was said by an eminent Cambridge professor that you could not see the University for the colleges ; and from the educational as well as the material standpoint the saying was true. Before then private tutors largely usurped the place which should have been filled by lecturers and professors ; and, except the comparatively few whose courses had some relation to degree studies, professors had few undergraduate auditors. In the eighteenth century many of them were non-resident : others, who were resident, did not lecture. Gray, the poet, never once lectured as Professor of Modern History. Watson, who from 1782 to 1816 combined the Regius Professorship of Divinity with the bishopric of Llandaff, lived chiefly at Windermere, and appointed a hack to perform his lectures. Infirmity or the excuse that there was no available classroom was accepted as valid ground for the pretermission of the duties of a chair. When Edward Daniel Clarke was appointed to the new Professorship of Mineralogy in 1808 there was no place for him to lecture in : so Martyn, Professor of Botany, obligingly gave up to him his room

NEWNHAM COLLEGE

in the Botanical Garden, which he did not require himself.

Before 1860 experimental science, other than in physics, was almost entirely excluded from the under-graduate's course of study. Charles Darwin, who resided at Christ's from 1828 to 1831, said that the study of Paley's *Evidences of Christianity* was the only part of the academical course which was of the least use to him in the education of his mind. Francis Bacon, in his *Advancement of Learning*, recognised a main defect of university education in his day.

Certain it is that unto the deep, fruitful and operative use of many sciences, specially natural philosophy and physic, books be not only the instrumentals. . . . There will hardly be any main proficience in the disclosing of nature except there be some allow-ance for expenses about experiments, whether they be experiments appertaining to Vulcanus or Daedalus, furnace or engine, or any other kind. And therefore, as secretaries and spials of princes and states bring in bills for intelligence, so you must allow the spials and intelligencers of nature to bring in their bills : or else you shall be ill advertised.

Not until Bacon had been more than two centuries in his grave did the University appreciate the wisdom of his counsel. Not until the scientific hegemony had altogether passed away from the older universities did Cambridge awake to its neglect of the knowledge which is not supplied by books alone. To the influence of Darwin and the present example of three of its professors, Sedgwick, Henslow and Humphry, it owes its rehabilitation in the kingdom which was peculiarly its own in the days of Caius, Harvey and Ray. The solitary lecture-room in the Old Botanic Garden has given place to the vast and ever-growing mansions of science, mechanical and natural : and in the grounds of Downing, where the torch of the New Learning was faintly re-lit in 1800, a Salomon's

House has risen, ampler and more splendid than that of the philosophers of Atlantis, as pictured by Bacon, whose end was ' the enlarging of the bounds of human empire, to the effecting of all things possible.'

CHAPTER VII

ERASMUS AND THE REFORMATION

> That glorious time
> When learning, like a stranger come from far,
> Sounded through Christian lands her trumpet, roused
> Peasant and king.
>
> WORDSWORTH

THE city of Bristol doubtless has its historians. Doubtless their hint has been to speak of the first settlement of the town, the rise of its commercial importance, the growth of its municipal liberties, its early rivalries with trading neighbours. The outlines of their work are so far sufficiently indicated to them. After 1497 a problem of some vagueness presents itself :—How far does the discovery and occupation of the American continent enter into the history of Bristol city ? Local patriotism may hesitate to claim for Bristol the merit of the enterprise of the Venetian Cabot.

At about the same date a similar problem suggests itself in the history of Cambridge University. Before 1500 let the candid historian admit that no very glorious things are to be spoken of it. Among the great educational adventurers of Europe it is a small trader. Oxford—not in the first rank of European universities—yet far surpasses it in lustre, and can claim a national consequence which as yet does not belong to Cambridge. And not Oxford only, but neighbour provincial towns, such as Bury Saint Edmunds, eclipse it in point of material splendour. In the half-century which follows this is all changed. Cambridge is trading its wares to lands unexplored by Oxford. At Oxford itself the staple of Cambridge scholars is set up in the cathedral-college of Christ Church, and what Balsham borrowed from Merton is repaid with more than interest to Wolsey. It is a Cambridge doctor who brings together the universities of Christendom to pronounce verdict on the Papal authority in the matter of King Henry's divorce. Henceforth Cambridge is assured of foremost rank among European universities. It steps into the place hitherto held by Oxford and holds it unchallenged for a century after the Reformation. Cambridge statesmen, Burleigh, Walsingham, Wentworth, Cromwell, for a century will control the nation's affairs. Cambridge divines, Cranmer, Parker, Grindal, Whitgift, Bancroft, for a century will occupy the See of Canterbury in a succession which is only broken by the interregnum of the Oxford Cardinal Pole. New worlds of science will be discovered by Cambridge explorers, Bacon and Harvey. Thomas Smith, Ascham and Cheke will transfer to Cambridge the primacy in Greek scholarship which Selling, Grocyn and Linacre first brought to Oxford. From Spenser to Milton it might almost be said that all the fresh springs of English verse were in Cambridge. Let there be no arrogancy in the boast. The spark that lit this lustre came from other lands, and *Non nobis* is a psalm which Cambridge need not be ashamed to repeat. To Erasmus Cambridge owes something more than Bristol to John Cabot.

The redundance of this Cambridge energy in the fields of state-craft, religion, science and letters does intimately belong to the history of the University. It powerfully re-acted on residents within the academic pale. Not to understand it is not to understand Cambridge. But in the compass of this book the story cannot be contained. In the second and third volumes of Mr. Bass Mullinger's History—surely, since Ascham's *Scholemaster*, the noblest record ever written of the mind that created England anew in the Reformation age—you may read how Cambridge thought and learning grew to fill all the spaces of England, and struck root in regions wider yet. Here I am only concerned with the Cambridge environments of some few of the men who gave lustre to the University in the century which was ushered in by the teaching of Erasmus—the friends whom they knew there, the rooms and courts on which they looked. Except Cambridge and Oxford there are no towns in England where at each turn we can look upon the veritable surroundings, comparatively unchanged by time, which were familiar to the eyes of men whose names are consecrated in the national history.

The turret-chamber of Erasmus at Queens' and the court which it looked down upon are an admirable example of the pious care with which buildings associated with great memories have been preserved at Cambridge. Milton, of course, knew the place, and perhaps Erasmus in his study was in his mind when he wrote :

> Or let my lamp at midnight hour
> Be seen in some high lonely tower,
> Where I may outwatch the Bear
> With thrice-great Hermes, or unsphere
> The spirit of Plato.

As Erasmus and Milton knew it the place remains to-day. Only the walls, now weathered and autumnal in hue, were very new and bright when Erasmus settled there in December, 1510 ; for the second court of Queens' had barely stood then for fifteen years. There must have been something in its aspect to remind him of his native Holland. After 1500 brick became the characteristic building material of Cambridge colleges, as stone always was at Oxford. But it was a novelty when it was employed at Queens', and bricks, if not actually imported from Holland, were regarded as Flemish in origin. Nothing could more precisely recall to the great scholar his own Rotterdam than the long river-front of the college, with its walls descending abruptly into the canalised waters. His study, in the south-east corner of the court, and the neighbour chambers which were probably his, were ' the fairest chambers in the ancient building '; so it stands on the record of a fellow of the College in 1680.

To one of them is a square turret adjoyning, in the upper part of which is the study of Erasmus ; and over it leads. To that belongs the best prospect about the colledge, viz. upon the river, into the corne-fields and countrey adjoyning. So yᵗ it might very well consist with the civility of the House to that great man to let him have that study. His sleeping room might be either the Vice-President's, which lookes into the hall and chief court, or, to be near to him, the next. The room for his servitor that above it, and through it he might goe to that studie, which, for the height and neatnesse and prospect, might easily take his fancy.

We may picture him pacing the college walk, on the opposite bank of the river, which has long been known as Erasmus' Walk, or taking horse for his exercise and riding about the market-hill, as the bookseller, Garrett, once his host, remembered and in after times told Ascham.

So far as we may judge from the scanty records of his stay in Cambridge, Erasmus was a highly honoured

THE PRESIDENT'S LODGE, QUEENS' COLLEGE

visitor and not a little petted and pampered. The degree of D.D. was conferred on him in 1506, four years before he settled at Cambridge. He was appointed to the only public readership then existing in the University—that of the Lady Margaret in divinity. Bishop Fisher was all kindness to him, and, though himself no Greek scholar, was keenly interested in his criticisms on the Greek Testament. It was Fisher who invited him to Cambridge, and Fisher—though he had resigned the Presidency three years before—no doubt procured him hospitality at Queens'. There, one might suppose, he mixed in an eminently congenial society. Henry Bullock, a fellow of the College, Latinised by Erasmus as Bovillus, was, on Erasmus' own testimony, an enthusiastic 'Grecian' and an intimate friend and correspondent in later years. Fawne (Phaunus), his successor in the Lady Margaret's chair, and Whitford, both of the same society, were other friends. In the University several men who later won eminence were numbered among his associates : John Brian, of King's, who asserted the claims of Greek Aristotelianism over those of the Aristotle of the medieval schoolmen : Robert Aldrich, of the same college, who was Erasmus' fellow-traveller on the famous journey to Walsingham : and John Watson, a fellow of Peterhouse who had travelled in Italy and afterwards was Master of Christ's, a man described by Erasmus as pious without pride, courteous without levity, strict without severity : there is a pleasant letter of his, inviting Erasmus to his country rectory of Elsworth, a few miles distant from Cambridge.

These and others mentioned in his letters were men of culture whom Erasmus was glad to count among his friends. And yet, if some of the letters which he wrote from Cambridge to his Italian friend, Ammonius—then settled in London—are to be taken seriously we must suppose that he was in perpetual ill-humour with the place. They are full of amusing complaints. *If* it be the fact that the loss of a letter directed to Ammonius is the fault of the local letter-carriers *then* the Cambridge townsfolk are boorish even beyond their boorish countrymen. It rains night and day, and the price of firewood is going up—no wonder, when there is such a demand for the burning of heretics. There is not a soul in Cambridge—what a University !—that at any price can be got to copy out his *Icaromenippus* in a decent hand. Cambridge beer is bad. Parenthetically one might remark that Francis van Horne in the early years of Henry VIII was vending beer from his brewery between the Bridge and Magdalene : might not a Batavian wholesomely quench his thirst there ? The wine is not much better : will Ammonius send him some Greek wine, and take care that it is not too sweet ? Unhappily, when the wine is dispatched the carrier drinks half of it, and fills up the barrel with water : the result to Erasmus is an attack of the stone. The place is not altogether displeasing—in summer-time, at least, better than London, where they have the plague : but one must tout if one expects pupils and fees. His lectures on the grammar of Chrysoloras attract few hearers : their fees amount to nothing : what is to be extracted from men with empty pockets ? Besides, Erasmus is resolved to lecture gratuitously. Cambridge is horribly expensive (and can Ammonius, Colet, anybody, spare a loan ?) : in less than five months since his first coming he has spent twenty nobles and only earned one — a lecture fee, which he would rather have declined.

With these half-peevish, half-humorous complaints of its eminent guest Cambridge need not greatly concern itself. Erasmus was not a little vain and exacting of admiration : he was a confirmed grumbler and, as Colet pleasantly tells him, a shameless beggar. The badness of the Cambridge beer is a pretext for asking his friend for a present of the Greek wine which he had learnt to love in Italy. The scantiness of his lecture fees need not have troubled him if his habits had been less sybaritic. Cambridge gave him the best it had, and its *nudi homines* might well stand agape at the Dutchman's wealth and extravagance. His readership brought him in £13 *per annum*, four times as much as Fisher received as President of Queens'. He drew £20 from his sinecure rectory of Alderton, in Kent. Warham added another £20 from his own purse, and Fisher gave him a pension of 100 florins : and besides all this he was liberally furnished with money by his patron, Lord Mountjoy.

Gibbon once shot an epigram at the University, which he despised even more than his own, that Erasmus learnt at Oxford the Greek which he taught to Cambridge. If the epigram were true in fact it might be supplemented with the truthful corollary that Cambridge retained what it learnt and Oxford forgot what it taught : but it is not true. Erasmus knew small Greek when he went to Oxford in 1498, and, on his own showing, he knew little more of it when he went away in 1499. He is proud of the fact that in Greek he was ' self-taught,' and his knowledge of it was mainly acquired in the interval of eleven years before he began his residence at Cambridge. In Italy, not at Oxford, he made the acquaintance of the brilliant Oxford ' Grecians,' Grocyn,

More and probably Lily.   Writing in 1519 he says pointedly :

> England has two universities, by no means unknown to fame, Cambridge and Oxford.   Greek is taught at both, but peaceably at Cambridge, since the head of that school both in learning and religious life is John Fisher, Bishop of Rochester.   But at Oxford, when a young man of no common learning delivered an admirable discourse in Greek, a barbarian fellow in a public harangue with loud and bitter taunts railed on Greek letters.

Once again in 1521 he contrasts the attitude of the two Universities to the new learning :

> In the University of Cambridge, instead of sophistical arguments, their theologians debate in a sober, sensible manner, and depart wiser and better men.   The University of Oxford, owing to certain monks, at first fought against the improvement in letters, but has been coerced by the authority of the Cardinal and the King.

In fact, Oxford, as usual on the losing side, fought bitterly in the obscurantist cause.   In its streets ' Grecians ' were mobbed and hounded down by an army of ' Trojans.'   More, whose services to learning were rewarded at Cambridge with the dignity of High Steward, noted with bitter contempt the foolish intolerance of his own University, quoting the Latin proverb : " The Trojans learn wisdom too late."   In 1519 he addressed a letter of serious admonition to the University authorities, drawing their attention to the example of Cambridge.   " At Cambridge, which you used to outshine, even those who do not learn Greek, drawn by common zeal for their University, make, each of them, a contribution for the stipend of the Greek reader, which is greatly to their credit." His warning was followed by a letter addressed to the University by the King, forbidding under severe penalties the molestation of students of Greek.

Wolsey founded a chair of Greek in the following year. "So the brawlers were silenced," says Erasmus.

The Divinity School, where Cambridge first heard the accents of Greek from the lips of Erasmus, since 1857 has been absorbed in the University Library. It is still known as the Old Divinity School, and occupies the ground floor under the Catalogue Room, formerly the Regent House of the University. No view of its interior exists even in the debased condition to which it had been reduced before 1857. Though its architectural pretensions may have been slight it was a very large room, capable of accommodating an audience of two hundred at the least. When Erasmus was at Paris his Greek classes had always been well attended, and the contrast of the echoing solitude of the school at Cambridge must have been chilling. Nor can it be said of his few pupils that any of them were men of commanding genius. The great scholars and divines who gave lustre to Cambridge in the Reformation age belonged to a generation which had never heard the voice of Erasmus.

Not by his lectures but by his written work the great Dutchman created Cambridge. It was his *Novum Instrumentum*, a critical edition and translation of the Greek Testament, published at Basel in 1516, but mainly prepared during his residence at Cambridge, which, far more than the writings of Luther, awoke the Reformation in England. Cambridge was ripe for the religious revival before Luther had nailed his theses on Wittenberg church door. The same occasion which called forth Luther's protest against the papal indulgences, in the same year (1517) produced a similar defiance at Cambridge. The proclamation of indulgences sent out by Leo X had been forwarded

Nicholas Ridley, in 1521 an undergraduate on the eve of 'determining,' owed his education to his uncle, a prebendary of St. Paul's and a devout Catholic. To him, as to Cranmer, the future was dark, the present a time for silence and questioning. Stephen Gardiner, then a young Bachelor of Law, may well have been an approving participator in the spectacle : he shortly afterwards became Wolsey's secretary.

But among the younger men who may have witnessed the burning of Luther's books were not a few earnest adherents of the ' German ' teaching, many of whom in later years ratified in the flames of martyrdom the protest which was silent when the warning fire was lit in 1521. In or about that year they formed themselves into a loosely organised society, somewhat recalling the Holy Club of Whitefield and the Wesleys at Oxford, and destined to achieve a yet mightier work for the emancipation of religion from the shackles of dead form. It was dangerous to meet in the colleges, where diligent search was made by the Cardinal's agents for the condemned books. Their gatherings took place in quasi-secrecy in an inn called the White Horse which occupied a site between the back parts of the present Bull Hotel and King's College, with a narrow frontage to the High Street. This inn came to be known as ' Germany ' among the enemies of the new sect, and it was chosen because it could be privately entered from the Backs by a door in the lane called Plute's Lane, extending from the High Street to Queen's Lane and bounding the site of King's on the southern side. The old inn was cleared away in 1823. All that is left of it is a beautiful specimen of woodwork consisting of three coved stalls with book-presses, elaborately ornamented, between them. They are now in the Archæological Museum, and tradition connects them with the name of Coverdale; but the style of the work shows that they date from a period a century later than the first Reformers.

Surely no site in the University itself compared in historic interest with this dark old inn, entered from the narrow alley, 'detestable and filthy,' of Plute's Lane; and deeply pathetic, in view of the after fate of so many of its members, were the secret meetings of the society of the ' Germans ' or ' Heretics.' Thither Thomas Farman, fellow and afterwards President of Queens', smuggles Luther's writings which he has hidden from the inquisitors in some corner of his college. With him comes John Lambert, a fellow of the same college : him the faggot and the stake await in Smithfield in 1538. Shaxton, fellow of Gonville Hall, President of Physwick's Hostel and in later life Bishop of Salisbury, gives weight and dignity to the assembly : he will be condemned to be burnt, but recant and save his life. All the clerks of Gonville Hall "savour of the frying-pan, speak they never so holily," says good-for-nothing Nix, Bishop of Norwich. Two others of the same society are present at the meetings—Edward Crome, who, like Shaxton, will escape the stake in Mary's reign by apostasy, and John Skip, who will die Bishop of Hereford. Tyndale, a martyr to the faith at Vilvorde in 1535, may have attended the early meetings, and from the house of the Austin friars at Cambridge came Miles Coverdale. Chief and president in the discussions at the White Horse was the Prior of the same house, a notable man, Robert Barnes.

Barnes was still a young man, twenty-six years old, when Luther's books were burnt. From the Augustinian

10

house at Cambridge he passed, as Ridley did, to the University of Louvain, then famous for its college of the three learned languages, established under the influence of Erasmus. Returning to Cambridge he lectured in the hall of the Augustinians on the Latin classics and the Epistles of Saint Paul. A man of learning and dialectical skill, he spoilt all by the intolerance of his enthusiasm and the rancour of his invective. In a sermon at Saint Edward's church, on the Sunday before Christmas Day, 1525, he attacked the Cardinal and the Bishops and clergy generally in terms of the utmost licence. Saint Edward's was the church where, at another Christmas season, four years later, Latimer delivered the first of his famous Sermons on the Card. It adjoined that part of the Market which was the Butchery or Butcher's Row, and the address of Barnes was accommodated to the calling of his audience, consisting largely of butchers, and bore a sidelong reference to the Cardinal's reputed lowly origin. The pastoral staff, said he, was more like to knock swine on the head with than to take sheep—" a foolish thing," said Fisher, " to preach before all the butchers of Cambridge." The Vice-Chancellor, Natares, inhibited Barnes from preaching and summoned him to answer the articles alleged against him on the subject of his sermon. The case was heard in the Schools, but the trial was interrupted by an incursion of the students, who insisted on their right to be present at the hearing. Proceedings were taken up a few days later at the lodge of Clare, but Barnes refused to revoke his statements. Next he was summoned to the presence of the Cardinal himself, in London. Wolsey treated him with smiles and good-humoured indifference. " What, Master Doctor, had you not a sufficient scope in the Scriptures to teach the people, but that my golden shoes, my pole-axes, my pillars, my golden cushions, my crosses did so sore offend you that you must make me your butt amongst the people? We were jollily that day laughed to scorn." In the issue Barnes abjured and was sentenced to free custody in the house of his own order at Northampton. Thence, by spreading a report that he had drowned himself, he managed to escape, first to London, then to Antwerp, and so joined Luther. He returned to London on Cromwell's invitation, for a time enjoyed high court favour and actually undertook the accuser's part against Lambert, his old companion at the White Horse. Lambert's fate overtook him after Cromwell's fall, in 1541. " A noisy, vain man," says Froude : but his bravery at the stake atoned for the weakness of his life.

Among younger men—bachelors and undergraduates —who found their way to the secret meetings at the White Horse a few notabilities deserve to be mentioned —John Rogers, the first of the Marian martyrs ; John Frith, Tyndale's assistant, burnt at Smithfield in 1533, whose examination before the Bishops is said to have converted Cranmer to the views of the Reformers ; and Matthew Parker. The most interesting personality in the group, the founder and inspirer of the movement, was Thomas Bilney.

' Bilney, little Bilney,' ' the blessed Saint Bilney,' as, with a tender irony, he was called by Latimer in a day when he had long been dead, was a curious and pathetic personality. He had strange antipathies and some points of littleness in his character which corresponded to his stature. But his earnestness, simplicity and enthusiasm were of the stuff that attracts and binds. He was a Norfolk man, and, as a Norfolk man should be, a member of Trinity Hall ;

and, as a Trinity Hall man should do, he graduated in Civil and Canon Law. A canonist of the type prescribed by Bateman might seem of all men to be least likely to head the crusade against popes and prelates. In truth, though Bilney made two notable converts among his students—Thomas Arthur, afterwards a fellow of Saint John's, and Sir William Paget, afterwards High Steward of the University—he could hardly have lighted on a college so attached, by the conditions of its statutes and the character of its leading members, to the traditions of medieval churchmanship; and, unfortunately for Bilney, his Protestantism took the form of insistence on the corruptions prevailing in the high places of the Church. The visitor of the College was ' blind bishop Nix ' of Norwich, a representative of prelacy in its most unregenerate form. The Master was Stephen Gardiner, ' smooth, treacherous and plausible,' the cruel author of the Six Articles. One of the fellows was Thomas Thirleby, who afterwards, as Bishop of Ely, assisted at the degradation of Cranmer. It happened that Thirleby, who ' kept ' in the rooms below Bilney's, was in the habit of playing on ' the recorder.' The prejudice of Andrew Fairservice against the use of ' kists of whustles ' was not stronger than Bilney's dislike of music of all kinds, and especially in the services of the Church; and, as often as Thirleby began to play, Bilney betook himself to prayer, as if to resist the Evil One.

In his early years at Cambridge he sought refuge from the tortures of a super-sensitive conscience in fastings, vigils and penances, as prescribed by the mechanical religion of the time. The New Testament of Erasmus brought him ' marvellous comfort and quietness.' There is in the library of Corpus a Bible which once was his. Its annotations and interlineations show how carefully he had studied it. A humble-minded, affectionate man, he conveyed inspiration where men greater and more learned would have failed to win confidence. Foxe admits that at his death he had not been brought into the full daylight of the Protestant confession—that he still held with mass, confession and the authority of the Church of Rome. But no man wrought more powerfully for the ends of the Protestant Reformation. Both Barnes and Lambert owed their conversion to him. Parker was enthusiastic in his devotion to him as his spiritual master. His most signal victory was over Latimer, a man considerably senior to him in years and once as strenuous in the cause of the traditional faith as he afterwards became in that of spiritual freedom. "By his confession," said Latimer, "I learned more than in twenty years before." Together the two might be seen in their daily walks about the Castle Hill, which from the circumstance came to be nick-named 'Heretics' Hill.' Together they visited the criminal and the sick in the Castle gaol and the Cambridge spital-house.

Perhaps the election of Gardiner to the mastership of his college, in 1525, made Cambridge an undesirable place of residence for Bilney; but the compulsion of his conscience drove him to seek a wider mission-field. He left Cambridge in that year, and among his own people in Norwich diocese and in the greater and more perilous world of London he spread the new gospel. At first he had episcopal licence for preaching; but his denunciation of relic and image worship and his re-jection of Mariolatry caused him to be arrested on a charge of heresy. At London, before Wolsey and the Bishops of London and Norwich—the latter being Nix—he was examined along with his fellow-collegian,

Arthur. After many refusals he was at last induced to abjure, and for a time was imprisoned in the Tower. Then, in 1529, he was released and returned to Cambridge. But his sensitive temperament was tortured with reflection on his apostasy. He fell into such despondency that his friends were afraid to leave him, night or day. For two years he endured this misery. Then, as Foxe tells us, " being fully determined in his mind, and setting his time, he took his leave in Trinity Hall, at ten of the clock at night, of certain of his friends, and said that he would go to Hierusalem, alluding belike to the words and example of Christ in the gospel, going up to Hierusalem, what time He was appointed to suffer His passion."

He departed immediately to Norfolk, and there preached at first privately in households, afterwards publicly in the fields. Then he went to the anchoress in Norwich and gave her a New Testament in Tyndale's translation. As a relapsed heretic he could expect no mercy at the Bishop's hands. He was arrested, carried to prison and condemned to burning. Many of his Cambridge friends went to Norwich to witness his martyrdom and bore witness to his constancy in death. In the army of marytrs there is none more noble, and none to be more honoured among Cambridge Reformers, than gentle Bilney, " the first framer," as Foxe calls him, " of the University in the knowledge of Christ."

So long as history is read and written the ethics of the divorce of Henry VIII will be matter for judgments as diverse as when it was first debated in 1529. The part which Cambridge played in the momentous question which determined the revolt from Rome belongs to national history ; but it even more profoundly affected the destinies of the University. For the first time in its history Cambridge stands forth as the exponent of national feeling, and for a century it remains so. So long as personal monarchy was in touch with the popular sentiment Cambridge was the University favoured by English sovereigns. Trinity is the monument of a king's gratitude, and with Trinity begins an altogether new chapter in Cambridge history.

The beginning of the story is old and familiar. Easter term, 1529, was dissolved on account of a visitation of the plague. Cranmer, a fellow of Jesus, was quietly engaged in tutoring two pupils, sons of a gentleman named Cressy, at Waltham Abbey. While he was there the King happened to visit the little town—grievously offended at the recent revocation of the suit for the dissolution of his marriage from England to Rome. It chanced that two of his attendants, Edward Fox, Provost of King's, and Stephen Gardiner, Master of Trinity Hall, were lodged in Mr. Cressy's house: they had just returned from their fruitless mission to Clement VII at Rome. The future Archbishop was a modest and retiring scholar, whose fame as an earnest student and teacher of divinity in the light of Erasmus' writings had hardly extended beyond his University. But he was an old acquaintance of his fellow-lodgers, and the three fell into familiar talk of the question which was agitating the King and the realm. It was then that Cranmer made the suggestion that the King should take the opinion of the learned men of his own kingdom without waiting for the 'frustratory delays' of the Papal Court.

Cranmer's suggestion was not altogether novel. In fact a proposal had already been made that the Universities should be consulted on the divorce question, and Cranmer himself had been nominated to represent

Cambridge on a commission. But coming at a time when the King was chafing at the frustration of his suit by its revocation to Rome it was eminently opportune. When Fox and Gardiner reported to Henry their conversation with Cranmer, " Marry," said he, " let him be sent for out of hand. I perceive that man hath the sow by the right ear."

In 1530, the year which witnessed Wolsey's fall and which, before its close, was to see the whole of the clergy of the land laid under a Præmunire, it was no light matter for a clerical body to disregard the King's will. Nevertheless, and though the result showed that opinion at Cambridge was sharply and evenly divided, the answer of the University may be said to have honestly conformed to the best opinion that could be obtained on a matter which had been provocatively complicated by Clement VII with extraneous considerations of policy. Nor was the decision actuated by merely servile considerations. In fact the King was displeased that the question propounded to the University was answered by it with a reservation which went some way to nullify its effect; and he was not less vexed that it did not go beyond its reference by denying the Pope's powers of dispensation. The question submitted to the University had ostensibly no reference to the particular case of the King. It was simply, " May a man lawfully marry his brother's wife, when that brother died without issue ? " It was purely a question for theologians and canonists, and implied no breach with the authority of the Pope. Of the King's party were orthodox Catholics such as Gardiner and Heath, afterwards Marian Archbishop of York, as well as Lutherans such as Shaxton and Latimer.

On February 16, 1530, the King addressed a letter to the Vice-Chancellor, Dr. Buckmaster, requiring him to submit the proposition, as above stated, to the consideration of learned men of the University and to inform him of the result of their deliberations. This letter was brought to Cambridge on a Saturday afternoon in the same month by Gardiner and Fox. Henry had better grounds for anticipating a favourable verdict from Cambridge than from Oxford, which had already received a similar requisition. Whatever doubts he may have entertained of the result were laid to rest by the intrigues of Gardiner and Fox. On the Sunday following their arrival a congregation was summoned by the Vice-Chancellor. It was attended by nearly two hundred Doctors and Bachelors of Divinity and Masters of Arts. The Vice-Chancellor called the Doctors apart and asked their advice. It was at once apparent that there was no agreement among them as to the selection of the delegates who should deliver the verdict of the University. There was great confusion. Strong exception was taken to certain graduates who were known to favour the King's desires. Seeing that no conclusion was otherwise probable, the Vice-Chancellor proposed that every man should deliver his vote in secrecy, but the opposition ' would in no wise agree.' Night had fallen and, nothing being determined, the congregation was continued until the next day at one o'clock. Then the Vice-Chancellor proposed a grace appointing by name twenty-nine Doctors and Masters to determine the question, with the proviso that whatever was decided by a majority of two-thirds of their number should be accepted as the final conclusion of the whole University. Violent opposition was raised to the constitution of the delegacy. At first the grace was rejected. When it was put a second time the votes on either side were equal. Finally, as Gardiner and

Fox reported the matter to the King, ' by labour of friends to cause some to depart the house which were against it,' a majority in favour of the grace was secured. Of the twenty-nine chosen the King was assured that he might depend on the votes of sixteen, and there were good hopes that the two-thirds majority would be secured by the adhesion of four others.

Vice-Chancellor Buckmaster wrote to his friend, Dr. Edmunds of Peterhouse, in much perturbation at his own part in the business. He delivered the University's answer to the King at Windsor. The King at first expressed great thanks, lauded the wisdom of the University and gave the Vice-Chancellor twenty nobles. But at a second interview, after ' casting a little holy water of the court ' in compliments, he intimated that he was ' scarce contented ' with the answer, though he was assured that it was the utmost that could be obtained. The Vice-Chancellor was ' glad to be out of the court, where many men did wonder on me.' Outside royal circles things were even worse. " All the world almost crieth out of Cambridge for this act, and specially of me," and the twenty nobles in his pocket were poor compensation for the loss of a benefice on which he had been counting. At Cambridge there was rioting. Parson Dakers of Saint Nicholas' Hostel— hostellers are always disorderly—assaulted Gardiner's servant, and, when arraigned before the unfortunate Vice-Chancellor for his conduct, ' did so order me as no man hath been ordered before,' refusing to submit to the Vice-Chancellor's jurisdiction on the ground that he had been familiar with Gardiner and Thirleby ; moreover, being ' commanded to ward,' he escaped from the bedell and disappeared. " And that night there was such a jetting in Cambridge as ye never heard of, with such booing and crying even against our

College that all Cambridge might perceive it was in despite of me."

From Loggan's draft of the Schools' quadrangle, taken about 1688, and from Dr. Stokes' account of *The Chaplains and the Chapel of the University*, we may realise something of the scene of the memorable debate which took place in the waning light of that February Sunday. The Regent House, or the New Chapel, as it was alternatively called, is now the Catalogue Room of the Library. It was the only place appointed by the statutes for the discussion and granting of graces, and, as its alternative name implies, it was also used for religious ceremonies. Even in Fuller's day it had ' something of chapel character and consecration, as wherein some University devotions were performed.' A portion of it, railed off from the rest, was called the ' small chapel,' and contained an altar, hung in 1523 with ' curtains of silk of orange colour and green.' Probably the small chapel was under the large Perpendicular window which Loggan's print shows in the eastern wall. A similar window was at the western end, overlooking the Old Court of King's, and in either of the flanking walls there were windows of stained glass containing, among other things, the arms of the Thorpes who had contributed to the erection of the building. In the middle of the room was a low screen dividing the ' Regent ' from the ' Non-Regent ' House. Graces were separately discussed in each House, and, if passed, proclamation was made at a door in the screen. The furniture of the two Houses was in appearance—some of it perhaps in material fact—identical with what may now be seen in the Senate House : a cushioned chair in the Regent House for the Vice-Chancellor, forms and settles in both Houses for the rest ; in the Regent

House a square table for the Proctors, and in the Non-Regent House another for the Scrutators ; and, just as in the Senate House, the ' Doctors' place ' was ' backed round with seats.' In place of the present plaster-ceiling there was a timber roof. The walls were wainscoted and hung with boards on which were inscribed the names of benefactors and of the keepers of the University ' hutches,' or loan-chests. Through the still existing door at the south-west end of the room Regents and Non-Regents passed out to the staircase— long since removed—which descended to the Schools' quadrangle. Thence through Rotheram's gateway— now to be seen at Madingley Hall—along the narrow East School Street, beset on either hand by town houses, they filed out into the High Street, opposite Saint Mary's Church.

CHAPTER VIII

SPENSER AND THE DRAMA

Those melodious bursts, that fill
The spacious times of great Elizabeth
With sounds that echo still.
TENNYSON

IN the first decade of the sixteenth century Ariosto
was writing his early comedies and was preparing
for his *Orlando Furioso*. In the same decade
Cambridge also had its ' poet '—so called in the
Grace-books of the time—and he also was an Italian,
named Caius Auberinus. His business with the
University was to write Latin letters of compliment
at twenty pence a letter—distressing evidence that
Cambridge had no creditable Latinist of its own. He
also delivered lectures on Terence in Long Vacation,
" and very dull they were, like the times he lived in,"
says a note in one of Archbishop Parker's books.
Such was the conception of poetry at Cambridge at
the beginning of the century which in its closing years
saw the production of the *Faerie Queene* and *Doctor
Faustus*.

The first gleams of poetry, worthy to be called so,
that illumined Cambridge were reflected from Italian
skies and were lighted by Petrarch and Ariosto. The
former inspired the sonnets of Sir Thomas Wyat, of
Saint John's, published after his death, in 1557, and nine
years later followed *The Supposes* of George Gascoigne,

of Trinity, adapted from Ariosto's comedy. It is not an unreasonable supposition that the awakening of song at Cambridge in the middle of the sixteenth century had a direct connection with the novel introduction of literary exercises in the curriculum provided for the scholars by Fisher in his statutes for Christ's and Saint John's. At Christ's the old routine of *trivium* and *quadrivium* was varied by the addition of Poetry and Oratory, and in the later statutes which he gave to Saint John's Fisher exacted that the students should compose weekly copies of Greek and Latin verse. It is needless to say that Fisher as little contemplated the cultivation of a native literature as a part of university education as Ascham and Bacon did in later times. The lapse of a century had made Chaucer's speech stranger to the comprehension of Fisher's contemporaries than that of Ennius ; and since Chaucer there had been no English literature. It was sufficient for the day that Virgil and Cicero were to have a hearing in the lecture-room along with Scotus and the Master of the Sentences. In the Trinity statutes of 1552 the part given to classical literature is greatly amplified. In Latin, Cicero, in Greek, Demosthenes, Plato, Homer and Hesiod are mentioned as authors to be specially studied. As the best imitations and translations of classical authors were Italian, the more ambitious students could hardly fail to add some knowledge of the poetry and prose of Italy to their store. So modern poetry begins for Cambridge with Saint John's and Trinity.

The verse of Wyat and Gascoigne has nothing in it that specially belongs to Cambridge. Of all Cambridge singers Edmund Spenser may be said to reflect most characteristically the influences of his university education. Though the breath of Cambridge is in all that was written by Milton and Wordsworth, it may be said of both poets, in the words which Wordsworth applies to Milton, that in their student days they 'dwelt apart' from the influences and conventions which ordinarily beset an undergraduate. To his student time at Cambridge Spenser largely owed his Puritanism, the Platonic and Aristotelian colouring of his poetry, and—though his art was never tongue-tied by the authority of university 'doctors'—the influences of the critical coterie to which he belonged.

He was matriculated, as a sizar, at Pembroke, in May, 1569, when he was about sixteen years old. He had previously been educated at the Merchant Taylors' School in London, then newly founded, where his master was the famous Richard Mulcaster. Spenser was the first of a line of Cambridge poets who had their schooling in London—Milton at Saint Paul's, Dryden at Westminster, Coleridge at Christ's Hospital. While at school he probably took part in the English plays, written by Mulcaster and acted before the Queen. No fitter master could have been found for the budding poet. Mulcaster was a classical and even an Oriental scholar, but, as a teacher, he was all for the emancipation of his boys from the 'thraldom and bondage' of the Latin tongue. "I love Rome," he writes, "but London better; I favour Italy, but England more; I honour the Latin, but I worship the English. I do not think that any language, be it whatsoever, is better able to utter all arguments either with more pith or greater plainness than our English tongue is."

A splendid confession truly! And the evidence of the success of Mulcaster's English teaching is that Spenser, when he left school, was already master of Italian and French, as well as the classical tongues. His first work, published anonymously, which appeared in the year when he left school, was a translation of the Visions of Petrarch, in rhyming stanzas, and of Bellay, the Calvinist poet of France, in blank verse.

Probably Pembroke was selected as the poet's college on account of the conspicuous Calvinism of its members. In numbers it was one of the smallest of the colleges in those days. Its undergraduates of all classes were thirty in 1564 and had increased to thirty-nine in 1573. But the memory of Nicholas Ridley attached to it a special reverence in the eyes of the stricter Protestants and elicited the Queen's salutation of it as *religiosa domus*. The tradition of advanced Protestantism was maintained in Elizabeth's reign under the successive headships of such eminent divines as Edmund Grindal (1559–1562), afterwards Archbishop of Canterbury, Matthew Hutton (1562–1567), afterwards Archbishop of York, John Whitgift (1567), afterwards Master of Trinity and Archbishop of Canterbury, and John Young (1567–1578), afterwards Bishop of Rochester. The high regard shown to Grindal ('Algrind') and Young ('Roffy,' an abbreviation for Roffensis) in the young poet's *Shepheard's Calender* is evidence alike of his Calvinistic principles and college patriotism.

The whole of the society of Pembroke, when Spenser was introduced to it, was housed in the Old Court, then the smallest court of any college in Cambridge. Most of the buildings of that court, which the memories of Ridley and Spenser should have rendered inviolate, have unhappily been swept away. The chapel— most ancient of college chapels at Cambridge—was the first to go, in 1690, when the Italian structure of brick, now the Old Library, was substituted for it. Loggan's view of the old chapel, taken just before its destruction, shows a large Perpendicular window in its west wall, facing Trumpington Street. Cold and bare the place may have been in the Puritan regime of Spenser's day, but cherubins and painted glass survived from the old time until they were broken and destroyed by Dowsing in 1643; and the pattern of the stalls, rood-loft, and 'candle-beam' was good enough to be copied in the chapel of Saint John's in 1516. The venerable hall of Mary de Valence was destroyed in 1875. Along with it went the range of chambers on the southern side of the court, and the picturesque lodge between it and the hall. The lodge overlooked the orchard where Ridley 'learned without book almost all Paul's epistles, as the walls, butts, and trees, if they could speak, might bear witness.' Of the college known to Spenser two parts only remain—the gateway in Trumpington Street, with the staircase adjoining it on the south side, and the range between the old chapel and the kitchen. There is a garret floor in this range which shows indications that once it was divided into 'studies'—spaces each about six feet square, separated from one another by wooden partitions, and each lighted by a small window. It is likely enough that one of them was allotted to the sizar-freshman of 1569.

In the little company of his fellow-scholars at Pembroke Edmund Spenser did not lack congenial friends. Two at least—each of them junior to himself by two years—had been his schoolfellows under Mulcaster. Of these, one was Thomas Dove, who afterwards became Bishop of Peterborough. The other was the learned and pious Launcelot Andrewes, who afterwards was Master of the College, and Bishop of Winchester. In communion with him the young poet must have found unfailing delight, for Andrewes saw mysteries in common things. " To observe the grass, herbs, corn, trees, any of the creatures, and to

11

contemplate their natures was ever to him the greatest mirth, content, and recreation that could be ; and this he held till his dying day." No doubt it was that joy in all things natural which made him perform his journeys between Cambridge and London on foot. Did Spenser share those delightful walks ?

Probably Spenser's most intimate friend among the Pembroke undergraduates was Edward Kirke, the ' E. K.' who annotated his *Shepheard's Calender*. He was a younger man than Spenser and graduated two years later, having then migrated to Caius. He was, we should suppose, a rather tiresome and pedantic youth. His comments, though they throw some incidental light on the poet's life after he left the University, are a gratuitous holding of a candle to the sun. But we may tolerate him for his Boswellian devotion to his friend, and respect the acumen which detected the new light before it dawned on the world at large. He belonged to the literary coterie which gathered about Gabriel Harvey.

Harvey, the ' Hobbinol ' of the *Shepheard's Calender*, was originally of Christ's, and took his B.A. degree there a year after Spenser was admitted at Pembroke. Soon after his degree he became a fellow of Pembroke and lectured on ' rhetoric,' which, in his case, meant chiefly Cicero ; and, as Ciceronian scholarship required, he was well versed in Italian literature. If we are to accept the verdict of his enemy, Thomas Nash of Saint John's, he was an arrogant pedant ; if we are to believe the testimony of some of the fellows of Pembroke, he was supercilious and unsociable. They complained that he ' cut ' them in the streets, that he was not ' familiar,' like a fellow, and deserted their company round the fire in the combination room after dinner and supper : perhaps it was to withdraw to

VIEW FROM NEWNHAM MILL

the company of Spenser and Kirke. One of his special
ill-willers among the fellows was Thomas Nevile—
magnificent Nevile, as Fuller calls him—afterwards
Master of Trinity and builder of the hall and Nevile's
Court there. He carried his malice so far as to non-
placet the grace for Harvey's M.A. degree.

Poor Harvey ! His little mannerisms—' the carrying
up of his gown, his nice gait in his pantoffles, the
affected accent of his speech '—live still in the unkind
portrait of Nash. Was he not the original of Pedantius,
' a concise and firking finicaldo fine schoolmaster,'
in the ' exquisite comedy in Trinity College ' ?   " Let
him deny that there was a Shew made at Clare Hall of
him and his two brothers," not without reference to
his English hexameters,

> Tarra rantantara turba tumultuosa Trigonum
> Tri-Harveyorum Tri-Harmonia.

Harvey was a prig but not altogether a pedant, and
his power of attracting and influencing men younger
than himself was not a quality which we associate
with a ' don.' His attempt to hobble the skirts of
Spenser's muse with the laws of Latin prosody seems
ridiculous to us whose ears are attuned to the matchless
melodies of the *Faerie Queene*. It was not ridiculous in
1579, when Harvey tried to wean young Spenser to the
metrical canons which the best learning of Cambridge
held to be infallibly correct. What of music was there
in any English verse yet written that could match
with the cadences of Horace and Virgil ? With such
master-work who would compare the stumbling metre
of Wyat, the ' fourteeners ' and doggerel that marred
even Surrey's work, or the tentative tunings heard in
Spenser's own *Shepheard's Calender* ? Who should
contest the judgment of Ascham and Cheke, pillars

of Cambridge scholarship, that ' our rude and beggarly rhyming ' showed ' small learning and less judgment ' in the poet ? Had not Thomas Watson, ' one of the best scholars that Saint John's ever had,' shown a better way in his translation of the *Odyssey* ? Had not his verses the very ring of the Homeric hexameter ?

All travellers do gladly report great praise of Ulysses,
For that he knew many men's manners and saw many cities.

If Harvey is condemned can we altogether acquit Philip Sidney, who thought English was ' fit for both sorts ' ?

Fortunately the battle of English prosody was not decided on the field of Cambridge. The hexameter was in full retreat when Nash turned his guns upon Harvey in 1592. Let it be remembered of Harvey that, when the first books of the *Faerie Queene* came from the printer's hands in 1590, Hobbinol prefaced them by a noble palinode in the rhyming stanzas which he had once banned, wherein he did homage to the ' deep scanning skill ' of his poet friend. He lived to a great age and died in 1630. That very year, and in his own first college, Christ's, a young Bachelor of Arts, in sixteen rhymed lines, did honour to the memory of a greater ' heir to fame ' than Edmund Spenser. Did Harvey read them ? And, looking back on his student days, did he realise that within the compass of his lifetime English poetry had grown from the cradle to a stature rivalling that of Greece and far surpassing the grandest work of Rome ?

Nash, who took his B.A. degree sixteen years later than Harvey, belongs to a generation which knew not Ascham and had scant reverence for bookmen of the Holofernes type. The so-called ' University wits ' who were Shakespeare's contemporaries were denizens of Bohemia, a 'turba tumultuosa' who took their learning and the joyousness of student life from Cambridge and Oxford, but, for the rest, were Londoners. And very disreputable characters they were in the estimation of the ruling precisians, whose barren theomachies went far to banish wit from the universities in the closing years of Elizabeth.

Among the 'roaring boys' of London who went out from Cambridge shortly before the Armada year, three we recognise as chief—Robert Greene of Saint John's (B.A., 1580), Thomas Nash of the same college (B.A., 1586), and Christopher Marlowe of Corpus (B.A., 1584). Greene and Marlowe, but not Nash, proceeded to M.A., and, as residence between B.A. and M.A. was then exacted in order to obtain the latter degree, the three must have been at some time contemporaries at Cambridge. At Cambridge perhaps they never met ; but in London, Nash, at twenty-two, was addressing ' the Gentlemen Students of both Universities ' in a preface to Greene's *Menaphon*, and, literally to his death, he was Greene's friend. Was it not after a debauch on pickled herrings and Rhenish wine in company with Nash that poor Greene came to his end ? There is generally a moral for the Puritan fabulist in the deaths of these literary outcasts, and the tale told once of Greene was effectively repeated about that ' merry meeting ' of Shakespeare and Jonson which only Jonson survived.

Without crediting scandalous inventions, we cannot doubt that the lives of Greene, Nash, and Marlowe were dissipated even beyond the Alsatian average. Nash, the longest liver of them, died at thirty-seven. Greene's dying hours were wrung with the retrospect of a mis-spent life, beginning at Cambridge. " Being at the

University," he says in his *Repentance of Robert Greene,*
" I light amongst wags as lewd as myself, with whom
I consumed the flower of my youth, who drew me
to travel into Italy and Spain, in which places I saw
and practised such villainy as is abominable to declare."
In one of his spiteful rejoinders to Nash, Gabriel Harvey
recalls Greene's ' fond disguising of [himself as] a
master of art with ruffianly hair,' evidently in a
students' play ; but the reproach coming from ' a
firking fine schoolmaster ' need not be taken as a
serious indictment. Nor need we think the worse of
Nash if, as Harvey says, ' a very Nash ' was taken as
a synonym for ' an untoward scholar.' Nash and
Greene were both excellent scholars. Greene's romances
are overlaid with classical allusion and ornament to
the point of tawdriness. Nash was enthusiastic in
his loyalty to Cambridge, and especially to his own
college—" that most famous and fortunate nurse of
all learning, Saint John's in Cambridge, a University in
itself ; shining so far above all other houses, halls,
and hospitals whatsoever that no college in the town
was able to compare with the tithe of her students ;
having (as I have heard grave men of credit report)
more candles light in it every winter morning before
four of the clock than the four of clock bell gave
strokes." For its erring children—Greene, tenderest
of romancers, Nash, gayest of humorists — Alma
Mater need have no thoughts that are not kindly and
reverential.

Kit Marlowe too was known to Greene in London
days ; but the two men were not friends. Greene
regarded him, as he did Shakespeare, with jealousy
as a younger and more successful rival. Of Kit we
like to think as the intimate of ' gentle ' Shakespeare,
as the ' dead shepherd ' of Arden. In the angry war

of pasquinades which filled the lives of Greene and Nash he took no part. The scandal attached to the story of his assassination in a Deptford ale-house possibly belongs to the apocrypha of outraged Puritanism. He was too outspoken a contemner of the Pharisees to escape their withering breath. The Machiavellianism with which he was charged by Greene was perhaps no more than a vehement protest against the formal pietism which smothered England, and particularly Cambridge, in the times of Whitgift. Faustus is Marlowe when he reviews the arid studies of the University, and dismisses them all for the magic which will make blind Homer sing to him and find heaven for him in the lips of Helen of Troy.

Marlowe, or Marlin, as his name is spelt in the College list of members and the University Grace-book, came from his Canterbury home to Cambridge in 1581. Matthew Parker, the great Archbishop of Canterbury and once Master of Corpus, gave his college endowments for the maintenance of two scholars to be nominated by the Dean of Canterbury from the King's School in that city. Marlowe was one of the first of these Canterbury scholars. Corpus, which had been almost the smallest of the colleges in 1564, had trebled its numbers under the rule and patronage of Parker. It is difficult to realise how densely peopled colleges were in the later years of Elizabeth. Corpus had ninety-seven occupants in 1573, all of them contained in the Old Court, except some who were lodged in the tennis court, recently adapted to serve as a Pensionary, and in certain houses, external to the court, which were fitted up as students' chambers. The butteries and the library, which are shown in Loggan's view and occupied the western end of the southern range, have given place to the new hall, put up in

1825 : otherwise, the buildings which presented themselves to Marlowe's eye remain much in their old condition. Fairly certainly we may identify the chamber in which he ' kept.' It was the ground-floor room on the right-hand side of the staircase now lettered R. It had served as a storeroom and had lately been fitted up for the Parker scholars. It is a large room, as college rooms go nowadays, and, no doubt, was shared by Marlowe with two or three other scholars. It looks diagonally across the court to the ivy-mantled oriel of the old hall. In that hall perchance Kit first learnt to ' bombast out a blank-verse ' in some college ' shew ' at Christmas-time. But concerning plays at Corpus in Marlowe's day history is silent, and the record of Marlowe's student life is a blank.

About the year of Marlowe's death (1593) Corpus admitted another famous playwright, John Fletcher. But with Fletcher we pass beyond the circle of the creators of English Drama. We turn to the question why it was that the Drama in its beginnings was linked with the Universities, and more particularly with Cambridge.

In the year 1598 Francis Meres (of Pembroke, Cambridge) published his well-known *Palladis Tamia*, which surveyed the position of poetry in England to the date of publication. In it he gives a list of twenty-eight writers of tragedies and comedies. Of those whom he mentions nothing is recorded of one, and the place of education of some others is doubtful. Ten were bred at Cambridge, six at Oxford, and one other, Sackville, seems to have been at both Universities.

In this book Meres shows an acquaintance with contemporary literature which is remarkable in a

OLD COURT OF CORPUS CHRISTI COLLEGE AS SEEN FROM MARLOWE'S CHAMBER

man who ended his days in a country living. His criticism is slight enough ; but he knows the books, and he knows a good deal of the writers—not only their printed work, but the unfathered plays which existed only in actors' copies and sonnets ' among private friends.' His summary is full enough to include the most recent publications as well as Chaucer and Lydgate : in the same sentence it links academic Legge with cockney Dekker. That in his comprehensive list so large a proportion should be university men is certainly noteworthy. But we must make allowance for the fact that Meres was himself a university man, and academic writers are pressed into his muster whose names were unknown to the audiences of the Curtain or the Rose. What more pertains to the connection of the Universities with the rise of the Drama is that play-acting of some sort was a very early feature of University life, and that, when the medieval church-plays passed away at the Reformation, stage performances, so far as they had a literary cast, hardly survived except in schools and colleges.

A discussion of the rise of the Drama in the Universities would take us far afield into the regions of Mystery and Morality, Boy-bishops and Feasts of Fools. At Cambridge the first that we hear of play-acting is in 1386, when the accounts of Michaelhouse contain an item of expenditure on an embroidered pall, six visors, and six beards for a ' comedy.' The title of ' comedy ' was indiscriminately applied in the fourteenth century to any kind of ' disguising,' and it is likely enough that the comedy of Michaelhouse was a religious play.

In the Elizabethan statutes of Queens' (1559) there is a remarkable provision. " Lest our youths should remain rude and unpolished in pronunciation and gesture, we will that the Greek professor [a college official, not the Regius Professor] and the examiner, each year, between the 20th of December and the beginning of Lent, shall provide for the acting in the College hall of two comedies or tragedies . . . and that each for his pains shall receive 6s. 8d. And if any of the scholars—unless he be a fellow-commoner—appointed by either of these two readers, refuse to act some part he shall be punished at the discretion of the President and these two readers." In schools and colleges, from time immemorial, it had been the custom to represent Latin plays at Christmas-time. The professed object of such exhibitions, apart from amusement, was the cultivation of colloquial Latin, which, it should be borne in mind, was, in theory at least, the ordinary medium of conversation in hall and class-room. From the Queens' statutes we may surmise that the plays represented were, at least some of them, in Greek, and the motive assigned for the enactment—the cultivation of correct pronunciation and appropriate gesture—indicates a more modern and just appreciation of the uses of the Drama.

In an original draft of the statutes of Trinity (about 1546) there is a chapter entitled *De Præfecto Ludorum qui Imperator dicitur*, which in an interesting way shows how the new humanistic aims of the sixteenth century legislators were grafted on the old tradition of celebrating Christmas by the antics of a Christmas Prince or Lord of Misrule. The statute directs that one of the Masters of Arts shall be placed over the juniors, every Christmas, for the direction of their games and festivities. He is to govern the whole society in hall and chapel, as a republic committed to his charge, by a set of laws which he is to frame in

Latin or Greek verse. His reign is to last during the
twelve days of Christmas and on Candlemas-day.
During that period he is to see that six spectacles or
' dialogues ' be presented, and his fee is to be forty
shillings. In the statutes ultimately given to the
College preciser ideas of discipline prevailed and the
Christmas Emperor, like the Christmas hobby-horse,
was ' forgot.'   In place of his licentious rule the College
lecturers are to exhibit comedies and tragedies, publicly
or privately, in the hall during the twelve days of
Christmas. Two lecturers are to be responsible for
each play, but the head lecturer is individually to
undertake one. In case they neglect their duties
they are each to pay a fine of ten shillings.

To play-acting within college walls and subject to
college discipline the authorities were kindly disposed ;
but the scholars were rigorously forbidden to attend
the stage exhibitions of professional actors. Witness,
in the code given to Peterhouse by Elizabeth's commissioners, the statute *Ne scholares se immisceant
inhonestis.* " Let them not attend the public shews of
jugglers or actors, or presume to be present at public
exhibitions in churches, a theatre or *stadia* "—by
which we are to understand such open air places as
Howes or Wandlebury, both near Cambridge and
commonly used for ' shews '—" unless perhaps, for
their recreation, and with due regard to decency, they
attend them for a short time ; lest otherwise the
reputation of the scholars be cheapened, to the danger
of soul and body and to the scandal of the whole
House, as often arises from such exhibitions."

In 1575 the University was authorised by the
Privy Council to inhibit ' the attempts of light and
decayed persons for filthy lucre to devise and set up
in open places shews of unlawful, hurtful, pernicious,

and unhonest games ' within a circuit of five miles of
the town ; and the prohibition was subsequently
interpreted as including plays. Yet the authorities
were constantly troubled with such unlicensed performances within the limits. Hired and abetted by
the mayor and townsfolk, the servants of the Earl of
Leicester, the Earl of Oxford, or whatever other noble
patron, were constantly pitching their wandering
stage in the yard of the Falcon, the Saracen's Head,
or some other inn. ' A bad kind of people ' they are,
say the Heads of Houses, ' who draw the students from
their books ' ; besides, it is likely that they will bring
the plague with them. Here, authorised by Lord
North, is one Dutton with his company in September,
1592, actually setting up his writings on college gates
to advertise a performance at Chesterton ; ' which
town,' by the way ' doth continually annoy our
University.' What does it serve the Heads to direct
the constable of Chesterton to stop the performances ?
Their charge is ' slenderly executed, or rather wholly
neglected,' and the interludes go forward in contempt
of the privileges of the University. We can imagine
John Fletcher creeping to that scandalous exhibition.
Possibly he acted in some inn-yard performance himself : at least Dominus Pepper of his college did so at
the Black Bear in 1600. Against him it was charged
that he " was seen with an improper habit, having
deformed long locks of unseemly sight "—we remember
that ruffianly hair of Robert Greene—" and great
breeches, undecent for a graduate or scholar of orderly
carriage ; therefore the said Pepper was commanded
to appear presently, and procure his hair to be cut or
powled ; which being done, the said Pepper was then
suspended *ab omni gradu suscepto et suscipiendo*."

Of the student-plays acted at Cambridge in the last

half of the sixteenth century the number and the kinds
were endless. Most common, as was natural, were
the Latin plays of Plautus, Terence, and Seneca. Greek
tragedies and comedies (sometimes in Latin garb) were
also in use. Dr. Dee, one of the first fellows of Trinity
and in later life famous as an astrologer, records that,
when he was Greek lector, he exhibited before the
University in the hall of his college the *Pax* of Aristophanes, " with the performance of scarabeus his flying
up to Jupiter's palace with a man and his basket of
victuals on his back ; whereat was great wondering
and many vain reports spread abroad of the means
how that was effected."

On other occasions the subject was religious, and,
after the breach with Rome, the abuses of papacy
furnished material for numerous plays. Of this class
was the celebrated comedy, *Pammachius*, written in
Latin by the German, Kirchmeyer, and acted at Christ's
in 1545. Though the acting edition was bowdlerised
by the omission of such passages as reflected most
severely on Roman misdoings, the performance was
highly censured by the Chancellor, Bishop Gardiner.
On other occasions English history supplied a theme
for Latin plays. In Emmanuel library there is a
manuscript copy, with the actors' names, of the once
famous tragedy of *Richard III*, written by Dr. Legge,
Master of Caius, but acted at Saint John's in 1580—a
play which, in the estimation of Sir John Harington,
in his *Apologie for Poetry* (1591), ' would move, I think,
Phalaris, the tyrant, and terrify all tyrannous-minded
men from following their foolish, ambitious humours.'

During the five days of Elizabeth's stay at Cambridge
in 1564, besides a round of visits to the colleges, she was
' entertained ' by interminable sermons, disputations,
and addresses, both in prose and verse and in all the

learned languages, including Hebrew and 'Caldee';
likewise by not less than three plays. The first was
the *Aulularia* of Plautus, which was acted in King's
chapel on Sunday evening. A great stage was erected
in the ante-chapel, "containing the breadth of the
church from the one side to the other, that the chapels
might serve for houses [*i.e.* tiring-houses]. Upon the
south wall was hanged a cloth of state for her majesty.
In the rood-loft another stage for ladies and gentle-
women to stand on ; and the two lower tables, under
the said rood-loft, were greatly enlarged and railed for
the choice officers of the Court. When all things were
ready for the plays the Lord Chamberlain with Mr.
Secretary came in bringing a multitude of the guard
with them, having every man in his hand a torch-staff
for the lights of the play (for no other lights were
occupied) and would not suffer any to stand upon the
stage, save a very few on the north side. From the
quire door unto the stage was made, as 'twere, a
bridge, railed on both sides, for the Queen's Grace
to go to the stage, which was straitly kept." The
actors were chosen from all the colleges. The play
lasted until midnight.

At nine on Monday night she was present, in the same
place, at the play called *Dido*, written in hexameter
verse and acted by the students of King's. On
Tuesday she saw *Ezechias* acted in English. On
Wednesday great preparations and charges had been
made for yet another play, ' the tragedy of Sophocles,
called *Ajax Flagellifer*,' in Latin. But her majesty,
not unnaturally, was ' over-watched with former plays,'
and, to the great sorrow of the players and the
whole University, the representation did not take
place.

Once again, in 1592, Elizabeth proposed to honour

KING'S COLLEGE CHAPEL

the University with her presence. Since 1564, her majesty had made acquaintance with a native drama which she reasonably preferred to all the premeditated welcomes of 'great clerks,' and, through her Vice-Chamberlain, she asked that the University should perform a comedy in English. The Vice-Chancellor and the Heads were seriously disturbed by the request, as barely three weeks' notice of the visit was given. Humbly they represented that, desirous as they were to do anything to give the Queen pleasure, yet their actors had had 'no practice in this English vein' and were indeed very unwilling to act in English : furthermore, that they had no English comedies, and would not be able to make or translate one in the time allowed them. They submit that longer time is needed, and that Latin is to be preferred. The visit never took place. Possibly Elizabeth was already taken with the flights of Shakespeare and was of Jonson's mind—

> The merry Greek, tart Aristophanes,
> Neat Terence, witty Plautus now not please.

In 1592 the University authorities were evidently unaware that there was ready to their hand, if not a translation, an adaptation of Plautus' *Menæchmi* in the *Comedy of Errors*. Before the century was out *Hamlet* had been acted in the University. Speaking in the character of the player, Kemp, the scholar-author of *The Return from Parnassus* (1602), shrewdly contrasts the academic and the stage actors and writers. " Few of the University pen plays well ; they smell too much of that writer Ovid and that writer Metamorphosis, and talk too much of Proserpina and Juppiter. Why, here's our fellow Shakespeare puts them all down."

To the *Parnassus* trilogy we turn as a specimen of the fully developed English comedy which was represented in college halls in the last years of Elizabeth. Here there is no space to do more than allude to its famous predecessor *Gammer Gurton's Needle*, acted at Christ's in or about 1563. It was once held that this was the first English comedy, and that its author was John Still, at the time a fellow of Christ's, afterwards Master of Trinity and Bishop of Bath and Wells. But Dr. Peile has shown reason for believing that the ' Mr. S., Master of Art,' to whose authorship it is assigned in the printed copy of 1575, was really a certain William Stevenson, fellow of Christ's. Moreover the greatly superior play of *Ralph Roister Doister* was written by Nicholas Udall and performed, apparently by the Eton boys, at least twenty years before the Christ's play. *Gammer Gurton* is a homespun performance of some humour but no wit. But for the incontestable evidence of the title-page that it was acted before a college audience, we might ask, with Christopher Sly, whether this ' commonty ' was not ' a Christmas gambold ' to amuse rustics. It only interests us as illustrating the immense progress which college drama made between the first and the last years of Elizabeth.

The *Parnassus* plays, on the other hand, breathe everywhere the atmosphere of London and the tiring-house. Not in Cambridge among ' old drowsy academics ' must the pilgrim seek Helicon hill. The god Cynthius holds his court somewhere near Paul's Churchyard and the booksellers' posts, and the Muses speak the language, not of Homer, Ennius, or Virgil, but of Shakespeare. In the company of this unknown writer we feel that we stand very near indeed to ' sweet Mr. Shakespeare.' It is not only that his characters quote tags from *Adonis, Lucrece* and *Romeo* as things with which everybody is familiar, or that he knows, and assumes that his audience know, how Shakespeare 'purged' Ben Jonson in some way now only conjectural. At every turn we meet the 'fine-filed phrases' of Shakespeare, and the blank lines, except where they parody the rant of Marlowe and Kyd, have the ring of *Love's Labour's Lost*.

Of the three plays the last (which is the second part of *The Return from Parnassus*) was printed in 1606. It has been reprinted many times and is fairly well known on account of its references to Shakespeare. The others, together with this second part, were discovered in 1886, by the Rev. W. D. Macray, in a manuscript book once belonging to the antiquary Hearne and now in the Bodleian Library. The second part of *The Return* may be distinguished by the second title, which it bears in the 1606 text, of *The Scourge of Simony*. *The Scourge* was 'publicly acted by the students of Saint John's College in Cambridge,' and it is clear that the others were acted by them too. *The Scourge* was played in December, 1602, and *The Pilgrimage to Parnassus*, which is the earliest of the group, in December, 1597. Of the writer we can only surmise from internal evidence that he was a member of Saint John's, and that, failing to get his degree at Cambridge, he removed to a German university, took a 'silly poor degree there' and afterwards returned to Cambridge. Either his name or his county seems to have been Cheshire.

The three plays are no elaborated productions. They are described as 'Christmas toys,' and the prologue of *The Pilgrimage* proclaims it to be the fruit of three days' study. In point of wit and ingenuity there is little to choose between them. But, as

12

The Scourge is better known and, on the whole, is less characteristic of student life, I select the two earlier plays as examples of Cambridge drama in the days of Elizabeth.

Two scholars, Philomusus and Studioso, about to start on a pilgrimage to Parnassus hill, take counsel of the aged Consiliodorus. He warns them of the difficulties of the journey and the ill companions they will meet on the way. The first country that they come to is the Island of Logic—Logic being, after Grammar, the first subject of the *trivium* course and the ' Little-go ' of those days. It is full of craggy mountains and thorny valleys, much like Wales, and in it dwell two robbers, called Genus and Species, who ' take captive every true man's invention that come by them.' In this island they encounter a tipsy scholar, named Madido, who recounts his travel thither. He took shipping at *Qui mihi discipulus*, sailed to *Propria quæ Maribus*, and thence came to *As in Præsenti*, but with great danger ; for there were certain people there, called schoolmasters, who took him prisoner and put to death at least three hundred rods on his back. So he went on to Syntaxis, a land full of joiners, and came thence to the Isle of Prosodia, ' where are men six feet long,' not mentioned in Mandeville's chronicle. Madido scouts the suggestion that he should join in the pilgrimage : " There is no true Parnassus but the third loft of a wine-tavern, no true Helicon but a cup of brown bastard." Philomusus is almost persuaded by his pint-pot oratory ; but Studioso prevails with him to prosecute the journey. Next they come to the Land of Rhetoric, a delicious country, where Don Cicero sings like a nightingale in company with Muretus, Ascham and other learned men. Here they overtake Stupido, who has taken ten

years to get thus far and finds that Logic makes his head
ache. A Puritan uncle, ' who never wore cap or surplice
or any such popish ornament,' has counselled him to
abandon the study of Rhetoric, Poetry and Philosophy,
as there is no sound edifying knowledge in them.
" You cannot see a rhetorician, a rimer or poet, as
you call it, but he wears such diabolical ruffs
and wicked great breeches, full of sin, that it would
make a zealous professor's heart to bleed for grief."
Studioso is half-disposed to join Stupido's ' pure
honest-seeming company ' ; but this time it is the
livelier Philomusus who insists on continuing the
quest.

Next they come to the pleasant Land of Poetry ;
and here they find Amoretto reading Ovid and celebrating his Corinna in lines that have the unmistakable
trick of Shakespeare in his salad days.

> Love keeps his revels in Corinna's brows,
> Dances levaltos in her speaking eye,
> Dies and is buried in her dimpled cheek,
> Revives and quickens in her cherry lips,
> Keeps watch and ward in her fair snowy chin
> That no rough swain approach or enter in.

And so forth. Philomusus and Studioso are for a time
seduced from the pilgrims' way by this fleshly poet.
When they come to their senses Studioso cries out
on ' poetry's fair baits ' : Philomusus, the Muses'
friend, is wiser.

> O do not wrong this music of the soul,
> The fairest child that e'er the soul brought forth.
> For who reads poets with a chaster mind
> Shall ne'er infected be by poesy.

Rather crestfallen, they emerge in the rough Land of

Philosophy. Here they fall in with an ' old school-fellow,' Ingenioso. He is making haste to quit the ' griggy barbarous country,' which, he says, is pitifully out of silver. " I talked with a friend of mine that lately gave his horse a bottle of hay at the bottom of the hill, who told me that Apollo had sent to Pluto to borrow twenty nobles to pay his commons : he added further that he met coming down from the hill a company of ragged vicars and forlorn schoolmasters, who, as they walked, scratched their unthrifty elbows, and often put their hands into their unpeopled pockets, that had not been possessed with faces this many a day. There stood one digging for gold in a standish ; another looking for cockpence in the bottom of a pew ; the third tolling for silver in a belfry : but they were never so happy as Æsop's cock, to find a precious stone." He flatly declines to join the pilgrims. Hobson, the carrier, finds more money in the tails of twenty sorry horses than a scholar in two hundred books. So he bids them farewell, " and take heed that I take you not twenty years hence in a vicar's seat, asking for the white cow with the black foot, or else interpreting *pueriles confabulationes* to a company of seven-year-old apes."

So after four years' travel *The Pilgrimage* takes leave of the two searchers, resolute and hopeful still, at the foot of Parnassus.

In *The Return* the pilgrims have gone out from the regions of academic learning into a world which knows nothing of the scholar's trade. The play is longer and more carefully elaborated than its predecessor.

It opens with an admirable scene of fooling between Consiliodorus and his boy, Leonard, a clown who is quite capable of holding his own with Lancelot Gobbo.

Then we are introduced to the returning pilgrims. Their quest has ended disastrously. Studioso, the man of books, rails on ' the cosening arts ' at whose cold altars he has sacrificed his youth. Philomusus proposes that they shall bid adieu to Parnassus and wander in the world to reap their fortunes wheresoever they grow.

> Some thacked cottage, or some country hall,
> Some porch, some belfry, or some scrivener's stall
> Will yield some harbour to our wand'ring heads.

To them enters Ingenioso. He is now a bookseller's hack, ' affectionately bound to the right honourable printing house for his poor shifts of apparel.' However, he has hopes from a gouty patron, in whose praise he has composed ' a pamphlet that none is privy unto but a pint of wine and a pipe of tobacco.' The patron is a curmudgeonly person, who talks much of his favour for ' scholars.' " But, surely, of late the *utensilia* of potions and purges have been very costly unto me. For my own part I had not cared for dying, but, when I am dead, I know not what will become of scholars : hitherto I have besprinkled them prettily with the drops of my bounty." When Ingenioso has pronounced his little speech, ' with a hundred damnable lies of his liberality,' his Mæcenas " puts his hand into the pocket of a pair of breeches that were made in William the Conqueror's days, groping in his pocket with great deliberation, and while I stood by dreaming of the gold of India, he drew me out two lean faces (*i.e.* coins), gave me fiddler's wages and dismissed me."

To him, thus distressed, enters an old acquaintance, Luxurioso, who is a ' liquid scholar ' with a nose in a red suit of apparel of the Bardolphian pattern. He has served a seven years' apprenticeship to the printers, ' levelling of colons, squaring of periods, by the month.' A good horse would not have endured his Pythagorean diet of single beer and three *q*'s of bread—*q* is the buttery abbreviation at Cambridge for a farthing. Now he is off to London, ' for there is a great-nosed ballad-maker deceased, and I am promised to be the rimer of the city.'   Next we find him at a fair, accompanied by his boy, engaged to sing his ' pretty sonnet ' of Richard and Robert and the strange event that befell them as they went to market, with a rousing Jingo chorus that might have done credit to Autolycus.

Philomusus and Studioso, dunned by drapers, tailors and tapsters, fall to even humbler courses. Studioso is engaged by an old churl and his wife, mistress Avaritia, to tutor their son. The conditions of his indenture are that he shall have bread, beer and bacon enough, lie in hempen sheets on a good mattress —to keep him from growing pursy—wait at meals, work all harvest time, be dutiful to his pupil, and receive five marks a year and ' cast forlorn wardrobe ' that ploughmen would scarcely accept. Philomusus is ' beneficed with a sextonship and clerkship,' and the voice that might have been a poet's or orator's is ' employed, like a bellman's, in the inquiry of a strayed beast.'   " For my conditions, the hoydens, for want of further rhetoric, made them but few and contained them in these two, *Dig well* and *Ring well* ; ' and in so doing,' quoth our churchwarden, ' thou shalt gain not only our praise but also our commendations.' "

Studioso loses his situation because his pupil is very forward to have him gone, and complains to his mother. Philomusus is put out of office by a stuttering churchwarden because he neglects

CAMBRIDGE FROM SHEEP'S GREEN

to sweep the church, ring the bells and whip the dogs out.

Not less unhappy are the experiences of Ingenioso and Luxurioso. Ingenioso hires himself to write love verses for Gullio, a foolish, bragging captain who has a copious store of quotations from Shakespeare, which, like Justice Shallow, he passes off as his own 'fancies and goodnights.' Ingenioso is commissioned to write verses to Lady Lesbia in divers veins, and duly executes specimens in the styles of Chaucer, Spenser and Shakespeare. The last is selected by Gullio. "Let this duncified world esteem of Chaucer and Spenser; I'll worship sweet Mr. Shakespeare, and, to honour him, will lay his *Venus and Adonis* under my pillow, as we read of one (I do not well remember his name, but I am sure he was a king) slept with Homer under his bed's head." Unhappily Gullio insists on adding some Latin verses of his own, and Gullio's Latin is such as they speak in Padua and Rheims. "Why, it is not the custom in Padua to observe such base rules as Lily, Priscian," the grammarians, "and such base companions have set down: we of the better sort have a privilege to create Latin, like knights, and to say, Rise up, Sir Phrase." Lesbia has wit enough to see that the Latin is Gullio's, and that the Shakespearian cento is not, and she rejects his suit with scorn: so Ingenioso loses his job. Luxurioso too finds that the honourable trade of ballad-making is 'of base reckoning.' "So it hath been in ancient time, when Homer first set up his riming shop, one of the first that ever was of my trade." He proposes to begin life anew as a tapster in the Low Countries, and there drink himself as blind as Homer. Studioso and Philomusus resolve to try their fortune at Rome or Rheims. And so the play ends with the dismal reflection that scholars still must live in discontent.

Yes : discontent is, and is long to remain, the note of the Cambridge scholar. The old order which satisfied the medieval clerk is hateful to him : he cannot live the life of Sir Nathaniel, the curate, or Holofernes, the schoolmaster. The wide Faery Land ruled by Gloriana is stretched before him, and there are brazen castles to assault and dragons to destroy, if only he were furnished with the warlike steed and knightly arms. A golden world of Literature has dawned on Cambridge, but as yet there is no mansion in it for the scholar who has no money and no patron. The voices of Philomusus and Studioso, desperately bound for Rome or Rheims, might seem to be heard in the lament which Robert Wild, fifty years later, puts in the mouth of the scholar who is leaving Cambridge without reward or prospects.

In a melancholy study,
  None but myself ;
Methought my Muse grew muddy
    After seven years' reading
    And costly breeding
  I felt, but could find no pelf ;
Into learned rags
  I've rent my plush and satin ;
And now am fit to beg
  In Hebrew, Greek and Latin ;
Instead of Aristotle
    Would I had got a patten.
Alas ! poor scholar, whither wilt thou go ?

Into some country village
  Now I must go,
Where neither tithe nor tillage
    The greedy patron
    And parchèd matron
  Swear to the Church they owe:

Yet if I can preach
    And pray too on a sudden,
And confute the Pope
    At adventure, without studying,
Then—ten pounds a year,
    Besides a Sunday pudden.
Alas! poor scholar, whither wilt thou go?

    Ships, ships, ships I discover,
      Crossing the main;
Shall I go in—go over—
      Turn Jew or Atheist
      Turk or Papist
    To Geneva or Amsterdam?
Bishoprics are void
    In Scotland—shall I thither,
Or follow Windebank
    And Finch, to see if either
Do want a priest to shrive them?
    O no! 'tis blustering weather.
Alas! poor scholar, whither wilt thou go?

CHAPTER IX

MILTON AND THE COMMONWEALTH

Men whose life, learning, faith and pure intent
Would have been held in high esteem by Paul
Must now be named and printed heretics.

MILTON

S O far this has been a Book of Beginnings. Very
slightly it has sketched the beginnings of the
University in the days of John and Henry III;
of the colleges in the thirteenth and fourteenth
centuries; of Cambridge humanism, with Erasmus;
of the assertion of independence in religious thought,
with the White Horse reformers; of Cambridge
science, with Caius and Harvey; of Cambridge literature in the reign of Elizabeth. If the limits or the
plan of this book allowed it, a chapter should be given
to the origin of individualism in religious belief,
presently developing into nonconformity. From the
days of Whitgift, when Cartwright raised the standard
of revolt against the Elizabethan settlement, to those
of Sancroft, when the Toleration Act effected a de-
ceptive truce, the question which absorbed Cambridge,
even to the overshadowing of the constitutional crisis,
was that of the authority of the Reformed Church.

Neither with the beginnings nor with the long
continuance of the factious debate of that question
will these pages be occupied. The discussion of
'church-clothes,' whether material or mystical, would

take us very far afield from the aim of this volume, which is roughly to outline the growth of the University from the seed to the full-grown tree, and to note the spreading of those branches which bear wholesome fruit at the present day. With the parasitic growths that at times have marred the picturesqueness and fertility of the tree I do not propose to concern myself. Sectarian controversy at Cambridge, it may be hoped, is dead. While it lasted it was a disease in the flesh, which drained the life's blood of the University, and sapped the energies which should have been devoted to more profitable ends.

The question in its beginning was not a Cambridge one. It began with Zurich and Geneva, where the exiled Cambridge divines ' ate pulse ' in the days of Mary. When it was transplanted to England it rooted itself at Oxford not less stubbornly than at Cambridge. Nor had it an effectual ending. The religious ' settlements ' of the sixteenth and seventeenth centuries were no settlements : settlement only came from exhaustion or the external arms of Rome. The human battles of Greek and Trojan interest us because they end in victory or defeat. Achilles slays Hector, and then ' gone is Ilium and the great glory of the Teucrians.' Not so the wars of the gods. Athene and Diomed wound Ares ; but we know that Ares will live to fight another day, and all-powerful Zeus shows a minimum of concern.

For more than a century after the expulsion of the Puritan Cartwright from the Lady Margaret Professorship of Divinity (1570) Cambridge was engrossed in controversies which, so far as its proper work was touched, scarcely concerned it at all. When the dust of battle begins to lift we discern some great captains, Newton and Bentley, and the forward march is

resumed.   Until then the field is occupied by wandering
shadows, forcers of conscience, Arminian or Calvinist.
In the great questions concerning Church and State
the University was inevitably involved by external
forces ; but the questions did not begin with Cambridge, and, so far as they were solved at all, Cambridge
was divided in its voice, and did not make a pre-
ponderating contribution to the solution, as it had
done in the Divorce Question.

A disastrous symptom of the time was the sub-
ordination of all learning to controversial theology.
The decay, not merely of secular knowledge, but of
that classical study which was the armoury of the
early Reformers was not so much the outcome of
neglect as of policy.   The Puritans of either party
in the Cartwright dispute deliberately attempted to
remodel Cambridge after the pattern of Geneva—
' an elementary school and a seminary for ministers,'
as Mark Pattison called Calvin's university.   Whitgift,
for all that he had been Lady Margaret Professor,
knew no word of Greek.   When John Bois, one of
the translators of the Authorised Version, entered at
Saint John's, in 1580, " the knowledge of Greek," says
Mr. Mullinger, " had become almost extinct in the
former home of Ascham and Cheke."   In the same
college " the dicta of Calvin and Beza were habitually
cited as of authority inferior only to that of Scripture
itself, while the names of Ambrose, Jerome and
Augustine often served but to raise a half-contemptuous
smile."   At Trinity Puritan writers, such as Perkins
and Preston, were preferred to Aristotle and Plato.
Among the militant hot-heads of the Rebellion time
the prejudice against Greek and Latin developed into
a furious animosity.   The Westminster Divines, in
1644, prohibited the use of Latin, Greek and Hebrew

in sermons, as well as all citations of the Fathers.   In 1643, when Dr. Power, Lady Margaret preacher, attempted to deliver a Latin sermon in Great St. Mary's, as the duties of his office required, he was rabbled by a mob of soldiers who insisted that ' they knew no reason why all sermons should not be performed in English, that all might be edified.'

The very existence of the Universities was threatened by the Barebones Parliament, which was largely composed of Fifth Monarchy men. A proposal for the suppression of the Universities and all schools of learning was actually debated for some days, and only the dissolution of the Parliament by Cromwell prevented it from being carried. One wiseacre argued that " two colleges in each University should be set apart for such as shall wholly and solely apply themselves to the study of attaining and enjoying the spirit of our Lord Jesus, to which study needs few books or outward human helps, and none but the Holy Scriptures and such books as Jacob Behmen's should be used in these colleges, and all in English."   It was this proposal that was the occasion of the verses by some Cavalier scholar :—

> Wee'l down with all the Versities
>   Where learning is profest,
> Because they practise and maintain
>   The language of the Beast ;
> Wee'l drive the Doctors out of doors,
>   And parts whate'er they be ;
> Wee'l cry all Arts and Learning down,
>   And, hey, then up go we.

No dispassionate critic will maintain that Cambridge, at the close of the sixteenth and the beginning of the seventeenth century, was devoid of theologians whose attainments and scholarship were not unworthy of the reputation of the University. That some of the best learning of the country was to be found there is evidenced by the fact that four of the five representatives of England at the Synod of Dort (1618) were Cambridge men. But, looking over the list of Cambridge divines who took part in the translation of the Bible in the Authorised Version, one cannot fail to remark that not one of them could claim an eminence in scholarship which could match the learning of Ascham or Cheke, and, outside academic circles, hardly one of them is remembered at the present day. And the besetting fault of the best scholars of the time was that they were factious controversialists who, so far as they were able, dissociated themselves from the cares of teaching and discipline. In 1565, when the University was absorbed in the ' vestiarian controversy,' and a deliberate strike against the use of the surplice had been connived at by the authorities in Trinity and Saint John's, the Chancellor, Burleigh, wrote to the Vice-Chancellor deploring the factious strife, ' wherein the time once bestowed upon arts and sciences is frittered away in frivolous disputes.' Under Whitaker, Master of Saint John's and one of the most learned of Calvinist disputants, his own fellows complained that learning had been ' so discouraged as is incredible to be told.'

The High Church party, under Bancroft at Cambridge and Laud at Oxford, has the merit of having recognised and remedied, so far as remedy was possible, the low state of education and discipline which resulted from the hair-splitting controversies of the two Calvinistic schools, one of which accepted, the other rejected, the conditions which the State imposed upon the Church. Anarchy had been reduced to order, morals and discipline had been restored, and pedantry had given place to effective teaching before the Universities were overtaken by the renewed lawlessness of the Puritan rebellion of 1642. The reforms, no doubt, were mainly directed to the improvement of the intelligence and learning of the clergy, and they were accompanied by regulations as to ritual which were unnecessarily offensive to Puritan prejudice. They were extremely unpopular. England, in the first half of the sixteenth century, did not ask the Universities for learning, and it did ask for piety. Some indication of the unpopularity of the stricter regime introduced by Laud's followers at Cambridge, Cosin, Wren, Beale and Sterne, is seen in the numbers at the different colleges in 1641 compared with those given by Dr. Caius in 1573. The total of the University has increased from 1813, in the earlier, to 2091 in the later year : but the increase is more than accounted for by the addition, since 1573, of two new colleges, Emmanuel and Sidney. In 1641 both these Puritan colleges were very full. Emmanuel is third in order and rivals the numbers of Trinity : Sidney, in spite of its poverty and lack of space, is ninth. Magdalene, another typically Puritan college, has more than doubled its numbers since 1573. Caius, depressed by suspicions of papistry in 1573, has risen from the eleventh to the fourth place. Saint John's and Queens', Laudian colleges, maintain their numbers ; but Jesus, Pembroke and Peterhouse, all of them noted for their High Church temper, come at the bottom of the list and show a heavy fall in numbers.

Both at the earlier and later period Christ's maintained a high place in the order of colleges. It was third in 1573, and in 1641, though it had dropped below Emmanuel and Caius, it more than maintained its numbers. Its success was not due to compliance with the fashionable Puritanism but to the capacity of its teaching staff and to a quality of large-minded comprehensiveness in which Christ's, in the twentieth as in the seventeenth century, deserves to be regarded as the most Cantabrigian of Cambridge colleges. Its doors have ever been widely open to men of all creeds and parties, whose incompatible ideals seem to have been compatible with harmonious college intercourse. In 1573 the college was said to be tainted with Novelism, *i.e.* Puritan doctrine. Emmanuel, founded in 1584, was a graft of Christ's, and its founder, Mildmay, and first Master, Laurence Chaderton, were Christ's men, and to Sidney also Christ's gave its first Master, James Montagu. But the Master of Christ's in 1573 was Dr. Hawford, a decided Anglican, and among recent graduates of the college was Bancroft. There is a pretty story that in their student days Bancroft and Chaderton got engaged in a town-and-gown fight, and that when Bancroft's life was in danger he was rescued by Chaderton ; from which incident grew up a life-long friendship, and Bancroft, in spite of his rigid views of Church discipline, during his primacy could never bring himself to deal harshly with Puritan Emmanuel. If further evidence be sought of the charitable good sense of the society of Christ's in matters of domestic difference it may be found in a document signed by the Master and fellows in 1590 that " we whose names are subscribed do forgive and forget all injuries past whatsoever, and do promise to deal Christianly and friendly hereafter one with another in words and actions."

Not less in 1625, the year when Milton was admitted, than in 1590, Christ's was distinguished from other colleges by its comprehensive tolerance. Among undergraduates who were Milton's contemporaries was John Cleveland, the Cavalier poet—a man antithetical to Milton alike in his poetry and his politics. Four years junior to Milton was Charles Lucas, the bold defender of Colchester against Fairfax in 1648. The Master was Thomas Bainbridge, a learned, quiet man, who in the religious warfare of his day stood neutral—' taking a nap and sleeping at our distractions,' says a Roundhead news-sheet, the *Mercurius Britannicus*. Among the fellows the two parties were represented in about equal numbers. The principal tutors were Power, Chappell and Mede. Power's pupils, who, like their tutor, were thought too loose, were called Poweritans : Chappell's, who were considered to be too precise, were called Puritans : and Mede's, as observing the medium, were called Medians. Of Dr. Power we have had a fleeting glimpse in the year 1643, when, on his way to preach at St. Mary's, he was pursued by a mob of soldiers, crying, " A Pope, a Pope," and vowing vengeance if he ventured into the pulpit. Of the three men Joseph Mede was incomparably the ablest—famous in his time as logician, philosopher, mathematician, anatomist, philologian, and skilled in history and chronology— more famous to-day as the spiritual father of the Platonists, who shed lustre on Cambridge in the generation which followed him, and who prepared the way for the school of Latitudinarianism which took such deep root in Cambridge theology in the eighteenth century. We may believe that Mede's learning and liberality profoundly influenced young Milton : but Mede was not his tutor.

To William Chappell the charge of the young poet was committed, perhaps at the desire of his Puritan father. But Chappell, though a precisian, was far from being fanatical. In later life he was even suspected of Arminianism by the more scrupulous of the

13

party. He was highly respected by Laud, and, through his influence, was advanced first to the Provostship of Trinity, Dublin, afterwards to the bishopric of Cork. His reputation as a tutor stood even higher than Mede's : " No tutor in our memory," says Fuller, " bred more or better pupils, so exact his care in their education." That he was severe, even to harshness, in his treatment of Milton seems pretty clear : Milton implies as much in a Latin letter to his friend, Diodati, and, after his freshman year, he was transferred to another tutor. But the story that he was ' whipt ' by Chappell, as Dr. Peile has shown, is merely a gossiping invention. Chappell and Mede were intimate friends. Very likely Milton, as was a common practice of the time, ' kept ' in his tutor's chamber, and there we may picture the young poet listening eagerly to the ' mellifluous streams ' that issued from the mouths of the two scholars and ' watered all the schools ' of Cambridge.

We have to remember that Milton, like Darwin, entered at Christ's with the intention of being ordained. There is no reason to suppose that, in his earlier Cambridge days at least, he viewed Anglican cere-monies with any repugnance. Sincerity and matured judgment are not to be looked for in a student's exercise, but it is hard to think that the Latin elegiacs which Milton wrote in his second year on the deaths of Andrewes, the good Bishop of Winchester, and Felton, Bishop of Ely, were altogether conventional in their respectful admiration. In Christ's chapel he must have seen a ritual which was certainly not in accordance with the simplicity demanded by the severer Protestants. Mede, most tolerant of men, admitted that the chapel services were rather too ' regular ' for his private taste. Though, perhaps under compulsion, he preached ' for bowing to altars,' he did not himself conform to the practice. The ' pictures and angels ' which provoked the zeal of Dowsing in 1643 were yet unchallenged in Christ's chapel in Milton's day. Doubtless he often kneeled, with a quiet conscience, on the altar-steps of costly marble which poor Dr. Bainbridge, in his last days, was compelled to level : and the pealing organ, built in long-gone times before the Reformation, was still in its place, to dissolve him into ecstasies. In the pagan allegory of his *Vacation Exercise* the Christ's undergraduate expressed a religious emotion, born of music and mysticism, which never warmed him in the sublimities of his epic, when he sang how

> The deep transported mind may soar
> Above the wheeling poles, and at Heaven's door
> Look in, and see each blissful deity,
> How he before the thunderous throne doth lie,
> Listening to what unshorn Apollo sings
> To the touch of golden wires.

The rooms traditionally pointed out as Milton's at some time during his seven years' residence at Christ's are on the left-hand side of the principal court as you enter it from the street—the first-floor rooms on the staircase next the gate, and on the gate side of it. Wordsworth has recorded in *The Prelude* how, in his thoughtless undergraduate days, he visited the rooms, which were then occupied by an acquaintance : how ' in the innocent lodge and oratory ' of the ' temperate bard ' he ' poured out libations ' to his memory : and how, ' excited by the fumes of wine,' he ran through the streets in desperate haste to reach the chapel of his own college, Saint John's, before the bell stopped. We may accept the tradition which Wordsworth honoured in such an uncharacteristic way. But, whether the rooms were occupied by Milton before or after his degree, we may be certain that, according to the invariable usage, he shared them with other students—possibly also with his tutor. The chamber —now divided into bedroom and ' keeping ' room—was then partitioned into studies—the three windows suggest that there were three of them—and the middle space was occupied by the beds of the tenants.

Two of the windows look across the ' smooth-shaven green ' towards the hall, which, in its present restored state, probably fairly reproduces the room as it was familiar to the poet. There, in the summer of his third year (1628), was exhibited the ' shew,' to which Milton contributed the Latin speeches and riming couplets of his *Vacation Exercise*. The occasion, as he says in the heading to the printed copy, was one at which nearly all the youth of the University was present, and we must suppose that the selection of Milton as the College spokesman was a recognition of his superior learning and poetical abilities. In later life when he was taunted with an un-Puritanical addiction to theatres, he dismissed the charge with a gratuitous jibe at the stage performances of which he was a spectator in college days.

Many young divines, and those of next aptitude in divinity, have been seen oft in the colleges upon the stage, writhing and unboning their clergy limbs to all the antic and dishonest gestures of Trinculos, buffoons and bawds, prostituting the shame of that ministry, which either they had or were nigh having, to the eyes of courtiers and court-ladies, with their grooms and mademoiselles. There, while they acted and overacted, among other young scholars I was a spectator : they thought themselves gallant men, and I thought them fools : they made sport, and I laughed : they mispronounced, and I misliked : and, to make up the Atticism, they were out, and I hissed.

The disclaimer was perhaps a little disingenuous, if

FIRST COURT OF CHRIST'S COLLEGE

FROM MILTON'S CHAMBER

it suggested a disparagement of Shakespeare. How the young candidate for ordination was magnetised by the genius of Shakespeare we know from the lines which he wrote, two years after his degree, in preface to the second Folio edition of the plays, from the recurring echoes of his master in *Comus*, and the direct allusion in *L'Allegro*. But what Milton condemned was not Shakespeare's comedy but the badness of the acting and the impropriety of the performance of it by clerical actors before an audience of courtiers and ladies. His words seem to imply that *The Tempest* was acted on some state occasion when he was a young scholar. The King and Queen visited the University in 1632, just before Milton took his M.A. degree and left Cambridge. On that occasion two comedies were performed in their presence, *The Rival Friends*, by Hausted, a fellow of Queens', and *The Jealous Lovers*, by Randolph, a fellow of Trinity. But there is no record of the acting of a third play, and, as the royal visitors came and left on the same day, it is scarcely possible that more than two were exhibited. The occasion to which Milton refers seems likely to have been the visit of King Charles in 1628 : but there is no information about the entertainments provided on that occasion.[1]

By his contemporaries at Cambridge Milton was styled ' the Lady of Christ's,' and the name may have been suggested by that delicacy of feature which, we know, was Milton's in his young days. But, as undergraduate sobriquets are more apt to have a homely reference to some unesteemed singularity, it is at least

---

[1] It is just possible 'that, when he wrote ' Trinculos,' Milton was thinking of Trincalo, a clown in the play *Albumazar*, which was acted before James I in 1615. Perhaps *Albumazar* was revived for the entertainment of Charles in 1628.

as likely that he impressed his fellow-students by qualities which they deemed effeminate. It is conjecturable that to the raw youths who were his equals in age he seemed distant in manners and too conscious of his intellectual superiority. Writing in 1642 he makes much of the more than ordinary respect in which he was held by those ' courteous and learned men,' the fellows of his college ; and in a letter addressed to his former schoolmaster, Alexander Gill, he mentions with obvious pride that one of the fellows, who was long past the age for such trifles, had employed him to write a copy of Latin verses, to be recited at a philosophical disputation which his employer had to conduct at the Commencement. But among undergraduates, on his own showing, he was not popular. In an exercise spoken in the College hall in his undergraduate time he deprecates the malice shown in the faces of his auditors ; and in his letter to Gill he says that he has almost no companions in his studies.

We may well believe that the academic routine which monopolised the attention of an ordinary undergraduate had very little part in the reading of Milton. Though custom demanded of him the composition of Latin elegiacs, he seems so far to have shared the Puritan contempt of the learned languages that he regarded them as only ancillary to the study of his native literature. That seems to be witnessed in his *Vacation Exercise*, when he turns with relief from Latin to address his Native Language as the daintiest dish, which is served up last. The preference of his youth lasted to old age. As he writes in *Paradise Regained* :

> If I would delight my private hours
> With music or with poem, where so soon
> As in our native language can I find
> That solace ?

If we did not know as much from *L'Allegro* and *Il Penseroso*, we have the evidence of Milton's own statement, in 1642, that his delight in younger days was in the romances of Spenser and the Arthurian cycle :

> Of faery damsels met in forest wide
> By knights of Logres or of Lyones,
> Lancelot, or Pelleas, or Pellenore.

Did Milton love his university, as it was loved by poor, ' untoward ' Nash ? Were his thoughts of it in after life linked with memories of youthful friendships, as those of Coleridge and Tennyson were ? The stormy period which covered his middle life left little room for sentiment, and, when he looked back upon Cambridge then, it was with the hardened eyes of a partisan. In 1642 it seemed to him, watching from a distance the insidious encroachment of ' prelaty,' that Cambridge and the sister university were very sick indeed. " She vomits now out of sickness, but, ere it be well with her, she must vomit by strong physic." London he thinks a more honourable place to dwell in than his university, " which, as in the time of her better health and mine own younger judgment I never greatly admired, so now much less."

If Milton's diatribe of 1642 is a true expression of the feelings which he entertained for his Alma Mater in his younger days, the pastors of his youth, whose learning and courtesy he had once so warmly recognised, might rise up in the judgment and condemn him for ingratitude. But it is not true. Milton had other thoughts of ' old Damoetas ' in 1637, when he wrote *Lycidas*. Unless we take the impossible view that *Lycidas* was merely a conventional tribute of respect to the memory of an exemplary clergyman, we must suppose that a warm feeling of affection joined him to

Edward King, his junior by two years at Christ's. If we are to attach any meaning to his allegory it was not affinity in religious preferences so much as common literary interests which drew them together :

> He knew
> Himself to sing and build the lofty rime.

And Damoetas, whether he were Chappell or Mede or some other senior, loved to hear his song. The rural ditties, to which rough satyrs danced, may very likely refer to some college ' shew ' prepared by King. All the evidence that he left of poetical faculty consists of certain copies of Latin iambics and elegiacs contained in collections of verse with which it was the fashion of the University to celebrate royal birthdays and like occasions. They are tame, prosaic performances and suggest that in an imitative way he was working a vein which Milton had more successfully exploited. But in him Milton had an admirer and sympathiser, as Spenser had in Kirke. The figures dim inwrought in Camus' bonnet have a suggestion of mystical speculation, inspired by Mede and shared by King. Nursed on the self-same hill with Lycidas, Milton, in 1637, had a kindness for his college and university which time and after-prejudice outwore. Prejudice of an opposite kind turned Dryden's affections away from his nursing mother. That was not the fault of Alma Mater.

Strong physic, the regimen prescribed for the University by Milton in 1642, was already at work before the year was out. Yet Cambridge seemed to be in pristine health in March of that year, when it was visited by the King. A melancholic season it was in royalist affairs, as Clarendon testifies ; yet his warm reception at the University contributed something to raise the spirits of the King and his party. Charles left London, never to return until the last scenes of his life, on January 10. Early in March he was at Newmarket, and there received the fruitless petition of Parliament that he should return to London—the last overture for a peaceable settlement. Even when he was there the county of Cambridge was petitioning Parliament to purge the universities and to settle religion on Puritan principles. Least of all in the eastern counties might unhappy Charles look for sympathy and support. In the University only the bold winds as yet were speechless and the rack stood still. There, though short notice was given of the intended visit, Charles was welcomed with something of the loyal ceremony that had waited on Elizabeth.

On March 21, ' the best day of my life,' as he says, Joseph Beaumont, afterwards Master of Peterhouse, sat down to write to his father an account of the auspicious occasion. First, on a Saturday morning, between nine and ten, came the little Prince of Wales, afterwards Charles II, attended by lords and gentlemen of the Court. The parade of dignity with which the child of eleven was received by the grave seniors of the University might seem laughable, but for the presage of tears which it concealed. No circumstance of honour was omitted that the University could give. He was greeted with the inevitable Latin orations : he was solemnly created a Master of Arts, and invited to nominate any of his train for a similar honour : he was taken to King's chapel, ' where, at his entrance into the choir, I saw him say his prayers, of which he was so little ashamed that, in the midst of that multitude, he hid not his devotion in his hat.' Then, at Trinity, after dinner he sat through a comedy in

English, ' and gave all signs of great acceptance which he could, and more than the University dared expect,' and so returned the same afternoon to Newmarket. The comedy was *The Guardian,* written by Abraham Cowley, then a fellow of Trinity. Six months later Parliament enacted that the public exhibition of stage-plays should cease throughout the kingdom, and for twenty years the dramatic Muses were silent at Cambridge. In the ten years which followed the Restoration we hear of occasional stage performances by the University in presence of distinguished visitors ; but college play-acting, as a custom, died with *The Guardian.* Twenty years after its exhibition in Trinity the play was revived, in London, in an altered form and with the new title, *The Cutter of Coleman Street* ; and Samuel Pepys took his wife to see it, ' and a good play it is.'

On the following Monday, King Charles himself, with his son and retinue, drove over from Newmarket to visit Cambridge, and the Vice-Chancellor and Mr. Cleveland, now a fellow of Saint John's, had orations ready to welcome him. He visited Trinity and Saint John's, approving the chapel ornaments, and took ' a travelling banquet '—he was on his way to York—in the second court of the latter college, ' where he ate a little and gave the Prince good store to put in his pocket : then the noblemen and the rest of his followers made quick dispatch of the remainder.' ' Much content ' the King received from the doctors : but his visit lacked not ominous symptoms. Neither the sheriff nor any of the county gentlemen came to meet him, and ' women and others of the town followed his coach humbly and earnestly entreating that he would return to his parliament, or they should be undone.' Happy in the condescension of the King and the oppor-

STAIRCASE OF THE LIBRARY, ST. JOHN'S COLLEGE

tunity of showing its devotion to him the University lulled, or tried to lull, itself into a belief that all was yet well. On the Sunday following the visit, Holdsworth, Master of Emmanuel, preached at St. Mary's, and confidently assured his audience, " Never were the riches of the kingdom so great, its peace so constant, the state of it for all things so prosperous."

Very near, ' even at the doors,' when Holdsworth was preaching his Lenten sermon, was the ' two-handed engine ' seen in vision by Milton five years earlier. The ' hands ' that wielded it were furnished by the new Puritan foundation of Sidney. Edward Montagu, who later became known in history as the second Earl of Manchester, was admitted there in 1618 : he was a nephew of the first Master, James Montagu, afterwards Bishop of Winchester. Oliver Cromwell was admitted in 1616, but was removed from the College on his father's death in the following year.[1] The two men, whose quarrel over the New Model was the crisis of the war, were neighbours in Huntingdonshire, and successively represented the town of Huntingdon in Parliament : but as students they never met at Cambridge. In the Long Parliament Cromwell was member for the town of Cambridge.

The election of Cromwell, against strong royalist opposition, proved that Cambridge town stood with the rest of the eastern counties in vehement antagonism to the King. The University, on the other hand, divided on the subject of religion, was almost wholly royalist in feeling. Puritanism was decidedly stronger here than at Oxford : but the Puritan party, and

[1] Tradition says that Cromwell's chamber was that which is distinguished by a projecting window looking into Sidney Street, at the north-west corner of the College.

especially its leaders—such men as Whichcote, Henry More, Cudworth, Worthington, and even the Heads of Emmanuel and Sidney, Holdsworth and Samuel Ward—were men of tolerant views and in sympathy with the system of monarchy, if not with the King.

Between March, when the King passed through Cambridge, and August, 1642, when he raised his standard at Nottingham, active preparations for the inevitable struggle were being made on both sides. The townspeople obtained muskets and made targets of the windows of some of the scholars. The colleges sent for arms to London, and fifteen chests were brought in July. The mayor seized ten of them, and retained them ' for the safeguarding of the town ' : but the scholars of Trinity managed to get five chests into their college.

In June the King, then at York, wrote to the Vice-Chancellor requesting that the colleges, or any individuals in them, should supply him with a loan of money bearing interest at eight per cent., and to be repaid when the distractions of the kingdom should cease. In July he sent a further request that the colleges should send their plate to him, promising that it should be restored, or an equivalent paid, ' when it shall please God to end these troubles.' Both requests were met with a liberal and general response. A loan amounting, it is said, to £6000 was raised, and most of the colleges sent the bulk of their plate to the King by the hands of one of the proctors, John Poley of Pembroke. Lists of the pieces sent were made out specifying the weight of the silver. Most colleges sent everything that they had of value, except communion plate. Until the eighteenth century plate served as the reserve fund of a college. Every fellow-commoner was not so much requested as required to make a present of a cup or dish of silver, and when the college had to raise funds for building or other extraordinary purposes it was the usual thing to obtain them by sending some of its silver to the melting-pot. Exceptional pieces, such as the Lady Margaret's gifts to Christ's and Saint John's, or the drinking-horn and mazers bequeathed to Corpus by the guilds which founded it, were piously preserved from age to age : otherwise, neither associations nor workmanship increased the value. So it is likely that virtuosos of to-day have only to blame King Charles for anticipating the fate which would have attended the college treasure in ordinary course, even if it had not been requisitioned by the Parliament.

It is evidence of the fact that Puritanism in religion was not inevitably dissociated from loyalty to the throne that colleges such as Emmanuel, Sidney and Magdalene joined the rest in sending plate or money, or both, to the King. Five colleges apparently sent neither : they were Caius, Trinity Hall, Corpus, Saint Catherine's and Christ's. The Heads of these colleges were either neutral or known adherents of the Parliament, and, when the first ejections from masterships were made, in 1644, they contrived to keep their places. Cromwell's eldest son, Oliver, was at the time a pensioner of Saint Catherine's.

The transmission of the plate was not a business that could be contrived with secrecy. Mr. Mullinger pictures the scene which was to be witnessed in the first week of August : " The crates containing the plate standing in the chief quadrangle of the different colleges—the streets thronged with spectators waiting to see each convoy set forth—while a lively expectation of an actual encounter between Cromwell's soldiery and the royalist forces within the town itself added not a little to the excitement that prevailed among the lookers-on." Cromwell thought it the better plan to intercept the convoys on their road to Huntingdon, and lay in wait for it with a band of rustics at a place called Lowler, or Lolworth, Hedges, the only spot on that bare road which is screened by trees. However, the troopers who were conducting the plate made a detour and escaped the ambush. On the Huntingdonshire border they were met by a party of the King's friends and thence made their way in security to York. But Cromwell succeeded in ' staying ' some of the plate before it left Cambridge and transmitted it to London. At King's the plate was ' loaden and ready to be conveyed to the King ' when it was intercepted by Cromwell's orders.

Three of the Heads, Beale of Saint John's, Sterne of Jesus and Martin of Queens', were chiefly instrumental in sending the loan and plate. During the same month of August, Cromwell stationed his soldiers about the chapels of these colleges during service, arrested the Heads and dispatched them to London, where, by order of the Commons, they were imprisoned in the Tower. Cromwell's behaviour, if we are to believe royalist recollections of the incident, was studiously offensive. When one of the arrested Heads made a request to be allowed time to put up some linen he replied ' that it was not in his commission.'

With the subsequent sufferings of the three Heads, the arrests of other ' malignants ' in the University and the sequestration of their belongings I do not propose to concern myself. The formation of the Eastern Counties Association and the fortification of Cambridge against an anticipated royal assault brought a train of disasters on the collective University. During the early months of 1643, it was subjected to a series of unwarranted indignities for which Cromwell must be held responsible. It was idle for the House of Lords to issue a ' Protection ' ordering that no person should presume to offer violence to any of the colleges, chapels, libraries and schools of the University, to interfere with divine service according to the rites of the Church of England, or to purloin or deface any of the belongings of the scholars. Cromwell treated the order with contempt. The colleges were garrisoned and suffered all the rigours of invasion in a hostile country. Carlyle sardonically draws a picture of ' confused brabbles between gown and garrison ' and ' college tippets, and on occasion still more venerable objects, being torn in the business.' Sane history, which does not concern itself with partisanship, may allow itself the expression of some disgust at the brutalities which ' the poor tapsters and town apprentices ' who constituted Cromwell's garrison wreaked on the quiet haunts of learning. In almost every college the bursars' accounts bear evidence to the wanton destruction made by Cromwell's men in students' rooms. Wainscot was burnt, furniture broken, books and properties stolen and sold for a tenth of their value in the market by ' a decayed hatter, a conventicling barber and a confiding tailor.' Treasuries were broken open, and at Saint John's ancient coins, valued at £22, were forcibly carried off. At Saint Mary's the Common Prayer Book was torn in pieces, and a beautiful cross, ' though it had not a jot of imagery or statue-work about it,' was defaced at the special instigation—so we are told—of Cromwell. Scholars ran the risk of being stoned as they walked the streets.

For some part of the vandalism committed in that

unhappy spring season the exigencies of war might be pleaded in excuse. The groves and orchards of some colleges were cut down and the timber sold. Six 'fair bridges' in college grounds were destroyed, and King's chapel was converted into a drill-hall. The materials lying ready for the rebuilding of Clare, and valued at £300 or £400, were used in the fortification of the Castle. Eighty soldiers were quartered in Pembroke. The occupants of the old court of Saint John's were driven out, and for sixteen months the place was made a prison 'for his majesty's loyal subjects.' One of the prisoners was the aged Samuel Ward, a good and able man, who was Master of Sidney in Cromwell's student-year, and, during the thirty-four years in which he presided over the College had won for it eminence and prosperity. Released from confinement when his health broke down, he died in his own college before the year was ended. When the election of a new Master was taking place and the fellows before election, according to custom, were receiving the communion, a body of soldiers 'violently plucked Mr. Pawson, one of the fellows, from the communion and threw him into a gaol in order to get a creature of their own at that election.'

Such is the picture—perhaps highly coloured—of Cambridge in 1643 which is presented to us by the *Querela Cantabrigiensis* and Walker's *Sufferings of the Clergy*. 'Agonised shrieks,' Carlyle calls the complaints of the sufferers, 'unmelodious hysterical wind, forgettable by all creatures.' They were no such matter. Cambridge, which, far more than Oxford, stood for liberty in religion and government, deserved other things from those whose watchword was Liberty. The excesses which Cromwell permitted were the outcome of a deep-seated hatred of discipline, learning and independence. William Dowsing, the ignorant clown who was charged by Parliament in 1643 with the duty of removing ' monuments of superstition ' from the churches and chapels of Cambridge, was a typical representative of the arrogant fanatics who knew as little of historical associations as they did of manners or ' Lating.' All that was noblest in Cambridge Puritanism revolted against the lawless violence of the zealots. Among the warmest adherents of Parliament not a voice in the University was raised in apology for it.

Dowsing took his authority from the Earl of Manchester, and Manchester was merely the agent of Parliament. In January, 1644, the two Houses passed an Ordinance for the Regulation of the Universities and commissioned Manchester to eject any persons whom he should judge unfit for their places, and to substitute in their room any other persons approved by the Westminster Assembly of Divines. In February it added a further proviso that special care should be taken that the Solemn League and Covenant should be tendered and taken in the University. Manchester's qualifications for the duty assigned to him were that he was at that time Major-General of the Eastern Counties Association and a member of the Assembly of Divines. He was a Presbyterian, and, though after the execution of the Earl of Holland in 1649 he was made Chancellor of the University, his claims to that distinction did not rest on the cultivation of which an academic degree is supposed to be the mark. He is described as ' a sweet, meek man,' and, though religion compelled him to an attitude of hostility to Charles, he was a pronounced royalist at heart, and detested the war. In December, 1643, he pleaded the cause of the University in Parliament, and obtained

14

from it a declaration that the revenues of the University and colleges—excepting such as, being payable to ' delinquent ' Heads and fellows, were handed over to the Sequestrators sitting at Cambridge—should not be sequestrated but administered by treasurers appointed by himself.

Manchester's task was at least performed with some regard for decency. In the proceedings which followed we hear nothing of ' scandalous living,' which had been one of the main charges brought by the ignorant section of the party against the Heads and fellows. The Commissioners for tendering the Covenant began their labours in March, 1644, sitting at the White Bear Inn, opposite Trinity Gate. The oath to be taken of course involved renunciation of episcopacy. Every resident office-holder was summoned, and ample notice was given in order to secure the attendance of such as might be absent from Cambridge. A large number declined the summons and were incontinently ejected. Of the sixteen Heads nine were displaced in 1644 and one in 1645 : two who were not ejected in 1644 died in the following year. At Sidney a new Master, favourable to Parliament, had been elected in 1643 by the forcible intervention of Cromwell's soldiers in the manner already described. Of the remaining three Heads Batchcroft of Caius was expelled in 1649 and Rainbowe of Magdalene, for refusing the Engagement, in 1650. The only Master who remained undisturbed until the Restoration was Love of Corpus. Though he bowed to the Covenant and the Engagement, singularly enough, he bore the character of being a loyal churchman and in 1660 was advanced to the deanery of Ely.

The fellows in the several colleges seem, for the most part, to have followed the lead of their Heads. About one hundred and eighty were ejected—the larger part of the total number—and their effects were sequestrated and sold. At Queens' the whole society was ' outed ' : at Jesus and at Peterhouse, in each case, all but one : at Pembroke nineteen, at Saint John's twenty-nine, at Trinity about fifty. Trinity Hall and Saint Catherine's were the only colleges which were untouched. Among the Heads and fellows who were ejected were ten who after the Restoration became bishops. The list also includes four poets—Crashaw and Beaumont of Peterhouse, Cleveland of Saint John's and Abraham Cowley of Trinity.

The Commissioners were put to great straits to supply the places of this great crowd. As a matter of fact, they did not attempt to fill them all at once. Many fellowships were unoccupied even until the Restoration : to others they nominated at intervals, as they could find suitable men of Presbyterian views among recent graduates. The virus of prelaty was widespread in the larger colleges. Eight of the nine Heads appointed in 1644 were supplied by the relatively less distinguished foundations of Emmanuel, Saint Catherine's and Magdalene : Emmanuel alone furnished six. A Scotchman, Young, who was not a graduate of the University, was thrust on Jesus in violation of its statutes. Most of the new Heads proved to be capable as administrators, and Whichcote (King's) and Cudworth (Clare) were deservedly honoured for their learning and ability : Tuckney (Emmanuel) is also rememberable as a scholar. But the other Heads, and the fellows on whom the Commissioners hastily laid hands, were, with hardly an exception, obscurities.

Time brought in its revenges. The weapon which Parliament forged in 1644 broke in its hands when it was needed for other uses in 1649. After the King's execution a new test was required of all graduates in the Universities and of all who were proceeding to degrees. As oaths and adjurations were repugnant to the conscience of Puritan England, this took the form of a simple declaration—or Engagement, as it was called—' that I will be true and faithful to the Commonwealth of England, as the same is now established, without a King or House of Lords.'

This was a double-edged instrument. It was a menace to the prelatical loyalist, and it dealt an intolerable wound to the dominant Presbyterians. The strong national sense of the Scottish people insisted on the visible tokens of its unity and autonomy—a king and a hierarchy of its own choice. In order to secure the Scottish alliance, in 1643, Parliament hastily and unadvisedly accepted the Covenant and imposed it on the nation. Manchester, himself a Presbyterian, had filled Cambridge with Presbyterian Heads and fellows. To earnest reformers the spirit of religion was all in all, the outward forms as nothing. To Milton it seemed that the Presbyterian hierarchy ' envied, not abhorred,' the sins of the Prelate Lord, and that the new tyranny was as bad as the old.

So in June, 1650, a new Committee of Regulation is sitting in the White Bear Inn. Again the mandate goes forth that every office-holder in the University is to attend and take the pledge : and again, by absence when their names are called, many of them tacitly accept the sentence of ejection. But Dunbar battle is not yet fought : the Scottish army is threatening : and Cromwell this time is all for a peaceable settlement among the Puritan bodies, if he can get it. He was at Cambridge on his way north on June 29, and assured the Vice-Chancellor and Heads that proceedings would not be pressed against those who declined the Engagement. The situation was altered by the victory at Dunbar (September 3). "The man in the north," *i.e.* Cromwell, writes Sancroft, ten days after the battle, " hath done his business and comes back triumphant : we must look for impositions of a higher nature and under far stricter penalties." Henceforth there is no mercy for the Presbyterian monarchist. "The Revolution, like Saturn, devours its own children." The Earl of Manchester was displaced from the Chancellorship to which he had been elected in 1649. In all, three Heads and about fifty fellows were expelled in 1650–1651, and sporadic ejections followed until 1654. A few of the ejected were royalists who had escaped the winnowing of 1644. One such was Sancroft, the Archbishop of days to come : so far he had retained his fellowship, though, like Whichcote, he never took the Covenant. In 1650, when the threat of the new conscience-forcing overhung the University, he writes : " I almost long to be displaced that I may hide my head in some hole so obscure whither our jolly conquerors may scorn to descend to seek me." Most of the sufferers were Presbyterians, and their places were filled by Independents.

In December, 1654, Cromwell is Lord Protector : the constitution established in 1649 is established no more. The royalist cause is irretrievably ruined—so it is to be supposed. Parliaments, Long and Little, have disappeared, and ' no dog barked ' at their departure. Lacking the voice of parliamentary partisans religious rancour is dying out, and a passion for peace fills the nation. Not least vehement in that desire was the Lord Protector. " Israel has been brought out of Egypt through a wilderness, by many signs and wonders, towards a place of rest." Within three weeks of his formal assumption of the supreme power he repealed the Engagement.

The last years of the Protectorate were years of quietude to Cambridge : but the quiet came of exhaustion, if not of despair. Puritanism had outworn its ideals of high thought and clean-living : lassitude and recklessness were its legacies to the after age. Hear the testimony of two men, very different in character, who returned to the University at the Restoration after some years of absence. Samuel Pepys, who describes himself as ' a great roundhead ' in his young days, was entered at Puritan Magdalene in 1651. Returning in February, 1660, he found there the same old ' dons ' who, having swallowed Covenant and Engagement, were now dozing in the sunlight of restored royalism : the same, yet not the same. " I went to Magdalene College to Mr. Hill, with whom I found Mr. Zanchy, Burton and Hollins, and took leave on promise to sup with them. To the Three Tuns where we drank pretty hard and many healths to the King : then we broke up, and I and Mr. Zanchy went to Magdalene College, where a very handsome supper at Mr. Hill's chambers, I suppose upon a club among them, where I could find that there was nothing at all left of the old preciseness in their discourse, especially on Saturday nights ; and Mr. Zanchy told me that there was no such thing nowadays among them at any time." William Sancroft tells us of the state in which he found the pure house of Emmanuel when he returned to it as Master in 1660. In matters of Church and State there is outward conformity. But Hebrew and Greek learning are out of fashion there as everywhere. " I find not that old genius and spirit of learning in the college that made it once so generally famous." At Jesus, in the decade following the Restoration, the

A COURTYARD OPPOSITE MAGDALENE COLLEGE

serious and scholarly John North, afterwards Master
of Trinity, found himself, as a fellow, in the society of
' grave and empty seniors ' whose refuge from *ennui*
was in ' the insipid pastime of bowls, or less material
discourse, such as town-tales, or punning and the like.'
The seniors were the recruits of 1644 and 1650.

CHAPTER X

NEWTON AND BENTLEY

Vivida vis animi pervicit, et extra
Processit longe flammantia moenia mundi,
Atque omne immensum peragravit mente animoque.

LUCRETIUS

AFTER 1660 Cambridge, as Oxford, ceases to be a national emporium of learning : it becomes an implement of State. The Act of Uniformity, passed in 1662, by an Anglican Parliament, in opposition to the wishes of the King, required that all Masters and fellows of colleges and all professors and readers in the Universities should subscribe a declaration of conformity to the liturgy of the Church of England. Subscription to the Thirty-nine Articles was again exacted of every one who was admitted to a degree : it had been first imposed in 1616, and was abolished in 1641. In the days of Elizabeth, when the common enemy of every section of Protestantism was Rome, there was a party within the limits of the Anglican communion which was in warm sympathy with the stricter Reformers, and the Puritans had grudgingly accepted the restraints of the Act of Uniformity, with a prophetic assurance that the day would come when they could reconstruct the Church on their own model. That day had since come and now was past, and the party which had known power was little disposed to accept the old fetters. Henceforth, for a century and more, the Protestant Nonconformist seldom knocks at the University gates. Within the gates, in spiritual matters, there is silence and sleep—it might seem to be the sleep of death. Only at intervals dim phantoms—Deism, Methodism, Arianism, controversies Whistonian and Bangorian—stir the sleeper and force him into inarticulate cries, not greatly heeded by the world outside the gates.

Though religion at Cambridge in the post-Restoration period was without the informing spirit which could stir the emotions of the nation and build new outposts of the faith, the absence of party dissidence at first gave a new impulse to religious speculation and to the science of Theology. That age was ushered in by the splendid visions of the Platonists and the erudition of Pearson. The following century was illuminated by the eminent names of Law and Paley. But confined as it was to the defensive lines prescribed to it by its alliance with the State, Cambridge Churchmanship, throughout the period, was timid and apologetic. With the exception of Bentley the occupants of the two chairs of divinity were men who left no name for origination or scholarship.

As, in the age which we have reached, Religion at Cambridge lacked the right Promethean fire, so undoubtedly did Literature. Even if we put out of sight the solitary, commanding figure of Milton, all Cambridge sings in Caroline days. It is a confused concert, for the most part academic, intellectual and 'conceited'; surpassing the Elizabethan choir in volume of sound, but not rivalling it in melody. "The words of Mercury are harsh after the songs of Apollo." But the number and variety of the performers is prodigious. Among them we count Herbert and Crashaw, the poets of mystical religion; Cleveland

and Cowley, representing cavalierdom in its lighter vein ; republican Wild and Marvell ; didactic Quarles and Phineas Fletcher ; More and Joseph Beaumont, the Platonists ; Herrick and Suckling, reflecting romance and Shakespeare ; Waller, anticipating the mechanical smoothness of Pope. During the second quarter of the seventeenth century Cambridge, as Mr. Gosse says, was ' a hot-bed of poetry.' After 1660, and until the new flowering of poetry with Gray, of prose with Sterne, it was a desert. Except Dryden, who preferred Athenian Oxford to his native Thebes, Cambridge has no name in the literature of that day to rank with the secondary writers of pre-Restoration times.

At the cost of some severance from national sentiment Cambridge turned from the profitless arena of theological polemics to the fields of Physical Science and Mathematics which it was to annex as its special domain in centuries to come. England and its Universities, already preoccupied with the problems of government in Church and State, had turned a deaf ear to the suggestions which Bacon had thrown out in his *Advancement of Learning* (1605) for the endowment of research in Natural Philosophy and Physics. It began to dawn on certain thoughtful minds in the days of the Protectorate that the Universities in their exclusive reliance on dogmatic teaching and traditional methods of education had forfeited their rightful place among the great centres of European learning. The discoveries of Copernicus and Galileo had brought no lessons to England. Even Milton's ample conception of a liberal education, as expressed in his *Letter to Samuel Hartlib*, does not reach beyond ' the historical physiology ' of Aristotle, Theophrastus, and Seneca's ' Natural Questions.' Chemistry is not so much as alluded to : his scant recommendation of the study of ' physic ' is limited by the proviso that it be not ' too tedious ' : and ' proceedings in nature and mathematics ' are oddly to be helped by the experiences of hunters, fishermen, gardeners, apothecaries and such-like persons.

John Hall of Saint John's in 1649 wrote a pamphlet on the *Reformation of the Universities* in which he acutely pointed out the deficiencies of the academic teaching of his time. Among other things he says :

> Where have we anything to do with Chimistry, which hath snatcht the keys of Nature from the other sects of philosophy by her multiplied experiences ? Where have we constant reading upon either quick or dead anatomies, or ocular demonstrations of herbs ? Where any manual demonstrations of Mathematical theorems or instruments ? Where a promotion of their experiences, which, if right carried on, would multiply even to astonishment ? Where an examination of the old tenets ? Review of the old experiments and beliefs which gull so many junior beliefs, and serve for nothing else but for idle priests, to make their sermons more gaudy ?

Hall, like other young republicans, was sickened by the monopoly of teaching arrogated by the Church. John Dell, Master of Caius, in his *Reformation of Learning*, and John Webster in his *Academiarum Examen*—both works published in 1654—emphasised Hall's plea for the encouragement of experimental science. Webster, referring to the subject of mathematics, expresses his fervent wish ' that this so noble and excellent a science, with all the parts of it, both general and special, vulgar and mystical, may be brought into use and practice in the schools.'

On the Continent it was the philosophy of Descartes which, more than any other thing, exploded the old systems of university teaching. With Descartes the issue concerned with Man's relation to God, which had hitherto engaged the schools, was changed to the consideration of Man's relation to Nature. His outspoken contempt for priest-regulated education, his rejection of the Aristotelian logic, canonised for the service of the Church, and his declared resolve to accept nothing as known which did not commend itself to reason gained for him warm supporters among the republicans of England and Holland, but in more hesitating and religious minds suggested the doubt that he was either a Jesuit or an Atheist. The strong attraction which he exerted on the younger minds of Cambridge, as well as the suspicion in which he was held by the older generation of scholars, is revealed by what Roger North of Jesus tells us of his course of reading in undergraduate days (1667–1670), when he was under the tuition of his brother John.

As to study, I followed my own appetite, which was to natural philosophy, which they call physics, and particularly Descartes, whose works I daresay I read over three times before I understood him. And at that time new philosophy was a sort of heresy, and my brother cared not to encourage me much in it.

The study of mathematics was universally recognised in the curriculum of medieval Universities. The earliest University statutes at Cambridge require that the candidate for Inception in Arts shall attend lectures on the subject for three whole years. But mathematics, as the term was understood in the Middle Ages, included a variety of loosely connected matters. Geometry included cosmography, in connection with which Pliny was the standard authority. Arithmetic was associated with the mystical properties assigned to numbers by Pythagoras. Astronomy was treated on the lines of the Ptolemaic system, and included astrology and the ' natural magic ' which was a part of the stock-in-trade of Chaucer's Doctor of Physick. Architecture and Music were treated as sciences closely related to mathematics. The figure of Melencolia, sitting rapt among the symbols of her art—the tools of building, the blazing star, the globe, the magical number-square, etc.—allegorically conveys the meaning which in Dürer's day was attached to the heterogeneous science of mathematics. In early Reformation days its professors rested under the suspicion of being ' conjurers ' or ' nigromancers.' Even in the seventeenth century, after Sir Henry Savile had given life to the study at Oxford, Hobbes —who never learnt Euclid there—tells us that geometry was regarded as ' art diabolical,' and careful fathers refrained from sending their sons to that University ' lest they should be smutched with the black art.'

Though in the later years of Henry VIII the University of Cambridge maintained a lecturer in mathematics the little importance attached to the study is shown by the fact that in times of financial stress his salary was suspended in order to pay the lecturers in Hebrew and Greek. In the scheme of undergraduate study prescribed by the statutes of Elizabeth mathematics were altogether omitted. Oxford found a home for the study fifty years before it was officially recognised at Cambridge. The Savilian professorships of Geometry and Astronomy were founded at Oxford in 1619. So small was the encouragement given to mathematical science at Cambridge that Seth Ward of Sidney and Wallis of Emmanuel migrated to the sister University in 1649, and were there appointed respectively to the chairs of Astronomy and Geometry. Wallis, writing of his Cambridge student days, says that " mathematics were scarce looked upon as academical studies, but rather mechanical. And among two hundred students in our college I do not know of any two—perhaps not any—who had more mathematics than I, which was then but little, and but very few in the whole University. For the study of mathematics was at that time more cultivated in London than in the Universities." The Royal Society, founded in 1662, consisted at first almost exclusively of Oxford men—Lord Brouncker, Wren, Wilkins, Petty, Sir Kenelm Digby, Boyle, Hooke, as well as Ward and Wallis. The Ashmolean Museum, established in 1677, and at that time chiefly connected with Natural History, was the first museum of science erected at an English University.

When they were at last recognised the new studies took strong and immediate hold at Cambridge. The Lucasian Professorship of Mathematics was founded in 1664, the Plumian of Astronomy in 1707, the Professorship of Chemistry in 1703, that of Anatomy in 1707. Isaac Barrow was the first Lucasian, Roger Cotes the first Plumian Professor. Vigani, who was the first Chemistry Professor, had begun to teach at Cambridge as early as 1683. It was long ere the University recognised the need of classrooms and laboratories for its Professors of Natural Science. Trinity found ' a lumber hole,' as Bentley described it, to serve as a lecture-room for Vigani : and the same college provided Cambridge with its first observatory. It was constructed, shortly after 1706, over the Great Gate, and remained there until its destruction in 1797.

In the central space of the antechapel of Trinity, at its western end, stands Roubillac's noble statue

> Of Newton, with his prism and silent face,
> The marble index of a mind for ever
> Voyaging through strange seas of thought, alone.

STATUE OF NEWTON

IN THE ANTE-CHAPEL, TRINITY COLLEGE

Beneath the statue are inscribed the words, adapted from those applied by Lucretius to Epicurus :

NEWTON, qui genus humanum ingenio superavit.

On either side, like lesser divinities, are the seated figures of Bacon and Barrow : in front are ranged those of Whewell, Tennyson and Macaulay. His portrait, on the wall beyond the dais, faces us on entering the hall, neighbouring the colossal figure of Henry VIII on the right, as Bacon does on the left. Ranged on the side walls we see, in long array, the portraits of the greatest of great Trinity's sons— Bentley and Porson, Dryden and Byron, Thackeray and Tennyson. Among them all we feel that Newton is the real Genius of Trinity, the man whose mind is still at work to inform Cambridge studies and students of to-day.

Newton was born at Woolsthorpe in Lincolnshire— the same county which gave Tennyson to Trinity. His schooling—interrupted by a spell of farming—was got at Grantham. As he developed a genius for solving problems and making mechanical models, a clerical uncle, who had himself been educated at Trinity, recommended that he should be sent there, and, accordingly, he was entered there as a sub-sizar in 1661, at the age of eighteen. We are told that, before he began residence, he had read Sanderson's *Logic*— which in those days was used as an introduction to mathematics—and Kepler's *Optics*. In September in his first year he happened to purchase at a bookseller's stall in Sturbridge fair—Cooks' row in the fair being then a notable mart of books—a book on astrology. As he found that he could not understand it without the knowledge of geometry and trigonometry, he purchased a Euclid, and, when he had mastered it, proceeded to read the *Clavis Mathematicae* of Oughtred (of King's), which was then the ordinary textbook on arithmetic, and the *Geometry* of Descartes. Of his undergraduate studies we know little until his third year, when he began to attend the lectures of Isaac Barrow, who in that year became the first occupant of the Lucasian chair of Mathematics. He mixed little in undergraduate society and complained that his neighbours in college were disorderly. His genius was so little noted that he failed to obtain a scholarship until 1664. In the following January he took his B.A. degree and in 1667 was elected a fellow of Trinity. Two years later he succeeded Barrow as Lucasian Professor.

It would take more space than the limits of this book allow, and exceed the powers of its writer, to set forth in any intelligible detail the discoveries which made the name of Newton illustrious. "It is almost impossible," says Mr. W. W. R. Ball in his *History of Mathematics*, "to describe the effect of his writings without being suspected of exaggeration. If the state of mathematical knowledge in 1669 be compared with what was known in 1687" — the date of the publication of the *Principia* — "it will be seen how immense was the advance. In fact, we may say that it took mathematicians half a century to assimilate the work which Newton had produced in those twenty years."

Newton resided in Trinity until 1696, when he removed to London. In 1701 he resigned the Lucasian chair, and in 1703 he was elected President of the Royal Society : he was re-elected annually until his death in 1727. In 1687, when James II attempted to compel the University to admit one Alban Francis, a Roman Catholic priest, to the degree of M.A., though he declined the oath of supremacy, Newton was appointed one of the delegates to represent the objections of the University before the Ecclesiastical Commissioners. His share in the proceedings led to his election as member of parliament for the University in 1689. The two offices of President of the Royal Society and parliamentary representative of the University, which were associated in Newton, were again combined by the most eminent of his successors in the Lucasian chair, Sir G. G. Stokes, in 1887.

Lovers of Thackeray will remember that, when Mr. Esmond was entered a pensioner of Trinity, 'comfortable rooms were provided for him in the great court, close by the gate, and near to the famous Mr. Newton's lodgings.' There are many staircases in Cambridge consecrated by memories and tradition, vaguer than memories, that cling to great names, but I do not think that there is any one of them which, if departed greatness ever revisits the scenes of its youth on earth, can boast such grand, ghostly company as that which is numbered C and stands next the Great Gate and between it and the chapel. Thackeray knew the staircase, for it was there, in the ground-floor rooms on the right, that he 'kept' in undergraduate days. The opposite rooms were once Macaulay's. The set above Thackeray's were occupied in recent times by Lightfoot, Bishop of Durham, and by Jebb, the Greek scholar. This set from early days was always assigned to a fellow, and there is clear evidence that it was Newton's from 1679 until 1696.

The picturesque front of the college, between the gate and the chapel, as it existed when Loggan's view was taken, about 1688, was altered to its present appearance in 1856. Between the college and the street, in the days of Newton and Loggan, there was a

15

garden, considerably larger than the present lawn, enclosed by an embattled wall of brick and laid out in square beds with intervening walks. It is mentioned in the Junior Bursar's accounts as 'Mr. Newton's garden.' A wooden lean-to contained a small room, annexed to the first-floor set, and a staircase which descended from it to the garden. Of the rooms which once were Newton's we are fortunate in possessing a description written by Bentley's grandson, Richard Cumberland, the dramatist, who was entered at Trinity in 1747. At that time they were occupied by Richard Walker, Vice-Master of the College, well remembered as Bentley's supporter in his quarrel with the fellows and for the 'Walker, our hat' incident of Pope's *Dunciad*. Of him Cumberland says :

He frequently invited me to his rooms, which I had so often visited as a child, and which had the further merit with me as having been the residence of Sir Isaac Newton, every relic of whose studies and experiments was respectfully preserved to the minutest particular, and pointed out to me by the good old Vice-Master with the most circumstantial precision. He had many little anecdotes of my grandfather (Bentley) which to me at least were interesting, and an old servant Deborah, whom he made a kind of companion, and who was much in request for the many entertaining circumstances she could narrate of Sir Isaac Newton, when she waited upon him as his bedmaker, and also of Dr. Bentley, with whom she lived for several years after Sir Isaac left college, and at the death of my grandfather was passed over to Dr. Walker, in whose service she died.

Walker left an inventory of the furniture in the rooms, but it does not appear from it whether any of the articles contained in them descended to him from Newton. But two properties which were there in Newton's time have some interest for us. The first was the celebrated triangular glass prism, shown in Roubillac's statue. Newton purchased it at Sturbridge fair in 1666, in order to investigate the phenomena of colours. The other was the reflecting telescope, constructed by himself, which is now in the possession of the Royal Society. The observatory on the top of the adjoining gate-tower was not erected until after he had left Cambridge ; but he had some sort of observatory in his own rooms.

In these chambers we must conceive Newton as living, in company at one time with a sizar-pupil who acted as his *famulus*, or domestic servant, and assisted him in his calculations ; at another with a fellow of the College, John Wiskins, to whom he bequeathed his chamber-belongings. Though he mixed little in society, the figure of the Trinity philosopher was familiar to every resident in Cambridge. The portrait of Ritts shows him in his habit as he lived— an untidy personage, carelessly wrapt in a morning-gown, his long locks of prematurely white hair drooping negligently about his face. Stories are told of his absent-mindedness ; how he startled ' dons ' and undergraduates by appearing in hall without bands, or at Saint Mary's in a surplice : how, on some rare occasion when he was entertaining his friends, he left them to get some wine, and, forgetful of his errand, was found after lapse of time working out a problem : how, one winter morning, he left on his table books and papers of experiments ' which he had been twenty years of making,' and found, on returning from chapel, that they had been burnt by a candle which he had left alight near them ; whereat ' he was so troubled that he was not himself for a month after.' His simple, religious character awoke the profoundest reverence in those of his contemporaries who could but dimly appreciate the profundity of his intellect.

Richard Bentley, whatever his faults—and they were many—'loved a man,' and among his friends none was more revered than Newton. So early as in 1692 we find the two in correspondence on the subject of Newton's recently published *Principia*. The Boyle lectureship 'for proving the Christian religion against notorious infidels' was established in 1691, and Bentley was the first lecturer appointed by the trustees. The last three lectures of the course which he delivered dealt with the evidence derived from 'the origin and frame of the world,' and Bentley, frankly discarding the system of Descartes which was then generally accepted, resorted for his armoury to the novel doctrine of Newton. In the letters which passed between the two—still preserved in Trinity library—Bentley asks and receives the advice of Newton for the most profitable method of studying the *Principia*. Later, in 1697, a letter from Bentley to Evelyn tells us that a small party of friends, including Evelyn, Sir Christopher Wren, Locke and Newton, was in the habit of meeting, once or twice a week, at Bentley's lodgings in London. It was Bentley who induced Newton, in 1709, to issue a new edition of the *Principia*, superintended by Cotes. And, when Newton died, Bentley wrote an epitaph for his monument in Westminster Abbey.

We shall not appreciate either the extent or the limitations of the service which Bentley rendered to Cambridge and to scholarship unless we realise what that Cambridge generation was like in which his spirit grieved for the forty odd years of his contentious mastership. Emphatically it was a Saturnian age of lead; more particularly so in the realm of classical learning. The scholarship which entitled Cambridge to a place among European repositories of classical culture died with Pearson, of whom Bentley nobly said that the very dust of his writings was gold. In an age which counted Gay and Young among its principal poets the historian of Classical Scholarship may find the names of some mediocrities to fill the gap of more than a century which lies between Pearson and Porson. Wasse, Markland and Taylor were friends of Bentley, and in his lifetime and under his influence produced creditable work which is not wholly forgotten. But among the enemies of Bentley at Cambridge—with the exception of Conyers Middleton—it is impossible to point to one who made any effectual contribution to the store of classical knowledge. If proof were necessary to show the stagnation of learning in the eighteenth century it lies in the melancholy list of the occupants of the Greek chair from the date of the death of Barnes in 1712 until the election of Porson in 1792. In the literature which it was their function to expound it may be said of all of them—seven in number—that they were ' sadly to seek '; and, except that some of them attained a thin notoriety as antiquarians or playwrights, not one in his lifetime had a reputation which reached beyond the University radius. Of one of them—W. Fraigneau, of Trinity, who became professor in 1744—Gray uncharitably says that in his inaugural lecture he ' made an Apology for Socrates an hour long in the schools, and all the world, except Trinity College, brought in Socrates guilty.'

What were the subjects on which these professors lectured, or whether they lectured to undergraduates at all, is not a matter of any consequence. Moderate as their own proficiency was, they might be pardoned if they did not accommodate their teaching to the lowly standard of attainment possessed by the undergraduate

the scholars or students have some of them an old professor or fellow of a college, whom they call tutor, who instructs them, the noblemen or other men of fortune, called fellow-commoners, admitting the poor, who serve them as *famuli*, to attend with them." The only things to attract were the libraries—treasures neglected, except by a few persons. In a single German university you might find more men of learning than in all England.

The first college visited was Trinity. In Uffenbach's opinion the chapel is very handsome, well lighted and long, but somewhat narrow. Of the hall he can only say that it is very large, but ugly, smoky, and smelling so strong of bread and meat that it would be impossible for him to eat a morsel in it. The library could not be handsomer or more convenient. The floor is inlaid with black and white marble, the cases are all of oak, with very artistic carvings, and the arrangement of the bookcases so as to make 'little closets' is an excellent device. " But," he adds, " of books we saw none this time, except such as the librarian showed us of his own accord. For it is my general custom in the first instance to confine my attention to what the librarian regards as most remarkable and to his observations upon it : but afterwards I search for myself, having often found far better things for myself, owing to the ignorance of many librarians, which one cannot but wonder at and deplore."

Passing by Clare, which pleased him on account of its fine, new buildings, he next visited the library of Saint John's, where he found the books more tidy than he had found them elsewhere in England. At King's chapel he duly admired the elegance of the stonework, but saw nothing marvellous in the fact that the roof was supported without pillars. He greatly admired the organ—'small and yet of a deep and extremely pleasant tone.' The library, contained in one of the side chapels, had nothing of interest, and there were no manuscripts — which seemed to him a thing incredible.

The next day was principally spent in examining the books and manuscripts in Trinity library. "From thence we went to the Greek's coffee-house, so called because the host is a born Greek. There we read all the journals and other news which may be seen there. I was specially pleased with the *British Apollo*, a sheet of which is published weekly by some scholars : all manner of curious questions in every faculty are there discussed. I found it more solid and better than the *Athenian Oracle*, which otherwise is of the same kind, and some volumes of which I bought in London. In this coffee-house, particularly in the morning, and after three o'clock in the afternoon, you meet the chief professors and doctors, who read the papers over a cup of coffee and a pipe of tobacco, and converse on all subjects ; and thus you can make their acquaintance. For here they are universally far more polite than scholars in London and elsewhere, and are also delighted to see strangers, fewer of whom come to Cambridge than to Oxford." Then, with Dr. Ferrari, he went to a concert at Christ's, but he comments that, 'though they make so much ado about music,' the performance, both vocal and instrumental, was very poor.

The following morning was spent at Caius. The librarian was absent, but somebody managed to produce the keys of the room where the manuscripts were kept—"a miserable garret under the roof, which could have been very little or not at all visited, for the top step was buried in pigeons' dung, and the manuscripts lay thick with dust on the floor and elsewhere about the room in such disorder that, though there was a written catalogue of them there, I could find nothing at all, and was even doubtful whether I could handle any for the dust, especially in our black clothes, though I should very gladly have searched for one or two."

In the afternoon Uffenbach called on Dr. Bentley, Master of Trinity, " who has built himself an excellent house, or wing, to live in, so that he is as well lodged as the Queen at St. James's, or better. The rooms ar every large and of extraordinary height, the floors curiously inlaid with all kinds of wood, the panels in every room very fine (as now in England tapestry is no longer in fashion, but all is panelled at great cost), the window-panes of extraordinary size, and the windows themselves very large and high. He has been greatly reproached for this building, since he endeavoured arbitrarily and without consent of the fellows to eject a fellow, who as doctor of laws occupied the rooms of a doctor of medicine. Many controversial pamphlets have appeared on the subject, filled with personalities, which do no honour to the otherwise famous and very learned Dr. Bentley, but rather serve to degrade him and to scandalise many honest folk. And so indeed I heard many complain of his extreme arrogance, though he tries to be very polite to strangers, and, for an Englishman, speaks good and tolerably intelligible Latin. He is a man somewhat more than forty years old, rather tall and spare and red in the face." Bentley ' talked big ' of his own forthcoming edition of Horace, scorning all other editions. He spoke strongly of the ' Gallic impudence of Le Clerc, the Swiss-Dutch scholar who had ventured to assail his notes on the Tusculan Disputations—' a versatile but shallow man,' as

THE UNIVERSITY LIBRARY AND KING'S COLLEGE CHAPEL

Professor Jebb characterised him, 'who had touched the surface of philosophy and was ambitious of figuring on the surface of classical literature.'

Magdalene was the next college visited. It is described as "a very old and mean building : the library, which stands at the top under the roof, is also very small, and may consist of perhaps 600 volumes. All the books, with hardly one exception, are entirely overgrown with mould."

Next day Uffenbach's first visit was to the University schools and library. The latter is in two mean rooms of moderate size, one of them half empty. The printed books were ill arranged and in utter confusion. The librarian, as usual, was absent, but Uffenbach was fortunate enough to find Mr. Baker, librarian of Saint John's, a friendly and learned man, by whose help he saw several things : " for otherwise the maid, who had opened the door, and was with us, would have been able to show us but little." He estimated that the library contained 6000 to 8000 volumes. He saw the celebrated Codex Bezæ, and underrated its antiquity. He saw also " a good number of ancient and modern coins, lying all covered with dust, without any order, in a deep, poor drawer, unlocked and left open." Afterwards he visited Mr. Baker's own museum in Saint John's. Baker received him with great politeness, and " spoke of all manner of scholars in Germany and Holland and of their works, with which he has a considerable acquaintance—a very rare acquirement in an Englishman, as they are very seldom at home in any part of the world except England. He is a very gentle, modest and well-bred man, who might have held high offices, if he were not a Jacobite and non-juror." Queens', the last college in the day's round, is spoken of as an old, mean building, not much better than Magdalene, but the library, though small, contained some good books.

At Clare, which was visited next morning, Mr. Laughton, a fellow of the college and University proctor, showed him the library. He was an agreeable man, who spoke French well, and the library was distinguished from others by containing books in Italian and Spanish. The most delightful treat of all his visit awaited Uffenbach at Christ's, where he called on Dr. Covel, the Master. "He is over eighty years of age, but from his briskness one would scarce set him down at sixty. He understands all sorts of languages and is singularly courteous, which he owes, no doubt, to his many travels. For he has not only resided long in Holland, Germany and Italy, but also as chaplain with an English ambassador at Constantinople, where he procured incomparable Greek codices and coins." The whole of the afternoon was spent in seeing Dr. Covel's collection of books, prints and coins. An uncommon curiosity among the printed volumes was a translation of the ancient Brahmanic texts, the Puranas, in seven volumes, by a member of the college, John Marshall.

On Sunday Uffenbach dined with Dr. and Mrs. Bentley—the gentle lady whose praise was in the mouths of her husband's bitterest enemies. In deference to her the conversation was on nothing more serious than Germany and Holland. On another day came a more detailed investigation of the University library, where the attendant—in the absence of the librarian—observing Uffenbach's interest in a codex of Josephus, was kind enough to tear off a leaf and present it to him as a curiosity. At Sidney, which he describes as an old but tolerably fine building, the chief curiosity was a petrified or incrusted skull from

Crete. At Trinity Hall the library, like the rest of the college, was very mean and contained nothing of note. At Emmanuel, which, he says, is tolerably large and well built, the books were respectable in number but in entire confusion. At Peterhouse, ' new and well built,' the library was in a poor room of moderate size, and the manuscripts were so buried in dust that the librarian was forced to send for a towel, for Uffenbach to wear as a pinafore, that he might not dirty himself too much : after all, they were ' sorry stuff.'

Revisiting Saint John's, he found the manuscripts in a small, dark, poor room. At Pembroke, a college ' neither large nor fine,' nothing of special note was discoverable, and at Catherine Hall, ' a large and fine building,' the library contained only 300 or 400 books and a single manuscript. Benet College ' is one of the ugliest colleges, lying among the houses, so that one cannot see it, and must approach it by a mean entrance.' This college has the choicest manuscripts of all, but they can only be seen with great difficulty, and are contained in a small, dark, very ugly room over the chapel. Jesus College resembles a monastery. In the court stands an exceedingly large walnut tree, measuring 96 feet across from side to side. The hall is elegant, and the library, though small, contains many good books. Of Christ's library it is remarked that the room is poor and the person who showed it was unaware whether it contained any manuscripts or not.

Uffenbach's visit lasted eighteen days. Of Cambridge town he can only say that, apart from the colleges, it is one of the sorriest places in the world.

Richard Bentley, born in 1662, was, like Ascham, a Yorkshireman, and, like Ascham, was entered at

Saint John's, whither he was sent, on the death of his father, at the very early age of fourteen. Of his undergraduate life nothing is known. He was debarred from election to a fellowship at his own college, since only two fellowships could be held by Yorkshiremen, and they were already occupied. But the college recognised his ability by appointing him to the mastership of Spalding School in Lincolnshire. After a year spent there he was engaged by Stillingfleet, Dean of St. Paul's and a former fellow of Saint John's, to act as tutor to his son. In this capacity he continued for six years (1683–1689), and, when Stillingfleet was advanced to the see of Worcester, Bentley accompanied him thither. The Bishop was a discerning patron and a man of learning ; moreover, he possessed a noble library which was of inestimable service to Bentley. He accompanied his pupil to Oxford in 1689, and resided there for a year, availing himself of the advantages of the Bodleian library. In 1692 Stillingfleet procured him a prebendary's stall at Worcester. In 1693 he was appointed keeper of the King's library at St. James's, and from 1696 lived in the rooms assigned to the librarian in the palace. On February 1, 1700, he was installed as Master of Trinity.

If the University was in ' a bad state,' as Ferrari described it in 1710, perhaps no college in it had declined more visibly than Trinity since the mastership of Isaac Barrow (1673–1677). Partly this was due to the relaxation of discipline under two easy-going Masters, Dr. North and Dr. Montagu : partly it was the result of the evil system of filling the fellowships by nomination of the Crown, without regard to merit. In the reign of James II every fellowship had been so filled. Though the system of mandate elections passed away with the Revolution its ill influences remained, and in

THE LIBRARY, ST. JOHN'S COLLEGE

1700 the College had altogether forfeited its intellectual pre-eminence. Except Newton, who resigned his fellowship in 1701, not one of the fellows had any claim to distinction in learning or culture.[1]

For the torpid society over which he was called to preside, Bentley, arrogantly conscious of his own ability and accustomed to the intellectual stir of London, displayed from the first an immeasurable contempt. Warfare began almost immediately after his appointment. The *casus belli* was the Master's lodge. ' Mean and old' many of the college buildings seemed to Uffenbach, and, no doubt, they were suffering from neglect : no doubt also, they were dark, cold and inconvenient. During the century which began with Bentley's mastership many of these old buildings, and especially Masters' lodges, were completely transformed. Sash windows and improved fire-places, for burning coal, were introduced : ceilings became fashionable : marble chimney-pieces were substituted for common stone : panelling took the place of tapestry, and garrets were converted into rooms. Immediately after Bentley's appointment the society sanctioned the renovation of the lodge, which was admitted to be in serious disrepair : but unfortunately it specified no limit of expenditure, and no contract was made. The repairs and alterations were carried out at Bentley's discretion, and the College was left to pay a bill vastly in excess of what he had led it to expect. The fine staircase, which remains as a monument of his conceptions of magisterial dignity, was a special rock of offence. When the bursar remonstrated

---

[1] Professor Jebb says that the Trinity fellows were ' not ideal students, yet, on the whole, decidedly favourable specimens of their kind.' He is speaking of the time after 1700, when such men as Cotes, Middleton and Colbatch were fellows.

Bentley said that ' he would send him into the country to feed his turkeys.' The junior bursar demurred to paying for a hen-house which the Master had put up, and Bentley arbitrarily stopped his commons ; and, when murmurs arose, he grimly observed, " 'Tis all but child's play : I am not warm yet." Acting on long-neglected provisions of the statutes he penalised the fellows by fining them for absence from chapel and compelling them to take degrees in divinity and to perform daily exercises in the hall. " Have you forgotten my rusty sword ? " he cried, referring to the powers which the statutes gave him of preventing fellows from leaving the College. Two of the fellows he actually expelled.

Another subject which was made matter of grievance was the restoration of the chapel. Bentley, when he first became Master, commissioned the well-known Father Smith to build a fine new organ ; and, in order to house it worthily, he proposed that the chapel, which was then in a dangerously dilapidated state, should be re-edified and suitably fitted up. Thirty years previously Dr. Barrow in his mastership had raised a subscription of £18,000, mainly by donations from members of the College, for the erection of Wren's magnificent library. Bentley adopted the precedent then set, and himself subscribed £200 to the chapel restoration. He induced the majority of the fellows to forgo the whole of their dividends for the year 1703–1704 for the same purpose—sufficient evidence that, with all their faults, they had the good of the College at heart. But the expenditure incurred was three times as great as the amount of the sums contributed, and the College found itself in serious financial embarrassment. To the remonstrances of the fellows Bentley roughly replied that " he expected their complaints, but that it would be all the same twenty years hence." To meet the deficit he attempted to abolish college feasts—a measure which the fellows interpreted as a device for making them pay for his domestic extravagance. Finding that they were in the habit of discussing their grievances in the combination room, he tried to prevent them from using it and to convert it into college rooms.

For years the fellows digested, with what stomach they could, the wrongs and insults with which the Master pursued them. In December, 1709, came the crisis. Bentley brought forward a proposal for a new division of the college income, on a system which would increase his dividend beyond what the statutes allowed. Even his supporters among the fellows were up in revolt. A violent altercation took place, and Bentley left the combination room angrily exclaiming, " Henceforward, farewell peace to Trinity College." Twenty-four of the fellows, acting on the suggestion of a legal member of the society, Serjeant Miller, then drew up and signed a declaration that it was desirable to refer the Master's conduct ' to those who are the proper judges thereof, and in such manner as counsel shall advise.' Bentley retaliated by declaring Miller's fellowship void. The Vice-Master replaced his name, and again Bentley struck it out.

In February, 1710, the fellows presented their petition and complaint to the Bishop of Ely (Moore) as Visitor, and Bentley, in a letter to the Bishop, answered their accusation by an offensive attack on them, alleging that their petition was ' the last struggle and effort of vice and idleness against virtue, learning and good discipline.' He claimed that the Queen was Visitor, and requested her intervention, trusting to the good offices of the Tory party, which was then

16

in power.   His appeal secured him a respite of three
years.   At last, in 1713, the ministry, on the advice
of its law officers, decided that in matters concerning
the Master the Bishop was special Visitor, and authorised
him to proceed.

Not till May, 1714, did the trial come on.   It was
conducted at Ely House in London, and Lord Cowper,
an ex-Chancellor, and Sir Isaac Newton acted as the
Bishop's assessors.   Bishop Moore had been instrumental in obtaining the mastership for Bentley, had
appointed him Archdeacon of Ely and in other ways
had shown his sympathy with him in the past.   Nevertheless, one day he intimated in court his condemna-
tion of the Master's conduct.   Bentley's courage, for
once, deserted him, and he fainted in court.

The trial ended in July, and both sides anxiously
awaited the judgment.   Then a strange circumstance
brought the whole proceedings to an ineffectual end.
The Bishop caught cold in court, lingered in illness for
some weeks and died on July 31.   Next day the world
rang with the news of the death of Queen Anne : the
Tory ministry fell.   After the Bishop's death his
written judgment was found among his papers.   He
sentenced Bentley to removal from the mastership.
By such a hair-breadth he escaped deprivation.

Fleetwood, the new Bishop, declined to take up the
proceedings, except as a general issue involving the
conduct of the fellows as well as Bentley's.   Again
the fellows took up their weary cause, and petitioned
the Privy Council to decide who should act as Visitor.
Bentley's matchless adroitness and audacity turned
the tables on them.   He induced Miller to withdraw
from the proceedings and resign his fellowship on
consideration of receiving £528 for his costs in the
trial before Bishop Moore.   By consummate art he

induced the senior fellows to vote this sum to Miller. Nor was this all. He claimed, and got the seniors to allow him a sum of £500 to reimburse him for his own costs in the trial. He went further and prevailed on them to allow him a handsome sum for furnishing the lodge. Against a foe so astute, and with feeling so divided among themselves, the fellows found further collective proceedings hopeless. They dropped their petition.

But retribution waited still for the terrible Master, and the blow came from an individual. In October, 1717, King George visited the University, and, in his honour, thirty-two persons were presented for honorary degrees in divinity. Though no fees were payable for honorary degrees, Bentley, as Regius Professor of Divinity, made on each an extortionate claim of four guineas before he would proceed to their 'creation' as full doctors. Conyers Middleton, a former fellow, who had been presented by Bentley for the degree, astutely paid the exaction, and then sued him for the debt in the Vice-Chancellor's court. After months of delay the Vice-Chancellor issued a writ for Bentley's arrest. One of the esquire bedells was sent to serve it at Trinity lodge. Bentley received him with studied insolence, took the decree and refused to give it back. When the bedell called, next day, to recover it, he was actually locked in a room in the lodge for four hours, and returned without having seen the Master. Bentley made merry over the incident, and, a few days later, during an examination for fellowships, set as a theme for the candidates a line from Homer :

> Slay others, but from Hector stay thy hands.

The provocation was too great to be endured by

the Vice-Chancellor and Heads.   A grace was proposed
to the Senate, and passed by a majority of two to one,
depriving Bentley of his degrees.

The action was undoubtedly illegal.   Endless
pamphlets, appeals and actions for libel ensued, and
Bentley remorselessly hounded down his chief enemies,
procuring the imprisonment of one and a fine and
apology from another.   At last, in 1724, the Court of
King's Bench issued peremptory orders to the University to restore Bentley to his degrees.

Then followed a truce which lasted three years.
For eleven more years the battle with the fellows was
renewed.   In 1733 Bentley was again brought to
trial at Ely House before Bishop Greene, and, in the
following year, sentence was passed depriving him of
the mastership.   Again a difficulty arose.   The statutes
provided that the sentence of deprivation should be
carried into effect by the Vice-Master.   The Vice-
Master, Dr. Walker, was a warm adherent of Bentley,
and he stubbornly refused to act.   In vain the fellows
moved the King's Bench for writs to compel Dr.
Walker to act, to compel the Bishop to act, to compel
the Bishop to compel Dr. Walker to act.   Their application was finally rejected in 1738.   For four years
more the old man was left undisturbed.   He died in
peace in 1742, at the age of eighty, and rests in the
chapel which he had done so much to adorn.

This is not the place to record all that Bentley did
for scholarship, or to recall all the memorable incidents
in the battle of the books which centred round the
mythical Phalaris.   The minute criticism which he
introduced, and which, for good or for ill, was to rule
so despotically in Cambridge classrooms for more than
a century after his death, was in its essence a striving
after truthfulness.   It was derided at the time by

Pope and ' the wits ' as derogatory to the conception
of literature as an organic whole. It was not implicitly
accepted even by scholars, and, after Bentley's death,
there was at Cambridge an egregious Professor of
Greek, Francklin by name, who still regarded Bentley's
arguments as specious and the Letters of Phalaris as,
in the main, authentic. Porson at Cambridge, Wolf
in Germany, gave to Bentley his true place as the
greatest of English scholars and the pioneer in regions
before him untrodden. No greater mistake could be
made than to suppose that the tendency of his in-
vestigations was merely destructive or pedantic. To
him we owe that criticism which Pope would have
marvelled to hear called ' higher,' and which has
created for us a new theology, a new science of language
and a new literature. He achieved, what Pope and
Swift deemed an impossibility, the marriage of science
and literature. In the Cambridge poets, Wordsworth
and Tennyson, more perhaps than in any other, minute
Knowledge is the source and inspiration of Imagination. Swift, in his *Tale of a Tub*, deriding Bentley,
draws the character of the ' true critic,' ' the discoverer
of other men's faults,' descended from Momus and
Hybris. It is, unconsciously, a true estimate of the
value of the achievement of the modern Aristarchus.

The proper employment of a true, ancient, genuine critic is to
travel through this vast world of writings : to pursue and hunt
those monstrous faults bred within them : to drag out the lurking
errors, like Cacus from his den : to rake them together, like Augeas's
dung : or else to drive away a sort of dangerous fowl, who have
a perverse inclination to plunder the best branches of the tree
of Knowledge, like those Stymphalian birds that eat up the fruit.

CHAPTER XI

THE TIMES OF GRAY

Plain living and high thinking are no more :
The homely beauty of the good old cause
Is gone—our peace, our fearful innocence
And pure religion breathing household laws.

WORDSWORTH

IN March, 1742, when Pope published the fourth
book of the *Dunciad*, containing the memorable attack on the ' awful Aristarch,' Bentley
was dying : when it was reissued in the following
October, with the addition of Warburton's dull
buffoonery of ' Ricardus Aristarchus of the Hero of
the Poem,' the old lion was dead. Pope himself died
in 1744. Swift faded out of the world, where he had
been long forgotten, in the next year. Walpole's
ministry ended in 1743. The painful student of the
annals which are not history may remember that
Wilmington and Pelham were Walpole's successors in
the control of the national destinies : that Lord Stair
was at the same time directing the English arms in
the campaign of Dettingen : that John Potter was
archbishop of Canterbury : and that Colley Cibber
was poet laureate. If we remove our eyes from these
notabilities we may remark what is being done in
that same year, 1742, by some men with whom the
world is as yet slightly or not at all acquainted.
William Pitt, the elder, is member for Old Sarum and,

so far, outside government circles. Edmund Burke will not enter Trinity, Dublin, until next year. Robert Clive is on the point of sailing to Madras as a clerk in the service of the East India Company. John Wesley in Epworth churchyard is preaching his first sermons in the open air. Laurence Sterne is an obscure country parson. Thomas Gray will take his LL.B. degree in 1743. Samuel Johnson is a bookseller's hack. *Joseph Andrews* comes out in this same year, 1742—the first notable production of Henry Fielding; it is a travesty of *Pamela*, the publication of which, in 1740, introduced Samuel Richardson to the reading public.

To all men it was plain in 1742 that the days of the giants were past. *Vixere fortes* is the sombre text that underlies the scurrilities of the *Dunciad*, and Pope saw none to succeed the Augustans. Most hopeless to him seemed the prospect that the former light should be restored by the Universities.

> Art after art goes out, and all is night.

Mystery flies to Mathematics: Religion veils her fires: Morality expires unawares: Faith and Enthusiasm are gone.

> No public flame, no private dares to shine;
> Nor human spark is left, nor glimpse divine.

The eighteenth century opened at Cambridge with prospects of new conquest in the domain of science and scientific scholarship, which had been revealed to the University by Newton and Bentley. The true value of Bentley's work was not appreciated until a generation had passed away after his death, but before the middle of the century Newton had quite come into his own. At first mathematics held only an equal position with humanities in the prescribed studies, and it might have been expected that the classical scholar would have reaped the same advantage from a training in exact science that Bentley had gained from the *Principia*. Unfortunately this was far from being the case. By degrees mathematics asserted a paramountcy in the Schools which was inimical to every other branch of culture, and its own free development was thwarted by the extreme deference to Newton's laws, which were accepted as the final exposition of a divinely inspired creed. Under the influences of 'mad Mathesis,' as Pope had anticipated, the Muses lay 'held in tenfold bonds.' A Cambridge skit of 1774 says:

> See Euclid proudly spurns the Mantuan muse,
> While gentle Horace wipes Maclaurin's shoes.
> There Homer learns the theory of light,
> And tortured Ovid learns to sum and write.

In the half-century which followed Uffenbach's visit Latin went out of use as a spoken language, only surviving in the parrot jargon of the disputations in the Schools. In the society of the combination room, where foreign literature was virtually unknown and English authors before Dryden lay under the imputation of Gothic rudeness, a smattering acquaintance with Latin authors was still considered a mark of refinement. The composition of Ovidian elegiacs was an elegant relaxation, and Vincent Bourne's facile Latin verses were admired and imitated when Herrick and Herbert were forgotten names. No young lady of passable attractions, who visited Cambridge at Commencement time, could hope to escape the doubtful compliment of a Latin ode, in celebration of her charms, from the ingenious pen of the reverend Mr. Bavius, 'Englished' by his admirer and bottle-friend, Maevius, in stanzas which were an echo of Prior, in everything but wit.

In London society the ' don ' who affected superior cultivation was a familiar type. Chesterfield in *The World* has sketched such a character. He belongs to a club of gentry who have an academical love of the bottle, and the elegancy and delicacy of their conversation, in his opinion, is little short of that of the Symposium of Plato. Says Mr. Fitzadam, his guest at a meeting of the club :

We were of the same year of Saint John's College, in Cambridge. He was a younger brother of a good family, was bred to the Church, and had just got a fellowship in the college, when, his elder brother dying, he succeeded to an easy fortune, and resolved to make himself easy with it, that is, to do nothing. As he had resided long in college, he had contracted all the habits, prejudices, the laziness, the soaking, the pride and the pedantry of the cloister, which after a certain time are never to be rubbed off. He considered the critical knowledge of the Greek and Latin words as the utmost effort of the human understanding, and a glass of wine in good company as the highest pitch of human felicity. Accordingly, he passes his morning in reading the classics, most of which he has long had by heart, and his evenings in drinking his glass of good wine, which, by frequent filling, amounts at least to two, and often to three bottles a day.

The thin veneer of learning did not conceal the animal coarseness of academic society at Cambridge. Gray's letters bear copious witness to the universality of drunkenness. Poet Smart, a fellow of Pembroke, is always drunk : Gray's neighbours in Peterhouse terrify him by their drunken escapades : at the installation of a Chancellor the whole University, ' from the Chancellor to the blue-coat,' is ' very owlish and tipsy.' If we are to believe a contemporary satire, never was such eating and drinking since the days of Noah—

> Mere drinking, eating, eating, drinking,
> With no impertinence of thinking.

Time was when Cambridge was national in sentiment.

When it became, in fact, provincial it aped the manners of London society. Clubs, taverns and coffee-houses supplied the means of social intercourse which once had been limited to the college parlour ; and the old gravity of talk was displaced by idle gossip on the current affairs of a world to which, as yet, the ' don ' was a complete outsider. The coffee-house and the public gazette were newly introduced at Cambridge when Dr. North was an undergraduate, just after the Restoration. In his biography of his brother Roger North writes :

At that time, and long after, there was but one coffee-house, kept by one Kirk. The trade of news also was scarce set up ; for they had only the public gazette till Kirk got a written news-letter circulated by one Maddiman. But now [about 1725] the case is much altered : for it has become a custom, after chapel, to repair to one or other of the coffee-houses (for there are divers) where hours are spent in talking and less profitable reading of newspapers, of which swarms are continually supplied from London. And the scholars are so greedy after news (which is none of their business) that they neglect all for it ; and it is become very rare for any of them to go directly to his chamber after prayers without doing his suit at the coffee-house, which is a vast loss of time grown out of a pure novelty ; for who can apply close to a subject with his head full of the din of a coffee-house ?

The always engrossing topics of academic talk were politics and personalities—and they were hardly dis-severable. The mill of party politics clacked incessantly, but for the principles of government or the serious interests of the nation there was very small concern. If we may judge from the letters which Gray dated from Cambridge in 1746, very little interest was shown in the Pretender's raid into England. " We talk of war, famine and pestilence with no more apprehension than of a broken head, or of a coach overturned between York and Edinburgh." Cambridge had long parted with the character for Whiggery which, in contrast with Oxford, it possessed when Hanoverian kings were new. In parliamentary elections parties were evenly divided, and personal considerations overruled political predilection. Bentley stood with the Tories so long as Harley ruled : when he fell, he shamelessly went over to the Whigs. The unblushing quest for preferment with which all clerical 'dons,' truthfully or not, were credited in the middle of the century is the salient feature of the cynical but singularly interesting *Letters of a Royal Chaplain*, Edmund Pyle of Corpus and Clare, edited by Mr. Albert Hartshorne. Cole's estimate of some of the Heads is, even for Cole, extremely unflattering. Gooch of Caius, afterwards Bishop of Ely, ' was a man of as great art, craft and cunning as any in the age he lived in.' ' The art and design ' of Newcome of Saint John's ' lost its effect by its perfection.' Of Keene, Master of Peterhouse and Bishop of Chester, Horace Walpole records that his father, Sir Robert, gave him the rich living of Stanhope on condition that Keene should marry one of his natural daughters, but that he jilted her, and satisfied his conscience by giving her £600 a year out of the benefice. Masters of colleges were many of them men of humble origin and no breeding, and their insolence in office made them highly unpopular in college society. ' That old rascal,' Long, Master of Pembroke, was a special object of Gray's aversion. A fellow of Jesus, Thomas Nevile, in 1750, wrote a poetical libel, called *The Capitade*, which is particularly noisome in its reflections on the Heads, all and sundry.

Heavy-winged clerical vultures flapped about the Chancellor whenever he visited the University. On such an occasion Cambridge loved its Ode to the great

man—not Grub street better. For the installation
of the Duke of Newcastle, in 1749, the reverend Mr.
Mason, Gray's friend and biographer, composed a
blatant ode, and was cruelly disappointed that he
was not selected for the laureateship when Cibber
died, in 1757. A less ceremonious bard, in a satire
called *Cam, An Elegy*, had some painfully sincere
things to say about ' that ever-memorable hour that
gave Newcastle and the charms of power.'

> Each Fellow, quick as glancing thought,
> Quick as the glass, the circling ardour caught ;
> From heart to heart, from lip to lip it ran—
> But did they hail the *patriot, scholar, man* ?
> No—'twas the enchanting ministerial charm
> That struck each bosom with a wild alarm ;
> Each in idea grasp'd preferment's prize,
> While scarfs, stalls, mitres, danc'd before their eyes.

In 1769, when the Duke of Grafton succeeded the
Duke of Newcastle, it was Gray's turn to execute an
ode. He had no liking for the task—though he
volunteered his services—and he loved neither the
Duke nor his politics. But the Duke, then prime
minister, had appointed him to the professorship of
Modern History in the preceding year, and the ode
was meant to be a settlement of the debt.

> Sweet is the breath of vernal shower,
> The bee's collected treasures sweet,
> Sweet music's melting fall, but sweeter yet
> The still small voice of Gratitude.

That part of the composition was intelligible enough
to the Duke. How did he keep his countenance when
the poet dwelt on the disinterested sources of Granta's
admiration of the Chancellor who had mitres in his
pocket ?

> Not obvious, not obtrusive, She
> No vulgar praise, no venal incense flings ;
> Nor dares with courtly tongue refin'd :
> Profane thy inborn royalty of mind :
> She reveres herself and thee.

In truth, Gray's ode—some fine passages excepted—is a performance as grotesque as Pindarics on such a theme were bound to be. It did not escape ridicule at the time. A parodist was unkind enough to suggest an Epitaph on "the Churchyard Poet who has deviated from the principles he once profest.'

> Here rests his head upon the lap of earth,
>   One not to fortune, nor to fame unknown ;
> Fair science frown'd not on his humble birth,
>   And smooth tongued flatt'ry mark'd him for her own.
>
> Large was his wish—in this he was sincere—
>   Fate did a recompense as largely send,
> Gave the poor Cur four hundred pounds a year,
>   And made a dirty Minister his friend.
>
> No further seek his deeds to bring to light,
>   For ah ! he offer'd at Corruption's shrine ;
> And basely strove to wash an Ethiop white,
>   While Truth and Honour bled in ev'ry line.

With the example of indolence and self-indulgence set to them by their instructors it is not surprising that every contemporary account represents the undergraduate class as idle, grossly ignorant and almost incredibly brutal in their manners. In the letters of Gray they only figure in connection with scandals which the 'dons' either winked at or were too supine to correct. At this time the fellow-commoners were far more numerous in relation to the whole body of undergraduates than ever before or since. 'Empty bottles,' 'useless members,' 'licensed sons of Ignorance' they were called. "The order has a prescriptive right to idleness," says the *Gradus ad Cantabrigiam*, "and fashion has inspired it with an habitual contempt for discipline." Tennis and football had been among the healthy exercises of undergraduates in the sixteenth and seventeenth centuries. In the eighteenth century bull-baiting, horse-racing, cock-fighting, prize-fights and gambling were the fellow-commoner's refuge from boredom. One sentence from Gray is sufficient to describe the manners of these ruffians. "The Fellow-commoners (the Bucks) are run mad; they set women on their heads in the street at noonday, break open shops, game in the coffee-houses on Sundays." No fellow-commoner ever read for Honours: few pretended to read at all. What served reading when a degree was to be got without any pretence of it? Let Cowper, who knew Cambridge well when he lived at Huntingdon and his brother was an undergraduate at Corpus, speak for the discipline and intelligence of the youth of Cambridge about the year 1765:

> The schools became a scene
> Of solemn farce, where ignorance in stilts,
> His cap well lined with logic not his own,
> With parrot tongue performed the scholar's part,
> Proceeding soon a graduated dunce, . . .
> And he was competent whose purse was so.
> A dissolution of all bonds ensued;
> The curbs invented for the mulish mouth
> Of headstrong youth were broken; bars and bolts
> Grew rusty by disuse, and massy gates
> Forgot their office, opening with a touch;
> Till gowns at length are found mere masquerade;
> The tassel'd cap and the spruce band a jest,
> A mockery of the world.

Not all individuals or colleges were infected by the

virus. Cowper dwells on one noble exception—his dead brother—and that brother's college, Corpus, ' in which order yet was sacred.' Fortunately for England and for Cambridge in the coming generation, other students, in their several ways, were quietly working out their salvation, unregarded and uncontaminated by ' Comus and his midnight crew.'

The townsfolk must have congratulated themselves that the young savages let loose upon them were not more numerous. Throughout the University there was a calamitous decline in the number of residents, and still greater in the number of degrees taken. In the half-century, 1620–1670, the admissions to B.A. degree in each year—except during the civil troubles of 1642-1660—had always exceeded 200, and sometimes had nearly approached 300. Between 1750 and 1775 they only once reached 100. In most colleges nearly half the rooms were empty. In 1749 Gray writes to his friend, Wharton, " I wish you would send them (Pembroke) some boys, for they are grown extremely thin." In 1751 he writes, " The College, which had much declined for some time, is picking up again : they have had twelve admissions this year."

From Eton Gray came to Cambridge in 1734, at first as a pensioner entered at Pembroke ; but in July of the same year he transferred himself, as a fellow-commoner, to Peterhouse, of which college his uncle, Robert Antrobus, had been a fellow. His admission at Peterhouse followed, by just a year, that of Laurence Sterne at Jesus. It is likely that the two never met at Cambridge. Their characters and tastes were poles apart, and, if it had not been so, academic caste put a wide gulf between the sizar of Jesus and the fellow-commoner of Peterhouse, Eton-bred and the friend of the prime minister's son. Perhaps when

Gray wandered into the entrance court of Jesus he may have seen Sterne sitting there under the great walnut tree which Uffenbach described. There tradition presents him to us in the company of John Hall Stevenson, who described the tree in some verses printed sixty years later—the two engrossed in the humours of some broad monastic tale. For the rest, Jesus has no remembrance of Laurence Sterne, though of it he had kindly thoughts in later life, and presented it with the portrait of his great-grandfather, Dr. Sterne, the royalist Master of the College whom Cromwell sent to the Tower.

At Eton Horace Walpole and Gray with two other boys, Thomas Ashton and Richard West—the 'Favonius' of Gray's correspondence—had formed a little circle of their own which got to be known as 'the quadruple alliance.' Ashton went to King's in 1734 and Walpole followed him thither in the next year. West—the only man who quite succeeded in thawing Gray's constitutional chillness — went to Christ Church, Oxford. Almost the only touch of personal feeling in Gray's poetry is contained in his sonnet on West's death in 1742.

In his own college he seems to have made no friends, and for companionship he went to the college on the other side of the street. So much did he identify himself with Pembroke that he dates his letters from that college, and to him 'over the way' is, oddly, not Pembroke but Peterhouse. In his correspondence with West he makes no mention of his tutor (the reverend George Birkett) or his lecturers, and it may be conjectured that they were sagacious enough to leave so clever a pupil pretty much to his own devices in the matter of study—the more so as he soon ceased to read for a degree. With his Eton friends, Walpole

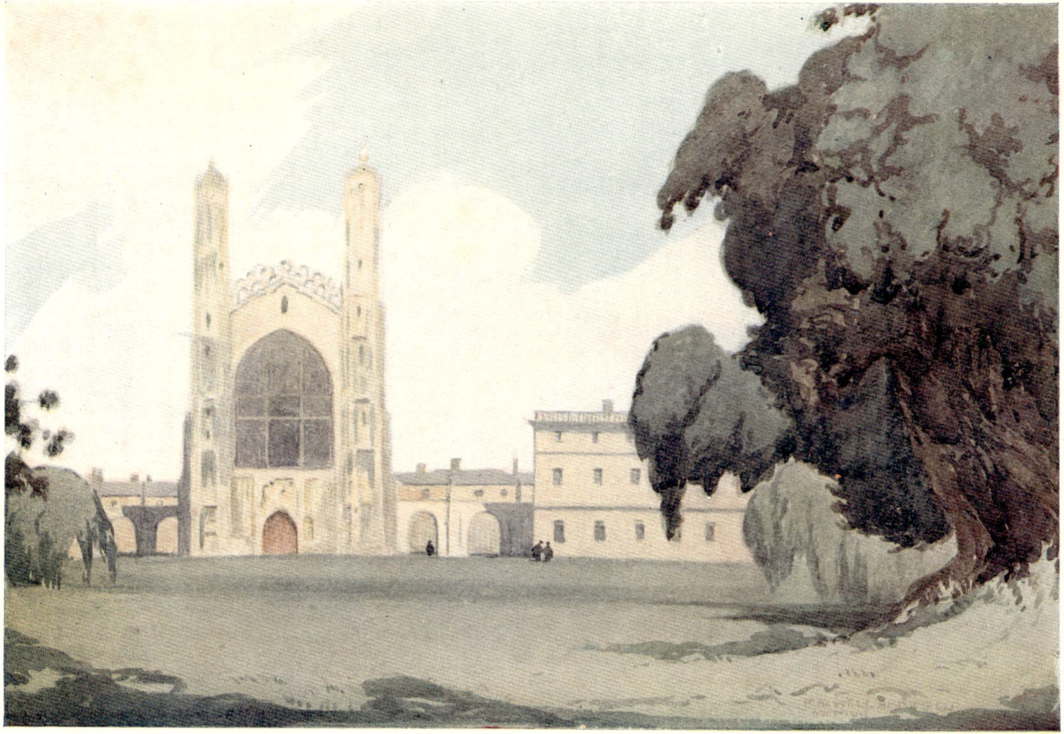

KING'S COLLEGE FROM THE BACKS

and Ashton, he kept up the old intimacy and often drank tea with the former—which in those crapulous days was a singularity.

In respect of tuition, Walpole was as badly served at King's as Gray at Peterhouse. Both had the most cordial detestation of the two principal ingredients in the Cambridge degree studies—logic and mathematics. Walpole professes that he was incapable of getting by heart even the multiplication table, " as blind professor Saunderson honestly told me, when I went to his lectures. After the first fortnight he said to me, ' Young man, it would be cheating you to take your money ; for you can never learn what I am trying to teach you.' I was exceedingly mortified, and cried ; for, being a prime minister's son, I had firmly believed all the flattery with which I had been assured that my parts were capable of anything. I paid a private instructor for a year, but at the year's end was forced to own Saunderson had been in the right." Walpole's tastes in study were as encyclopædic, and as superficial, in Cambridge days as they remained in after life. He attended professors' lectures on Civil Law and Anatomy, and had private teaching in Italian and in drawing.

Of Gray we know that, in these years, he was learning Italian—French he had learnt at Eton—studying the classics, and in particular Statius and Propertius, and writing Latin verses which got into print and remain a witness to a scholarship and poetical faculty remarkable in that age of Latin elegising. He did not ride, or even walk, and by his sedentary habits he laid the seeds of the gout which tormented him in later life. In Peterhouse he seems to have lived ' a solitary fly,' for he was constitutionally incapable of friendship, except in reminiscence. ' A dull man in every way,'

17

Dr. Johnson called him when he was in the height of his fame—which, as a literary judgment, seems a surprising thing to say. But of his own dullness—dullness of spirits and of interest in men and things present—poor Gray was always conscious. He shrank from exposing his feelings even in intimate talk, detested any reference to his poetry, and fortified himself in a cold precision of demeanour. The charm of his letters consists in the frankness with which he unbosoms himself to friends whom he loved the better for being remote. There is obvious sincerity in his oft-repeated expressions of dislike for Cambridge and its society. It is apparent in one of his earliest letters to West, dated December, 1736.

I have endured lectures daily and hourly since I came last ; supported by the hopes of being shortly at full liberty to give myself up to my friends and classical companions, who, poor souls ! though I see them fallen into great contempt with most people here, yet I cannot help sticking to them, and out of a spirit of obstinacy (I think) love them the better for it ; and, indeed, what can I do else ? Must I plunge into metaphysics ? Alas, I cannot see in the dark : nature has not furnished me with the optics of a cat. Must I pore upon mathematics ? Alas, I cannot see in too much light ; I am no eagle. It is very possible that two and two make four, but I would not give two farthings to demonstrate this ever so clearly ; and if these be the profits of life, give me the amusements of it. The people I behold all around me, it seems, know all this and more, and yet I do not know one of them who inspires me with any ambition to be like him. Surely it is of this place, now Cambridge, but formerly known by the name of Babylon, that the prophet spoke when he said, ' the wild beasts of the desert shall dwell there, and their houses shall be full of doleful creatures, and owls shall build there, and satyrs shall dance there : their forts and towers shall be a den for ever, a joy of wild asses.'

In March, 1739, Gray and Walpole started on a two years' tour in France and Italy, which opened Gray's eyes to the beauties and sublimity of natural scenery, and his mind to the interests of historical antiquity. In May, 1741, they quarrelled, and Gray returned alone to England. In the following November his father died, leaving a bare subsistence to his widow. She went to live at West End, Stoke Poges, with her widowed sister, Mrs. Rogers, and with the two ladies Gray lived until the winter of 1742. He had looked forward to a life of lettered ease, and was, indeed, unfitted by temperament for the active pursuit of a profession. At the age of twenty-five he discovered that his mother's means left no margin for his support, and he determined to return to Cambridge, partly with a notion of qualifying for a career in law, but mainly because there he could live cheaply, and among books. At one time he talked of migrating to Trinity Hall, but ultimately he returned to Peterhouse in 1742, and took a bachelor's degree in Civil Law.

At Peterhouse, as in his letters he never mentions any resident by name, we must suppose that he lived as solitary as before. In 1756, writing to his friend Wharton at the time of his rupture with Peterhouse and removal to Pembroke, he says of the former college that his rooms there were noisy and the people of the house dirty—' this is all that I would choose to have said about it '—and he refers Wharton to another friend, Stonehewer of Pembroke, for particular details of the circumstances.

Since Gray's first admission at Peterhouse the college had embarked on a somewhat ambitious addition to its buildings. After Wren had familiarised Cambridge with Italian designs in architecture the colleges were possessed with a mania for reconstructing their courts after the model of the great country seats of the nobility, which at this time were taking the place of Tudor halls and manor-houses. Partly the change was due to altered taste and the passion for correctness and elegance, which overruled even considerations of convenience. But in the main it was dictated by change of habits and the abandonment of the old collective life.

Conservative minds deplored the disappearance from rural England of the brave old houses where a lavish hospitality had been maintained, and scores of ' old fellows with blue coats and badges ' had inefficiently rendered the services which in the new era were better performed by a few footmen and pages. The ballad of " The Old and the New Courtier " (1660) pathetically contrasts ' the old hall hung about with pikes, guns and bows ' with ' the new-fashioned hall, built where the old hall stood, hung round with new pictures ' and ' with a fine marble chimney ' ; and ' the old buttery hatch quite worn off the hooks ' with the new one ' that opens once in four or five days.' In college life the change was even more marked. Now we begin to hear of ' bedmakers,' male or female, who discharged the duties once gladly rendered by sizars, who thereby earned the means of education and advancing themselves to positions of honour and usefulness in the University or the world. Henceforth the tutor, who had once lived and slept in the company of two or three pupils, shuts himself up in a solitary study, and asks to forget that he has any pupils at all. Two features, ominous to discipline, begin to appear. The Heads sever themselves from the society of the fellows, the fellows from that of the undergraduates. The arrogance of Bentley was only too faithfully copied by inferior Masters in the adornment and extension of their lodges. The history of the century is one of perpetual encroachment by the lodge on rooms which had once been tenanted by fellows and their pupils.

Peterhouse was the first college to set the evil precedent of removing the lodge altogether from the college precincts. A new house, on the opposite side of the road, was bequeathed to the College in 1725 as a residence for the Master. More and more, as the century advanced, the fellows withdrew themselves from the intimate, if turbulent, society of the hall to the privacy of the parlour. Parlourdom, with its petty interests and mean squabbles, fills Gray's letters; it fills Gunning's *Reminiscences* from Gray's time to the end of the Georgian reigns.

Not to be outdone by their Master, the fellows of Peterhouse, in the year 1736, decided on the erection of a new building adapted to the standards of comfort and privacy which the habits of the day made desirable. With this object they remorselessly removed a range of chambers on the north side of their court, erected not longer ago than 1632, and in its place put up a new building planned by Mr. Burrough, then a fellow, and later Master, of Caius. Burrough was an amateur architect, whose taste was accepted with the utmost deference by his contemporaries, and perhaps no single man has left a more permanent mark on the architecture of Cambridge than he. Under his unhappy influence and that of his successor, James Essex, the colleges assumed a tame, Italian mantle which was extravagantly admired until another generation of desecrators found merit in an even tamer masquerade of ' Gothic.'

Burrough's building was completed about the time of Gray's return to the college, and Gray was probably the first occupant of the rooms which remained his until 1756. They were on the top floor at the street end of the range. It is quoted as a mark of Gray's refinement, superior to his surroundings, that he used to cultivate a box of mignonette outside his window. Attached to the sill of one of the windows overlooking Little St. Mary's churchyard is an iron frame, intended for such a window-box, and tradition says that it was placed there by Gray.

Gray, in his second-floor rooms, had a dread of fire, which, in the then undisciplined state of the college, was certainly not unreasonable. In January, 1756, he wrote to his friend Wharton :

> I beg you to bespeak for me a rope-ladder, for my neighbours every day make a great progress in drunkenness, which gives me cause to look about me. It must be full 36 feet long, or a little more, but as light and manageable as may be, easy to unroll and not likely to entangle. I never saw one, but I suppose it must have strong hooks, or something equivalent, a-top, to throw over an iron bar, to be fixed within-side of my window.

The generally accepted story, quoted as fact by Mr. Gosse, is that in the following month of February, some fellow-commoners, who 'kept' on Gray's staircase, raised a cry of ' Fire,' late one night, outside the poet's room, having previously placed a tub of water under his window, and that he hastily descended by the ladder into the tub. Something of the kind probably did happen, though Mr. Gosse's version is in some respects clearly inaccurate.[1] Anyhow, we may believe that Gray keenly felt the indignity, and he justifiably resented the disregard of the incident by the Master, who called it ' a boyish frolic.' He transferred himself to Pembroke, where, as he tells Wharton, he was

[1] Mr. Gosse makes the poet hook his rope ' to the bar ' : but there are several bars, and they are not adapted to the purpose ; moreover, they are outside the window, not inside, as Gray's letters would make us suppose that they should be. Mr. Gosse has taken his tale from a silly book, published, many years after the supposed incident, by a Scotchman who knew nothing of Cambridge, and did not pretend that his story was more than a jest.

IVY COURT, PEMBROKE COLLEGE

(GRAY'S ROOMS IN THE LEFT HAND CORNER)

civilly received, and extremely well lodged, and as quiet as in the Grande Chartreuse.

In the quiet of Pembroke, Gray lived out his days until the end in 1770. In the old home of Spenser and Andrewes poetry and learning were still honoured. The chambers allotted to him were in the interior court, on the first floor of Sir Robert Hitcham's picturesque building, erected in 1659, and adjoined the dais end of the hall. They were afterwards occupied by William Pitt. Southwards the poet's rooms overlooked what was then the fellows' garden and the garden of the lodge. The latter is said to have been very beautiful in Gray's time. It contained a sheet of water, whereon the eccentric Master of that time, Roger Long, used to divert himself on a water-velocipede, to the amusement of Gray and the undergraduates. The same ' high and mighty Prince Roger, surnamed the Long, Lord of the Great Zodiack, the Glass Uranium, and the Chariot that goes without Horses,' also erected, on the side of the court opposite to Gray's rooms, a great hollow sphere of metal, eighteen feet in diameter, constructed by himself to represent the appearance, relative positions and motions of the heavenly bodies. This Zodiac room, says Gray—I presume, in mockery— poor, mad, shiftless Christopher Smart—at the time one of the fellows—intended to borrow for the acting of his comedy, *A Trip to Cambridge, or the Grateful Fair*. It was, in fact, acted in the hall. Though only a few fragments of it remain, we may infer from the quality of Smart's extant poems, not excepting his much vaunted *Song of David*, that it was as foolish an exhibition as Gray says that it was.

Except a few translations and fragments, all Gray's poetry was published during his residence in the University ; but, of course, the Elegy and the Eton

Ode owed their suggestion to other scenes than Cambridge. Had he taken the seed of his Cambridge scholarship to fructify in the free air and light of Stoke Poges, as Milton did at Horton, perhaps something as sweet and fresh as *Comus* or the *Sonnets* might have gladdened the desert air of the eighteenth century. But the confinement of the cloister froze the genial current of Gray's soul, as Milton's was checked by his years of political servitude. In the University, Gray told his friend, Nicholls, he had lost the versatility of his mind. His characteristic melancholy, says Bonstetten, who attempted in vain to pass the gulf that separated him from Gray's soul, was the unsatisfied demand of a repressed sensibility, existing under the arctic pole of Cambridge life.

Strange it seems that the first man to free English poetry from the conventions of the school of Pope, and to awake anew the varied melodies of Milton and the Elizabethans, should have been one who, to use his own phrase, was all his life a 'captive linnet,' In that respect, as in others, he is the counterpart of Collins, who, scarcely less than Gray, carries with him the academic atmosphere. But it may be said that the passage to the green fields of nature was made by a classical bridge. For half a century before Gray, poetry had been limited to the narrow confines of Latin 'heroic' verse—Virgil, Lucan, Statius—and Latin satirists. Greek literature was practically untouched; for in Pope's dressing Homer was a lay figure in Roman costume. Gray's first models were the elegiac poets, who, for all the artificiality of their phrase, expressed emotion, either individual or common to humankind. His Pindaric odes introduce the subjects which were most nearly allied to his academic studies, English History and Archæology. In the eighteenth century, when the cult of Heroic Verse was fading at the Universities, its place was largely taken there by the Ode, the Elegy, and the Epigram—all, of course, on the classical model. This was so far recognised at Cambridge that the first University prizes for classical verse composition were awarded for Greek and Latin Odes and Epigrams, and not for Latin hexameters. Greek tragic verse, so especially associated with the name of Porson, was not extensively cultivated until the next century, when the Porson prize gave it the stamp of University recognition. The practice of Greek iambic verse was the outcome of the change which came over English poetry at the end of the century, shown mainly in individuality in style and the expression of personal feeling. The medals for Greek and Latin Odes and Epigrams were established in 1774 by Sir William Browne, who had been a fellow of Gray's first college, Peterhouse. Though he survived Gray for four years, he was by birth his senior by a whole generation. It may be supposed that it was the eminence of his fellow-collegian in Ode-writing that dictated the form of composition which his endowment was intended to encourage. And it is worth observing, as an indication of the unforeseen results that may flow from such benefactions, that in 1792 the prize for the Greek Ode was won by a youth who was destined to give the Ode a new expression and importance in English literature—S. T. Coleridge of Jesus.

CHAPTER XII

COLERIDGE AND WORDSWORTH

Bliss was it in that dawn to be alive,
And to be young was very heaven! Oh! times,
In which the meagre, stale, forbidding ways
Of custom, law and statute took at once
The attraction of a country in romance.

WORDSWORTH.

GRAY died in July, 1770. William Wordsworth entered Saint John's in October, 1787, and took his B.A. degree in January, 1791, and, one month later, S. T. Coleridge was admitted at Jesus. A narrow flood of less than twenty years parts two continents—the one

A land where all things always seem'd the same,

the other a region of blood and fire and pillars of smoke, where, nevertheless, young men see visions and prophesy. What traders do we see embarked on the dividing sea, and what freight do they carry?

While he lived, Gray may have felt that the world of Cambridge was left to darkness and to him. When his solitary candle went out in Pembroke it was night indeed. In theology, in science, in classical or other literature it is impossible to remark one of the resident graduates of 1770 who planted seed that bore notable fruit for the world in his own or after times. Utilitarianism, associated with the names of Bentham and Priestley, was not a plant which grew originally on Cambridge soil, though it ended by overshadowing all the schools there.   No star approaching the first magnitude lights the wide gulf that separates Newton from the younger Herschel, or Bentley from Porson. The hope of Cambridge was in the men who were not old enough to remember Gray. .

Among the younger generation who graduated between 1770 and 1787 were a few who achieved greatness, and more whose names are significant for their association with new popular aims.   William Pitt, the younger, began residence at Pembroke in the spring of 1773, when he was barely fourteen, and graduated M.A., without examination, in 1776. William Wilberforce went to Saint John's in October, 1776, and Thomas Clarkson to the same college in 1780. Charles Simeon was admitted at King's in January, 1779, Richard Porson at Trinity in March, 1778, and Thomas Robert Malthus at Jesus in June, 1784. The last three became fellows of their respective colleges, and resided for a time, shorter or longer, in the University.

Cambridge may be modest about its part in shaping the characters and destinies of these eminent men. Pitt's age and the peculiar circumstances of his residence at Pembroke cut him off from ordinary undergraduate life, and left him free from the trammels of degree-reading.   His education was privately directed by his tutor, Pretyman—afterwards Pretyman Tomline and Bishop of Winchester—and, among other things, it seems that his attention was directed to the newly published *Wealth of Nations* of Adam Smith.   Needless to say, the science of Political Economy was generally unheard of by ' dons ' and their pupils in the eighteenth century. Though George Pryme lectured on the subject in 1816, and received the honorary title of Professor of Political Economy in 1828, no regular teaching was supplied by the University until Henry Fawcett was made Professor in 1863. Malthus, whose *Essay on Population* was produced after he had left Cambridge, had to seek a post at the East India Company's college at Haileybury.

For the Greek learning which gave Porson rank second only among English scholars to Bentley, it is certain that he owed little or nothing to his teachers at Cambridge. Markland and Taylor, who carried on the traditions of Greek scholarship in the University in the generation which succeeded Bentley, were dead when he was admitted at Trinity; and Parr and Twining, who, after them, almost alone sustained the reputation of Cambridge classicism, were non-resident. Owing to the conditions of ordination and celibacy which were generally attached to the tenure of a fellowship, and the smallness of the emolument to be derived from lecturing or private tuition, there was a general exodus from Cambridge of all that was ripest and most suggestive in scholarship, and some of the best work of this and the succeeding age issued from London or from country schools and parsonages. Porson's brilliant career at Cambridge, beginning with a Craven scholarship in 1781 and followed by the first Chancellor's Medal and a fellowship at Trinity in the following year, ended in 1792, when his fellowship lapsed owing to his refusal to take orders; and, though he was elected to the Professorship of Greek in that year, the stipend being only £40 per annum, he was compelled to seek a livelihood in London. During his lifetime a fund was raised for his benefit, and, after his death in 1808, the balance of it was devoted to the establishment of the Porson Scholarship and Porson Prize. Second in the list of Porson Scholars is the name of R. C. Jebb, which will always be associated with the drama of Sophocles, as Porson's with that of Euripides. With Bentley, Porson rests in the chapel of Trinity; and, as in the *Frogs* Aristophanes represents the dead Æschylus as welcoming the shade of Sophocles and giving place to him on his throne, we may imagine that the solitary spirit of Bentley was well content to ' make a room ' near him for the greatest of his successors.

It may be claimed for Cambridge that it prompted in Clarkson the enthusiasm which animated him in his battle for the abolition of the slave-trade. The University showed a creditable zeal in that cause, and addressed many petitions to Parliament on different aspects of the question between 1788 and 1830. Peter Peckard, Master of Magdalene, who was Vice-Chancellor in 1785, was amongst the earliest advocates of Suppression. He preached with warmth on the subject at Saint Mary's, and, instead of the usual ' bidding prayer,' he desired the prayers of the congregation for their brethren in the West Indies, labouring under galling oppression. In the same year he proposed as a subject for the Members' Latin Essay Prize, *An liceat nolentes in servitutem dare.* The prize was won by Clarkson, and his investigation of the subject led him to devote all his energies, throughout a life extending considerably beyond eighty years, to the abolition of slavery. Of good Dr. Peckard, otherwise unremarkable, may it be remembered ' at that day ' that he first turned academic thought from barren questions of party politics to the common ground of bettering human lot.

Unlike Clarkson, Wilberforce took from Saint John's

neither the philanthropy nor the evangelical principles which distinguished him in after life. As he had wealth as well as talents, some of the fellows were so stupid as to recommend him not to trouble himself about books, and he acted on their advice. He always kept 'a great Yorkshire pie' in his rooms for his friends, who were many; he sang, played cards and forgot the methodistical notions which his masters, Joseph and Isaac Milner, had implanted in him at Hull. Methodism and its shadow, Low Church evangelicalism, were things strange and little loved in the University in his undergraduate days. 'The Saints,' as they were called, were then confined to Magdalene, where temperance and tea-drinking prevailed and waked the derision of more convivial colleges. There was a suspicion among Magdalene men that their methodism was reckoned to their discredit in the Tripos. "A Maudlin man," said one of them, who was placed low in the senior optimes, "stands little chance in the Senate House. The world is not fond of seeing a religious man honoured."

Whatever injustice was done to the methodist mathematicians of Magdalene was removed, and the balance was even inclined to the other scale, when Isaac Milner was a Tripos examiner; for Gunning—who did not love Milner—says that he notoriously favoured his own college and Magdalene. Milner was entered, as a sizar, at Queens' in 1770, and became President in 1788. A Yorkshireman, as Bentley was, he had much of Bentley's rugged and overbearing character; but, by filling college offices with men subservient to his will, he managed to obtain an ascendancy at Queens' which Bentley never got at Trinity. Under his rule Queens' entirely changed its character. Its numbers were greatly increased, and the majority of the undergraduates were of the class denominated 'Serious Christians.' With Milner, Simeon and Professor Farish for leaders, evangelicalism gradually won for itself a position, first of respect, afterwards of dominance.

Charles Simeon, of King's, took his B.A. degree in 1783. As an undergraduate he was known for his strong religious convictions, and was a disciple of Henry Venn, at that time rector of Yelling in Huntingdonshire. Soon after taking his degree he became vicar of Holy Trinity church in Cambridge, and he continued his ministry there until his death. His views at first evoked the strong hostility of the parishioners and the undergraduates. The former ceased to attend the church, put locks on their pews, and even locked up the church, so that Simeon was obliged to get a smith to open the doors. For many years the street near the church was the scene of riotous gatherings at service hours. " In vain," says Gunning, " did Simeon, with the assistance of persons furnished with white wands, exert themselves to preserve order in the church ; in vain did Professor Farish, who as Moderator was well known and popular with the undergraduates for some years before and after he was Proctor, station himself at the outside door to prevent improper conduct to the persons leaving the church ; and, though one undergraduate, who had been apprehended by Simeon, was compelled to read a public apology in the church, the disturbances still continued." By his tact and singular gentleness Simeon gradually overcame the prejudice against him. His serious and commanding manner in the pulpit riveted the attention even of unsympathetic hearers. " Well, Simeon is no fool, however," said an undergraduate to his companion, on leaving the church. " Fool ! " was the answer, " did you ever listen to such a sermon before ? " In later life he became the object of something like adoration. It was the habit of religious parents, when they brought their sons to the University, to introduce them in the first place to him, that they might remain under his spiritual guidance. In 1831 as many as one hundred and twenty freshmen were so introduced to him. His rooms in Gibbs' building, at the top of the second staircase from the chapel—as Littlemore was in Newman's Anglican days—were the Mecca of many pilgrims. The iron rail, still fixed in the wall of the staircase and originally placed there to help him upstairs when he was an old man, went by the name of ' The Saint's Rest.' When he died, in 1836, he was attended to his grave in King's chapel by eight hundred University men.

The Evangelical Revival within the Church in its origin belonged as much to Cambridge as Methodism to Oxford. It began in the middle years of the century with isolated preachers such as Henry Venn of Jesus and Queens', and Berridge of Clare. Not less than Wesley's work it was in its essence a protest against spiritual deadness in the high places of the Church, the rational attitude of Church apologists, and the rejection on rational grounds, even within the Church, of dogmatic belief. In the days of the first two Georges ' Low Church,' which had nothing in common with the later Evangelical school, was perilously allied with Latitudinarianism, and Latitudinarianism was identified with the Court and Whiggery. The Evangelicals were perforce Tories. Unhappily the French Revolution seemed to timid minds to justify the belief that change was inimical to religion, and, for half a century after it, the leaders of the party assumed an attitude of unreasoning opposition to all reform of the University. To each proposal for the inclusion of nonconformists by the abolition of tests for degree or for their election to any college or university office they raised a dogged resistance which was all too long successful. But it stands to their everlasting credit that they purged the moral atmosphere of Cambridge, and awakened it to some sense of its responsibility to the nation in spiritual and social concerns.

Cambridge—and, for that matter, Oxford too—touched the bottom of its degradation during the time when Gray was resident. After 1770 very slowly it began to regain some of its lost ground. Very slowly the number of its residents grew. After 1775 the total of admissions to B.A. never sank in any year quite so low as one hundred. But no substantial advance happened until after Waterloo. As early as 1750 the Chancellor, the Duke of Newcastle, submitted to the Senate some regulations for the better maintenance of discipline. Violent animosity was excited among the laxer ' dons ' by this interference, and sheafs of pamphlets were the outcome. Riotous proceedings on the part of the undergraduates, abetted by certain graduates, followed when the new regulations were enforced. When one of the proctors attempted to disperse a meeting of ' dons ' and undergraduates, who were dining at a tavern, he was insulted by several of them who were fellows of colleges, one of the number being the Professor of Greek. The proctor complained to the Vice-Chancellor, and the accused persons were publicly tried in the Senate House. In the result they were reprimanded, and one of them, a fellow of Trinity Hall, was suspended from his degrees. The undergraduates behaved so riotously during the trial that sixteen pro-proctors were appointed to preserve

18

order. The older ' dons,' who formed the Non-Regent House in the Senate, were stiff in their support of licence. As a measure of retaliation these ' hot men ' attempted to stop all business, and, by way of menace, threw out in their House a *supplicat* for a M.A. degree.

Other reforms were attempted, but without result. That which might seem most reasonable was the institution of annual University examinations for undergraduates. Up to this time the only examination to which the candidate for degree was submitted took place in his third year. The ' Previous Examination ' was not instituted until 1824, and, as its name implies, was the only examination previous to that for the B.A. degree. It was originally taken in the second year. The proposal to establish annual examinations was made by John Jebb, a fellow of Peterhouse, in 1772. A syndicate was appointed to consider his scheme, and it was warmly supported by the Chancellor, the Duke of Grafton, but it was thrown out by both Houses in the Senate.

The Cambridge Tripos, the name and the thing, had a strange beginning and has gone through notable vicissitudes. The Triposes are now the examinations of candidates for Honour degrees. Until 1824 there was but one Tripos examination, and pollmen as well as Honour men took it. In the eighteenth century, besides Mathematics, it included ' Natural Religion, Moral Philosophy and Locke.' Those who deserved Honours were ranked in order of merit in three classes— Wranglers, Senior Optimes and Junior Optimes. The others, if they qualified for degree, were separately classed, also in order of merit, but were described as οἱ πολλοί, pollmen, or the multitude. The examination was conducted by dictated questions, which were separately given out whenever the examiners saw that any candidate had finished his answer to that last set.

The names, Tripos, Wrangler, Optime, are all derived from the disputations in the schools which, from the earliest days, had been the sole test of fitness for the B.A. degree. The tripos was originally a three-legged stool, on which, in sixteenth-century days, a certain ' ould bachilour ' sat on Ash Wednesdays, when ' questionists ' were admitted to be Bachelors of Arts. The questionist got his name from the ' question ' which he maintained in syllogistic argument as Respondent, or to which he raised objections as Opponent. The old bachelor's business was to dispute with the ' eldest son,' or senior questionist, of each college, as well as with the ' father,' who was a Master of Arts of the college and supported the question maintained by the ' son.' After the Restoration the old bachelor's part in the dispute degenerated into licensed buffoonery. His speech—dealing with personalities of a Fescennine type—came to be known as the Tripos speech, and the speaker was ' Mr. Tripos.' In process of time the Tripos speeches became compositions in Latin verse, which retained much of the old licence. About the year 1748 it became the fashion for the ' Moderators,' who presided over the disputations, to print the Tripos verses on the back of the list of candidates approved for degree—a practice which survived until 1894—and the list itself came to be known as the Tripos list.

A man who, as Respondent or Opponent, had acquitted himself well in the controversy in the schools was dismissed by the Moderator with the approving remark, " Tu quidem, domine, optime disputasti." Such a candidate deserved ' Honours,' and his name was ranked according to his merit in the class of

' Junior ' or of ' Senior Optimes.' Originally the Tripos list contained only these two classes of Honour men ; but in 1751 the distribution into three classes, which has continued ever since, was introduced, and the best men were distinguished from other Senior Optimes as ' Wranglers.'

The written examination in the Senate House was at first only supplementary to the ' Act,' as the disputation in the schools was called. In 1780 the Act, at least in the case of Honour men, was still a serious matter, which required much preparation and went far to decide the class order in the Tripos examination. Gradually its importance was overshadowed by the written test, and in the nineteenth century it dwindled into a mere form : but it survived until 1839, and in the examination for LL.B. degree until 1851. In the case of pollmen it became an almost nominal exercise. The discussion was conducted in Latin. The Moderator, occupying the pulpit, put up the candidates in pairs to dispute as opponents. " The Respondent said simply, *Recte statuit Newtonus*, etc., to which the Opponent as simply replied, *Recte non statuit Newtonus*. This was a disputation, and it was repeated as many times as the statutes required. The parties then changed sides, and each maintained the contrary of his first assertion." This ceremony called ' huddling ' was performed in the case of candidates for an ordinary degree who had not kept all the statutable exercises. Pensioners and sizars had previously undergone some more serious test, but ' huddling,' which was dispatched in ten minutes, was all that was required of fellow-commoners. The quality of the Latin on these occasions is illustrated by the story that a candidate who came into the schools in haste, without his academic bands, was admonished by the Moderator in the words, " Domine Opponens, non habes quod debes. Ubi sunt tui—Anglice—' bands ' ? " To which answer was made, " Domine Moderator, sunt in meo —Anglice—' pocket.' "

Henry Gunning, the well-known bedell and author of the *Reminiscences*, came to Christ's in October, 1784, three years before the admission of Wordsworth at Saint John's, seven years before that of Coleridge at Jesus. His descriptions of Cambridge during the seventy years of his residence are extraordinarily lifelike and outspoken. It is likely that he gives fairly accurate portraits of some of the men who were contemporary, as ' dons ' or undergraduates, with himself and the two poets. But his own character is so clearly, though unconsciously, revealed in his book that we may well hesitate to credit the truthfulness of his picture of Cambridge life as a whole. The *Reminiscences* were written when he was over eighty years of age, and were not published until after his death. They are prefaced by some rather unctuously pious reflections, and he protests his affection and gratitude to certain living friends and disclaims any feelings of animosity for injuries received in the past. If we are to believe the account which he gives of himself, he lived conscious of his rectitude in a society steeped in depravity of every kind. Among his associates he singles out a few as deserving of his respect and admiration, and candidly informs us, long after they had gone to their graves, of the obliquities of their youth. Of the rest he writes with a moral reprobation which contrasts rather pitifully with the particular knowledge of sordid details which it gratifies him to impart. Though he is an excellent raconteur, his nature was petty and venomous : he neither forgot nor forgave. In politics he was a Whig, and in his Tory opponents he saw nothing but what was unprincipled and ridiculous. On his election to the bedellship his colleague informed him that the duties of the office were twofold —to execute the statutes by violating them, and to carve well at table. As a parasite at the tables of many Vice-Chancellors during sixty-five years he had unusual opportunities for picking up gossip, and he spent the virtuous evening of his life in raking up malicious tales about dead hosts and fellow-convives.

At Christ's he was entered at the age of sixteen, when, as he says, he was ignorant of the first proposition of Euclid. There were only two other freshmen in his year at college, and they were not reading men. His tutor, Parkinson, very soon released him from attendance at his lectures, telling him that he would doubtless pass his time more pleasantly, and perhaps more profitably, in his own room. Fortunately for Gunning a Yorkshireman, named Hartley, who was a year senior to him in the College, gave him some voluntary assistance and encouraged him to read. His best time for reading, he says, was in September and the first half of October, when the fellows were absent from the College. In term-time he gave himself up to shooting, card-playing and the society of non-reading men of his own and other colleges. " Drunkenness was the besetting sin of the period, and many other vices followed in its train." The undergraduates are always drunk and disorderly. There are riotously drunken parties of graduates in the combination room of Christ's. The Senior Fellows of Trinity are ' notorious for their vices.' The new-made Bachelors entertain the fellows of their several colleges at supper : immense bowls of punch are emptied, and every one is compelled to sing or drink an enormous glass of liquor by way of penalty. On a certain memorable occasion, described by Gunning, the Vice-Chancellor, in company with one of the bedells, Beverley, and a fellow of Trinity, named Hole, drove to Burwell, on Mid-Lent Sunday in 1810. Custom prescribed that the Vice-Chancellor should preach in the parish church in the morning and attend service in the afternoon, when the Vicar occupied the pulpit. Between services the University party was entertained at dinner by the tenant of the University farm. In the afternoon, when the Vicar had departed to preach, the Vice-Chancellor asked, " What sort of preacher is Mr. Turner ? " to which the tenant replied, " For my own part, I would not go over the threshold to hear him preach." " If that be your opinion, who have had frequent opportunities of hearing him," said the Vice-Chancellor, " I am of your opinion too ; and we will remain and have a few more glasses of your fine old port." The Vicar, after waiting a considerable time for the Vice-Chancellor, was at last obliged to proceed without him. On the return journey the party was at first in high glee, and loud in their commendation of the tenant's ale and wine. But presently, as they were driving over Newmarket Heath, a furious quarrel arose between Beverley and Hole, in which the Vice-Chancellor came in for some unceremonious treatment. He stopped the carriage and insisted that Beverley should ride outside : Beverley, in turn, insisted that the others should get out and find their way on foot to Newmarket. Finally the whole party fell asleep, and the Vice-Chancellor thought it prudent next day to overlook the bedell's conduct.

Equally stupendous was the gourmandising of the ' don ' of those days. At Sturbridge Fair, in a dirty booth and at a rough table supported by casks, the

Vice-Chancellor and University officials dine on herrings, pork, plum-pudding, pease-pudding, a goose, an apple-pie and a round of beef, ' with ale and bottled porter in great profusion.' The celebrated Dr. Milner finds the best remedy for his weak digestion is to eat as much as he can, and at his Sunday dinners to members of the University the bottle circulates very freely. Another celebrity, the reverend ' Bob ' Collier, when on his way to dine with a friend in London, sees in a back court a notice hanging outside a cook's shop, ' A roast pig this instant set upon the table.' The temptation is irresistible. He orders and devours three quarters of the animal, and reluctantly leaves one quarter behind, as his dinner hour is approaching and his friend is punctual.

Wholesome exercise seems to have been almost unknown, whether to ' don ' or undergraduate. Cricket, football, rowing and athletic exercises generally are not so much as alluded to by Gunning, though from other sources we do know that undergraduates played cricket at Cambridge when Henry Venn was an undergraduate, about 1742. The disciplinary regulations of 1750 tended to discourage healthy amusements. The undergraduate was forbidden to keep a horse without the express sanction of the Master of his college ; to go out of Cambridge on horseback or in a carriage without his tutor's permission ; to possess a gun or sporting dogs under any conditions ; to frequent cricket-grounds or tennis-courts before noon. Under such conditions we are not surprised to learn that fellows of colleges ' of most convivial disposition ' committed suicide ; that one undergraduate is tried for the murder of a townsman, and another expelled the University for killing a fellow-student in a duel. As the microscopical observer of habits and

habiliments Gunning has his interest.   Vice-Chancellor
Lowther Yates in pantaloons: the elegant Mr. Foley,
of Jesus, who affected a scarlet coat because it was
denounced in the University statutes: 'ghastly'
Castley, of the same college, who enjoyed the humours
of a merry-go-round arrayed in a greatcoat of 'tolerably bright green,' are sufficiently diverting people.
And only surviving relatives need have been vexed
to be told in what company the reverend Dr. Kipling
rode on the Hills Road: by what devices Professor
Busick Harwood started a testimonial to himself:
or through what misadventure the Bursar of Trinity
invited the Master's wife to visit him in his college
rooms.

These are the things that were talked of over the
parlour punch-bowl and at the lower end of the Vice-
Chancellor's table. About intellectual movements
at Cambridge in his day Gunning has nothing to say.
He barely mentions Porson: he knows nothing of
Malthus, who was of his year: of Wordsworth we might
suppose that he never heard: Coleridge only interests
him for an escapade in the Senate House at the time
of Frend's trial. Religion provides him with some
anecdotes about Simeon and some jibes at 'the Saints.'
Of the remarkable outgrowth of Unitarianism at Cambridge in the last quarter of the century—if his silence
is evidence—he knows nothing at all. After his own
undergraduate days the undergraduates fade out of
his knowledge, except when they draw attention to
themselves by turbulence.

There is another picture of this late eighteenth-
century Cambridge in Wordsworth's *Prelude*—the
picture of its influences on a young soul, not great nor
greatly removed from the ordinary, but growing. It
does not blink the coarseness and vapidity of then-

present college life, which was all that Gunning knew ; but it tells us how the memories and associations of historic Cambridge, its material beauties and solemnities, and the sense of nearness to the great spirits of the past wrought on a receptive mind, and on one altar kept alive the fires of reverence and imagination. *The Prelude* was written between 1799 and 1804, and is the judgment passed by the mature man on his former self and his Alma Mater. The University by his ' own beloved Cam ' was always dear to Wordsworth, but he did not shrink, any more than Tennyson did, from telling it how its gold was become dim and its fine gold changed.

Wordsworth began his residence at Saint John's in October, 1787. His rooms, he tells us, were in ' a nook obscure ' in the first court, over the kitchens : they were, in prose fact, on staircase F, but since 1893 they have been absorbed by the kitchens.[1] From his pillow, on moonlight nights, he could look across to the ante-chapel of Trinity, where Newton's statue stood : and near him

> Hung Trinity's loquacious clock,
> Who never let the quarters, night or day,
> Slip by him unproclaim'd, and told the hours
> Twice over, with a male and female voice.

Dropped at the age of seventeen into a world utterly strange to the dweller among Cumbrian hills, the poet confesses that he spent his days much as other undergraduates did. He was

> Rich in monies and attir'd
> In splendid garb, with hose of silk, and hair
> Powder'd like rimy trees, when frost is keen,

---

[1] An inscription has been put in the large window overlooking the kitchen lane to record Wordsworth's residence in the rooms.

and his ' weeks went roundly on with invitations, suppers, wine and fruit,' in a thoughtless, freshman fashion.   He was happy in the companionship of other happy youths, for his heart ' was social, and loved idleness and joy.'   Nevertheless, from a sense of duty to his relations and a prudent regard to his worldly prospects he attended lectures : but they did not interest him, and in later days he reproached himself for not having followed his own bent in reading.

> I did not love,
> Judging not ill perhaps, the timid course
> Of our scholastic studies ; could have wished
> To see the river flow with ampler range
> And freer pace.

And the passions of the few eager students seemed to him pitiable and ungenerous.   Gray's soul had chafed at the bondage of mathematical work.   Wordsworth, unless he is ascribing to youth the judgment of his later years, says that even in Cambridge days he revolted against the tyranny of classics and the worship of phrase, at the expense of thought, which the minute study of them fostered—

> The dangerous craft of culling term and phrase
> From languages that want the living voice
> To carry meaning to the natural heart.

He adds the observation—singular in a poet—that he took pleasure in the rudiments of geometry—though he progressed no further than the threshold of the subject.

In the first terms of his college life he tells us that his ' imagination slept.'   The fellows who had pointed the way of idleness to Wilberforce were little likely to understand or encourage the dreamings of a youth

who showed small aptitude in their perfunctory trade.
Like other undergraduates he found rich pastime in
the spectacle

> Of the grave Elders, men unscoured, grotesque
> In character, tricked out like aged trees
> Which through the lapse of their infirmity
> Give ready place to any random seed
> That chooses to be reared upon their trunks.

Most he resented—as Southey resented at Balliol,
Oxford—the compulsory attendance at chapel.

> Was ever known
> The witless shepherd who persists to drive
> A flock that thirsts not to a pool disliked?

In its outward incidents Wordsworth's student life
was as ordinary, respectable and conventional as the
meekest freshman's. Among his Johnian acquaint-
ances he had no friend capable of influencing him, and
none who interested him in after life or need interest
us. He talked with his companions unprofitable
talk with no thought of the great issues that were then
being presented to the world or of the eternal problems
of existence. For all that he tells us in *The Prelude*,
the fall of the Bastille, which happened in his second
Long Vacation, waked no echoes in the first court of
Saint John's. The questions of the liberty of the individual and the order of society which were stirring
the thoughts even of ordinary men seem to have left
Wordsworth undisturbed. To him that dawn when it
was bliss to be alive and very heaven to be young did
not come until Cambridge days were done. In his
third Long Vacation (1790) he made a walking tour on
the Continent in company with a Welshman, named
Jones, who afterwards became a fellow of Saint John's
and settled in an Oxfordshire parsonage. Though they

BRIDGE AND GATEWAY, SAINT JOHN'S COLLEGE

landed in France on ' the great federal day ' when
Louis XVI swore fidelity to the new constitution, and
though they took part in the universal rejoicings which
attended the occasion, he ' looked on these things as
from a distance,' without intimate concern.   It was
the revelation of the sublimity of Nature, witnessed
in the Alps, and the beauties of the Italian lakes which
far more powerfully excited his imagination.

Not less at Cambridge, amid the trivialities of
college society, it was Nature and the solitude which
he made into a world of his own that quickened his
soul.   In ' the level fields ' that surround the town
he turned to earth and sky for solace in ' the injurious
sway of place or circumstance,' and to the very stones
of the highway he ' gave a moral life.'   To others this
passionate sympathy with living Nature, betrayed
occasionally in gesture or look, seemed a kind of
madness—' and so it was,' says he, ' if inspiration
sort with such a name.'   In his last months at Cambridge ' the Poet's soul was with him,' and he cherished
dreams of leaving behind him some monument that
pure hearts would cherish.   In his own picture we see
him rapt in ' sweet meditation, the still overflow of
present happiness,' as he wandered solitary in the
College grove on winter nights, until the porter's bell
sounded at nine o'clock to recall him to the courts.
Among the elms with which the so-called Wilderness
was planted, a single ash tree grew, green even in
winter with clustering ivy.   Often, he says, he stood
' foot-bound uplooking at this lovely tree, beneath a
frosty moon,' and conjuring up, as Spenser might have
done, ' bright appearances of human forms with super-
human powers.'

The ' Friend ' to whom *The Prelude* was addressed
was Samuel Taylor Coleridge, who began his residence

at Jesus in the October (1791) after Wordsworth took his degree and left the University. Deeply the elder poet regretted that in the days of his spiritual solitude at Saint John's he had missed the companionship of a soul so kindred.

> Not alone,
> Ah ! surely not in singleness of heart
> Should I have seen the light of evening fade
> From smooth Cam's silent waters.

In the retrospect of his own collegiate life he says that he has present before his eyes the after-sojourn of Coleridge in the same scenes, and thinking

> Of thee, the learning, gorgeous eloquence
> And all the strength and plumage of thy youth,

he sadly contrasts the inspired energy of the poet in those young days with the physical decrepitude of his middle age, and sorrows to think that, in altered circumstances, his own maturer age and calmer habits might have spared his friend a world of pain in the stormy course of his Cambridge life.

The university careers of the poet-friends were indeed as divergent as their temperaments in youth. Partly the difference is accounted for by the electrical storms in France, which spread even into the quiet atmosphere of Cambridge after Wordsworth left it. Wordsworth, who had been an eye-witness in under-graduate days of the dawning scenes of the Revolution, had looked upon them with the unimpassioned eyes of a spectator. Coleridge, who never set foot on France, was carried away into the vortex of republicanism. In 1789 all England, Whig and Tory, was joining in dithyrambs over the destruction of the Bastille. The Vice-Chancellor of Cambridge spoke of it as ' a subject

of triumph and congratulation.' In 1792 the Republic was declared, the Revolutionary war began
and the Edict of Fraternity was issued.   The wave of
anarchy threatened to submerge England, and Pitt
was grappling with the secret Revolutionary Societies.
The University aided the efforts of its representative
by an address to the King, denouncing ' the promoters
of anarchy.'   In the month of the September massacres
(1792) Coleridge tells ' a Young Lady '—Sara Fricker,
shortly to be Mrs. Coleridge—in a poem addressed
to her,

> Red from the Tyrant's wound I shook the lance,
> And strode with joy the reeking plains of France.

When he first came from Christ's Hospital to Cambridge Coleridge settled down, as Wordsworth says,
' in temperance and peace, a rigorous student.'   To
Jesus he was drawn by the prospect of getting a
scholarship on the foundation of Tobias Rustat, which
has opened the doors of the University to many a
poor youth who, like Coleridge, was the son of a
deceased clergyman.   In his freshman year he gained
a Browne Medal for a Greek ode on the Slave Trade
—the same subject which, seven years earlier, was
proposed for the Latin Members' Prize, when it was
gained by Clarkson, the emancipator.   In the next
year he was selected by Porson as one of four (chosen
out of seventeen or eighteen) to compete for the
Craven Scholarship, which then ranked with the
Chancellor's Medals as the highest distinction in
classics which the University bestowed.   Among the
four were the successful candidate, Samuel Butler,
who afterwards was the famous Shrewsbury headmaster
and Bishop of Lichfield, and Keate, who later was
headmaster of Eton. To fail against such com-

petitors was no humiliation; but insensibly the disappointment helped to turn the thoughts of Coleridge away from academic ambitions and the fellowship on which at first he set his heart.

The fame of the precocious learning and extraordinary fascination of Coleridge had preceded him from Christ's Hospital. 'The inspired charity-boy,' as Lamb calls him, to whose accents 'the walls of the old Grey Friars' re-echoed as, to the entranced admiration of casual passers, he 'unfolded the mysteries of Jamblichus and Plotinus,' or recited Homer and Pindar in Greek, drew about him the like groups of eager listeners at Cambridge. Though he was not to make acquaintance with William Wordsworth until three years had passed after he quitted the University, William's brother, Christopher, then an undergraduate and afterwards Master of Trinity, belonged to a literary society of which Coleridge was the moving spirit. From Christopher's diary we learn that at one meeting Coleridge 'talked Greek—Maximus Tyrius, he told us—and spouted out of Bowles,' whose sonnets the young poet admired much beyond their worth. At another time he hears Coleridge 'repeat some original poetry—he having neglected to write his essay'—a characteristic neglect. A former schoolfellow, C. V. Le Grice—of Trinity and a year junior to Coleridge—in a letter to the *Gentleman's Magazine*, written in 1834, just after the poet's death, gives an admirable picture of him in his rooms at Jesus.

He was very studious, but his reading was desultory and capricious. He took little exercise for the sake of exercise; but he was ready at any time to unbend his mind in conversation, and for the sake of this his room—the ground-floor room on the right hand of the staircase facing the great gate—was a constant rendezvous for conversation-loving friends. What evenings have I spent in those rooms! What little suppers, or sizings, as they were called, have I enjoyed, when Æschylus and Plato and Thucydides were pushed aside with a pile of lexicons, etc., to discuss the pamphlets of the day ! Ever and anon a pamphlet issued from the pen of Burke. There was no need of having the book before us. Coleridge had read it in the morning, and in the evening he would repeat whole pages *verbatim*. Frend's trial was then in progress. Pamphlets swarmed from the press. Coleridge had read them all ; and in the evening, with our negus, we had them *viva-voce* gloriously.

If the influence of Coleridge was radio-active on others he was equally sensitive to such influence himself, and the mention of Frend recalls a chapter in his undergraduate career which profoundly affected him in the days when his star was newest and brightest in the literary firmament. Things, material or spiritualised, had been Wordsworth's teachers at Cambridge : Coleridge took his lessons from psychology and man, as displayed in books or society. It was his fortune to come to Jesus at a time when the College counted among its graduates some men of marked individuality and magnetic influence. Among men immediately his seniors were Malthus, William Otter, afterwards Bishop of Chichester, and E. D. Clarke, the well-known traveller and archæologist. Coleridge probably never made their acquaintance at Cambridge, but the three had formed an intellectual circle which gave an energy to the College strongly contrasted with the inertness of the society of Saint John's. The Master, Dr. Pearce—who was also Dean of Ely—was an able man, humorous and kindly, who had a shrewd comprehension of the genius of Coleridge and acted a friendly part in his undergraduate troubles. Among past or present fellows who were still resident were three who powerfully impressed the young poet's views and imagination. These were Dr. Edwards, Robert Tyrwhitt, founder of the Hebrew scholarships and brother of the editor of Chaucer, and William Frend.

19

The names of these three men are intimately associated with the efforts, which had been sustained for some years before Coleridge came to Cambridge, to obtain the abolition of religious tests in the University. A grace was offered by Tyrwhitt to the Senate in 1771 for exempting Bachelors of Arts from subscription to the Thirty-nine Articles. It was rejected by the Caput, a body nominated by the Heads of Houses and possessing a veto on all graces that were to be presented to the Senate. Petitions were addressed to the House of Commons, one by graduates, another by certain undergraduates, requesting the removal of the subscription : they were rejected on the ground that it was competent for the University to apply a remedy without the interference of Parliament. In 1772 a grace was passed allowing an affirmation that the candidate for B.A. degree was *bona fide* a member of the Church of England to be substituted for subscription. In 1787 Dr. Edwards proposed the abolition of the affirmation, and he was warmly supported by Frend. The grace was rejected, and the matter slept until it was revived in the reign of William IV.

That the imposition of any form of test was ineffectual in attaining its objects was apparent in the fact that these three men were Unitarians. In the eighteenth century the Church, and especially at Cambridge, was saturated with Arianism. No barrier that it could erect could exclude even from its ordained priesthood men whose views were undisguisedly Arian. ' Josephus ' Whiston, Samuel Clarke, Conyers Middleton, John Jackson, John Jebb and Gilbert Wakefield were clergymen of this class. Towards the end of the century Unitarians—Jebb and Wakefield, for example —severed themselves from the body of the Church. Under the influence of Priestley they became generally

identified with the movement for Radical Reform.
Many of them—Frend and Edwards among them—
were suspected of corresponding with the National
Convention.

Tyrwhitt was a man of fifty-six when Coleridge
came to Jesus, and had resigned his fellowship ten
years previously on religious grounds, though he still
resided in College.   He was devoted to biblical research,
and his unaffected piety and warm charity made him
universally beloved.   His religious views were moderate, and he contributed liberally to the ' beautification '
of the chapel of his college, after the thin classical
pattern which was deemed elegant in those days.
Though he did not attempt to make converts to his
views the earnestness of his search for religious truth
awakened the interest of the undergraduates.   Frend,
who graduated B.A. in 1780, for several years was vicar
of Madingley.   He renounced his orders in 1787 and
published a statement of his new creed, addressed
to the inhabitants of Cambridge.   He retained his
fellowship, and in Coleridge's day was resident in the
College—deeply interested in the study of Hebrew
and engaged in translating the historical books of the
Old Testament for Priestley's new version of the
Scriptures.   Though his zeal was untempered he seems
to have lived on amicable terms with the rest of the
society.

In January, 1793, Louis XVI was executed : in
February war with France was declared.   A wave of
horror and dread passed over England.   Everywhere
was suspicion of traitorous correspondence with the
Revolutionary leaders.   A royal proclamation against
seditious writings was issued in May, 1792.   Magis-
trates and corporations eagerly lent their services to
the Government in bringing to justice the authors of

pamphlets calculated to promote disaffection. At this crisis, within a month of the French King's death, Frend published a pamphlet entitled *Peace and Union*, denouncing the war on the ground of the hardships which it entailed on the poorest classes. It went on to discuss political questions such as Parliamentary Reform, Triennial Elections, etc., which a year or two earlier had been debated without heat and nowadays would seem perfectly innocuous. But in 1793 the revulsion against political change was so strong that throughout the country advocates of reform on constitutional lines were convicted and sentenced to transportation for treasonable practices. It was, however, the flippant and contemptuous tone of Frend's remarks on the Christian religion which excited the strongest reprobation in the University, and especially in the evangelical party. Action was promptly taken by his opponents in Jesus and in the University. In both Frend had warm friends who supported him in the subsequent proceedings, though they did not share his views. Appeals to the Visitor of the College and to the court of King's Bench delayed the issue for some months. In the end both the College and the University passed a sentence of expulsion.

The example and influence of Edwards and Frend did much to confirm in Coleridge the political and religious sentiments which were awaked by the events of 1793. In one of his letters, written in 1794, he describes a tea-party at the house of Dr. Edwards, at which he discussed for six hours his ideal scheme of Pantisocracy and convinced the doctor of its impregnability. He showed his sympathy with Frend at the trial in the Senate House in an uproarious manner which called for the intervention of the proctor, though he contrived to escape punishment by changing places with an innocent bystander. In a letter to his clergyman brother he describes himself as being in a religious twilight, with too much vanity to be altogether a Christian, and too much tenderness of nature to be utterly an infidel.

His academic ambitions faded away, but he was an omnivorous reader. Metaphysics, poetry, travel, medicine, but chiefly politics and religion, all interested him by turns. He wrote a great deal of verse of kinds, some of which he inserted in a newly established Radical paper, the *Cambridge Intelligencer*. One piece, entitled, ' A wish written in Jesus Wood, February 10, 1792,' was addressed to Mary Evans, to whom he was at that time paying his attentions ; but he did not think it necessary to inform her that it was a literal translation of a Sapphic ode by Dr. Jortin, a former fellow of the College. Mostly the poetry of his student days was imitative, and its model was Gray—anything can be personified by capital letters. Ossian has his turn, and Verses to Young Ladies—which, with a change of name, were serviceably used on a variety of occasions—make up the rest. Cleverness and rhythmical ease are their only recommendation. We look in vain for any trace of the joy in nature, the self-interpretation, the romantic half-lights that belong to *Christabel*, *The Nightingale* or *Dejection*.

The clouds which gathered over his later life were already darkening his path. His Cambridge letters reveal the lack of resolution which was the disease of his life. His popularity in ' fast ' circles of undergraduates led to dissipation, debt and unavailing regrets. In November, 1793, he disappeared from the College, and for five months he was lost to his friends. Then a letter which he sent to friends at Christ's Hospital revealed that he had enlisted in the 15th Dragoons, and was in barracks at Reading. His brother, George, procured his discharge, and he returned to Cambridge in April. By the College authorities he was treated leniently and even kindly. They sentenced him to a month's ' walling ' within the College, but the Master, with a sagacious discernment of his scholarly abilities, added the penalty that he should translate the works of *Demetrius Phalereus* into English, and, wisely severe, took frequent opportunity of finding out from Coleridge how the work was progressing, as he intended that he should publish an edition. Coleridge says that his friends at Cambridge welcomed his return as that of a lost brother.

The kindness with which he was received touched his heart, and for a time he returned to his studies in a chastened spirit. But when he came back after the summer vacation he came in a spirit of declared revolt. " Since I quitted this room," he writes to his new-made friend Southey, in September, " what and how important events have been evolved ! America ! Southey ! Miss Fricker ! Pantisocracy ! " " The leading idea of Pantisocracy is to make men *necessarily* virtuous by removing all motives to evil—all possible temptation." The scheme, which presently became the talk of the whole University, was to take shape in a socialistic settlement in America. Coleridge, Southey and a third friend, Lovell, originated the project ; and, as it was an essential feature that each settler should be accompanied by a wife, Coleridge—unhappily, as the sequel proved—hastily engaged himself to Sara Fricker, whose two sisters were already engaged, one to Lovell, the other to Southey. Good Dr. Pearce was seriously disquieted by this new folly of the fatherless scholar in whom he had interested himself, and he was probably still more annoyed at the publication of *The Fall of Robespierre*, a three-act tragedy which bore the name of Coleridge on the title page, though he only wrote the first act, the second and third being by Southey. But the whole erection of Pantisocracy tumbled to the ground when, for the second time, Coleridge vanished from Cambridge, in November, 1794. Whether he had any motive beyond the desire to escape from a cage which had become intolerable it is hard to say. In the *Biographia Literaria* he deplores his hasty act. " In an inauspicious hour I left the friendly cloisters and happy grove of quiet, ever-honoured Jesus College, Cambridge." The man to whom Cambridge had most to forgive loved it with a depth of feeling that was unknown to Gray, who owed to it a life of case.

CHAPTER XIII

TENNYSON AND THE NEW AGE

Ye fields of Cambridge, our dear Cambridge, say
Have you not seen us walking every day ?
Was there a tree about which did not know
The love betwixt us two ?

COWLEY

IN 1828 the world was very old and on the point
of being very young. An old King reigned and
old ministers governed. Old poets and thinkers
and their thoughts went back to old days. The
great voices of the Revolution were hushed. Shelley
and Byron were dead. Coleridge in his 'Dodona
grove' at Highgate, Wordsworth in his Westmorland
stamp-office, were, for all present concernments, deaf
and mostly dumb. For the material age into which
they had survived they had much reproach but no
practicable counsel. Nevertheless young minds
pathetically sought them for guidance, and their
philosophic pieties passed into a creed. John
Sterling, fresh from his degree at Cambridge, made
pilgrimages to both in 1828. From the mild ecclesi-
asticism of the two old hermits Sterling, always
with reverence for their teaching, passed into the
new world by paths of his own. Arthur Hallam,
as he tells us in his poem on *Timbuctoo*, was
one of the youths who 'drank the sweet, sad
tones of Wisdom' from 'the good old man, most

eloquent, who spake of things divine' on High-gate Hill.

The generation which passed away at Cambridge between 1794, when Coleridge turned his back upon it, and 1828, when Alfred Tennyson and Charles Darwin were freshmen, was made illustrious by the University careers of some great, many eminent men. The mere list of them shows how far the University was removed from the aridity of the age which preceded the French Revolution. Among statesmen are to be counted : William Lamb, afterwards Lord Melbourne, of Trinity (B.A. 1799) : Palmerston, of St. John's (M.A. *jure natalitium*, 1806) : and Stratford Canning, entered at King's in 1806. In letters and poetry the chief names are : Byron, matriculated at Trinity in 1805, a year after his friend, John Cam Hobhouse : T. B. Macaulay, matriculated at the same college in 1818, and contemporary as undergraduate and fellow there with W. M. Praed : and the novelist, Bulwer Lytton, of Trinity and Trinity Hall, who matriculated in 1822. Among mathematicians and astronomers to this period belong the second Herschel, of Saint John's, and G. B. Airy, of Trinity, who were senior wranglers, respectively, in 1813 and 1823, and Charles Babbage, of Peterhouse, who was B.A. in 1814. Among men of science were Adam Sedgwick of Trinity, matriculated in 1804, William Whewell, of Trinity, matriculated in 1812, and Darwin's friend and teacher, J. S. Henslow, of Saint John's, matriculated in 1814. In the pre-Tractarian age the old religious issues were dead and the new problems were hardly yet recognised : yet among Cambridge divines should be mentioned Julius Charles Hare, of Trinity (matriculated in 1812), Hugh James Rose, of Trinity (matriculated in 1813) and Frederick Denison Maurice, of Trinity and Trinity

Hall (matriculated in 1823). In classical scholarship the name of Peter Paul Dobree, of Trinity (matriculated in 1800), who died too early to show the full measure of his ability, is the only one which deserves to be ranked with those of Elmsley and Gaisford of Oxford.

In this list the great preponderance of Trinity names will be remarked. Since Waterloo Cambridge had seen an extraordinarily rapid increase in the number of its members. Between 1810 and 1828 the numbers given in the Calendar had risen from 2469 to 5104. Trinity had shared in the numerical growth of the University, but not more than other colleges : its total membership had just doubled. But in intellectual eminence the College began to draw away from the rest of the University in an unmistakable manner. In mathematical study the other colleges fairly held their own. The high wranglers and Smith's prizemen, then as now, came from the smaller schools, and especially from those in the north of England, with which Saint John's had an intimate connection. But in classics, which since the beginning of the century had won an ampler recognition by the foundation of the Davies, Pitt and Porson scholarships, and by the institution of the Classical Tripos, in 1824, Trinity distanced all competitors. In the ten years, 1791–1800, of the Chancellor's Medals for classics, eight fell to Trinity, six to Saint John's and six to the rest of the colleges. In the ten years preceding Tennyson's matriculation (1828) fifteen were gained by Trinity, five by Saint John's and the smaller colleges did not gain one. Between 1806 and 1828 there were thirteen Craven scholars from Trinity, one from Saint John's, one from King's, and the other colleges were not represented. Between 1792 and 1867 five Trinity men successively held the Professorship of Greek.

Unquestionably the fame of such teachers as Porson, Dobree and Monk did much to attract classical talent to Trinity. But a more efficient cause was the great development, in the early years of the century, of the Public Schools, as they began to be called in distinction from local grammar-schools. After 1800 local schools, generally throughout England, suffered a decline in numbers, in social standing, and in efficiency, from which they did not recover until they were rehabilitated by the Endowed Schools Commission, after 1869. At Saint John's and the smaller colleges scholarships, until the Statutes of 1858 and 1882 in many cases liberated them, were generally limited to particular counties and schools, and in many cases were awarded without competition. At Trinity, with the exception of those attached to Westminster, they were open to the world, and it naturally followed that the richer, abler and more ambitious boy renounced the emolument which he might have for the asking for the uncertain but more glorious prospect of election at Trinity. Especially this was the case of the Etonians. The unprofitable privilege of exemption from degree examinations which King's still asserted closed the gates of that college to the more adventurous Eton scholars, and Trinity was the gainer. Among Etonians entered at Trinity in Tennyson's year were Arthur Hallam, Kinglake and his own brother, Frederick.

In the autumn of 1824, four years before Tennyson's admission, John Sterling began his residence at Trinity. Of the circle to which he belonged, as it lasted into Tennyson's time, it is worth while quoting Carlyle's description.

Their life seems to have been an ardently speculating and talking one ; by no means excessively restrained within limits ; and, in the more adventurous heads, like Sterling's, decidedly tending towards the latitudinarian in most things. They had among them a Debating Society called The Union ; where on stated evenings was much logic, and other spiritual fencing and ingenuous collision,—probably of a very superior quality in that kind ; for not a few of the then disputants have since proved themselves men of parts, and attained distinction in the intellectual walks of life.

Carlyle says that Sterling was the acknowledged chief in this Union Club, which included F. D. Maurice, Trench (afterwards the poetical Archbishop of Dublin), Kemble (the Anglo-Saxon scholar, son of the actor, Charles, and brother of Fanny), Spedding (editor of Bacon's works), Venables (of the *Times*), Charles Buller (the Liberal politician) and Monckton Milnes (afterwards Lord Houghton).

> The Union Club, of rhetorical fame,
> Was held at the Red Lion Inn,
> And there never was Lion so perfectly tame,
> Or who made such a musical din.

So sang Praed in 1823, when he, Macaulay, Bulwer and Charles Austin were its princes of debate. J. H. Moultrie too tells in blank verse of those ' nights and suppers of the gods,' when, after ' the keen conflicts of contending wits,' the leaders adjourned to his rooms, close by, to sup on oysters. Looking back in later life on those memorable scenes he shows in vivid picture the speech and fashion of those heroes : Praed, the Etonian, whose dexterous sword-play of subtle wit, keen sarcasm and reckless levity few could encounter : Macaulay, not over-scrupulous, breathing an atmosphere of argument, keen to detect error and stored with multifarious learning : and Austin, older than the others, of massive brow already furrowed with deep thought, an unconscious enthusiast, though to him the ideal was untrue, and his weight of understanding crushed imagination, feeling, taste and reverential faith.

Maurice and Sterling were jointly the founders of the famous society of ' the Apostles.' Arthur Hallam wrote to Gladstone concerning Maurice : " The effect which he has produced on the minds of many at Cambridge by the single creation of that society of ' the Apostles ' (for the spirit, though not the form, was created by him) is far greater than I can dare to calculate, and will be felt, both directly and indirectly, in the age that is upon us."

' The Apostles,' like other ' intellectuals ' of that day, were of course radical : but they eschewed party and reverenced the traditions and teachings of the past. They had regular meetings, as well as informal gatherings in the rooms of this or that ' Apostle,' where much coffee was drunk and much tobacco smoked. They debated politics, read together Hobbes, Locke, Bentham, Kant, etc., and discussed questions of religion, morality and psychology, the proposer of the subject standing generally before the mantelpiece. Essays were read in turn, and Alfred Tennyson wrote one on Ghosts, the prologue to which survives in his son's *Memoir* : but he was too shy to deliver it. He was ordinarily a silent member, and ' the society was content to receive him, his poetry and wisdom unfettered.'

Never perhaps in its splendid history has Trinity assembled within its walls such a glorious company as the friends of Tennyson in ' the dawn-golden times ' of his undergraduate career. With him came his poet-brothers, Frederick and Charles—the former a migrant from Saint John's, which had been the college of the Tennysons' father. Among the freshmen of 1828 who belonged to the Tennyson ' set,' besides Hallam, were W. H. Thompson, most intimate of interpreters of Plato, and afterwards Master of Trinity :

' Eōthen ' Kinglake : Alford, poet and Dean of Canterbury : and Edmund Law Lushington, who married
Tennyson's sister, Cecilia, and became Professor of
Greek at Glasgow. To the year above him belonged
Spedding, ' the wisest man I know,' as Tennyson
said, and Monckton Milnes. Henry Lushington, the
poetical brother of Edmund, and, like him, afterwards
a fellow of the College, and W. H. Brookfield, the
' old Brooks' beloved by Thackeray as well as Tennyson,
were freshmen in 1829, and to the same year belonged
Thackeray himself : but Thackeray's intimacy with
Tennyson came in later years. Edward Fitzgerald
was in his third year when Tennyson came up, and
John Mitchell Kemble, matriculated in 1825, was
still resident and linked Tennyson and his circle with
Maurice and the early ' Apostles.' Outside Trinity
Tennyson's friends were Charles Merivale of Saint
John's, historian of Rome and Dean of Ely : G. S.
Venables of Jesus, from whom Thackeray is said to have
drawn the character of George Warrington : and J. W.
Blakesley, the future Dean of Lincoln, at first of
Corpus but later a scholar of Trinity.

When the brothers, Alfred and Charles, ' came up '
in October, 1828, they occupied lodgings at 12 Rose
Crescent, but afterwards moved to 57 Corpus Buildings.[1]
Was it in one or other of those houses that their
friends acted scenes from *Much Ado about Nothing*,
with Kemble as Dogberry, Hallam as Verges and
Monckton Milnes as Beatrice, and that Beatrice,
collapsing on the sofa, broke it with her weight, and
lay, a mass of tumbled petticoats, on the floor ? Alfred,

---

[1] The house then numbered 12 was the last house in Rose
Crescent on the northern side. It is now added to the shop of
Messrs. Reed, silversmiths, which is at the corner of the Crescent
and the Market Place. The house still numbered 57 Corpus Buildings
is opposite the door of the Bull Hotel.

it seems, took part in such actings and was famous in
the part of Malvolio.   Hallam's rooms, as *In Memoriam*
has placed on everlasting record, were near the end of
' that long walk of limes,' on staircase G in the New
Court of Trinity.

Frederick and Charles, though the condition then
attached to the Classical Tripos that candidates should
have been classed in mathematics debarred them from
an Honours degree, were both good scholars.   Frederick
won the Browne Medal for a Greek ode in 1828, and
in the same year Charles gained a Bell scholarship.
Alfred had no academic ambitions.   In a letter of his
earliest college days we find him regretting that ' the
golden days of Faerie are over ' and that gossamer
dreams may not be consolidated into reality.   The
studies of the University he finds uninteresting and
matter of fact, and ' none but dry-headed, calculating,
angular little men can take much delight in them.'
Never, perhaps, had Trinity commanded a staff of
teachers in their way abler and more efficient than in
1828 : but none of them penetrated the recesses of
the shy student's soul.   His tutor was William
Whewell, whose rough dogmatism must have been
repellent to the poet, who, however, sincerely respected
him.   On a certain occasion when ' Billy Whistle,'
as Whewell was nicknamed, was hooted by the undergraduates in the Senate House, Tennyson raised a
cheer for him.   Whewell grimly smiled and invited
him to breakfast next morning.   Connop Thirlwall
and Julius Hare, who were classical lecturers, perhaps
never knew Tennyson.   In fact, by the ' dons ' he passed
wholly unobserved, and College and University faithfully performed their primary duty of not meddling
with a genius which they did not understand.   None
the less, what Tennyson did not owe to himself he owed

to Cambridge. What Carlyle wrote of the influences of Cambridge on young Sterling is even more applicable to Tennyson.

His studies and inquiries—diligently prosecuted, I believe—were of the most discursive wide flowing character ; not steadily advancing along beaten roads to college honours, but pulsing out with impetuous irregularity, now on this track, now on that, towards whatever spiritual Delphi might promise to unfold the mystery of this world, and announce to him what was, in our new day, the authentic message of the gods. His speculations, readings, inferences, glances and conclusions were doubtless sufficiently encyclopædic : his grand tutors the multifarious set of Books he devoured. And perhaps it was not the express set of arrangements of this unexampled epoch in this or any extant University that could essentially forward him, but only the implied and silent ones ; less in the prescribed ' course of study,' which seems to tend no-whither, than in the generous rebellion against said prescribed course, and the voluntary spirit of endeavour and adventure excited thereby. Certainly, if rebellion is unfortunately needful, and you can rebel in a generous manner, several things may be acquired in that manner—rigorous mutual fidelity, reticence, steadfastness, mild stoicism and other virtues far transcending your Greek accidence. Nor can the unwisest ' prescribed course of study ' be considered quite useless, if it have incited you to try nobly on all sides for a course of your own.

To Tennyson, deeply pondering on the ideas of the new age, the narrowness and dryness of academic teaching and the blindness of the teachers to every subject of human interest, to every new application of human knowledge was intolerably hateful. His indignant feelings found vent in a noble sonnet of 1830.

Therefore your Halls, your ancient Colleges,
Your portals statued with old kings and queens,
Your gardens, myriad-volumed libraries,
Wax-lighted chapels, and rich carven screens,
Your doctors, and your proctors, and your deans,
Shall not avail you, when the Day-beam sports
New-risen o'er awaken'd Albion. No !
Nor yet your solemn organ-pipes that blow
Melodious thunders through your vacant courts

THE HALL, TRINITY COLLEGE

At noon and eve, because your manner sorts
Not with this age, wherefrom ye stand apart,
Because the lips of little children preach
Against you, you that do profess to teach
And teach us nothing, feeding not the heart.

The sonnet was never included in his published
works.   The young idealist had his own clear notion
of what a University might be, and later, in *The
Princess*, expressed his notion of the teaching, old or
new, that should inspire.

A classic lecture, rich in sentiment,
With scraps of thundrous Epic lilted out,

as Tennyson himself might lilt them.   The lectures are
to include all the new learning that was sealed to
Cambridge in 1830—

all
That treats of whatsoever is, the state,
The total chronicles of man, the mind,
The morals, something of the frame, the rock,
The star, the bird, the fish, the shell, the flower,
Electric, chemic laws, and all the rest,
And whatsoever can be taught and known.

Tennyson saw his vision realised before he died.
He regretted the bitterness vented in his sonnet when
he witnessed his old University taking up the burden
of a really national education, touching the heart of
England and adapting itself to its living needs. Greatly
he rejoiced in his last years to know that the gulf was
bridged which in his young days had parted the teacher
from the taught.

From the first Tennyson's powers as a thinker and
a poet were recognised by those who were best able to
pronounce—his coevals. "That man must be a poet,"
said Thompson when he first saw him walk up the
college hall. On Fitzgerald he impressed himself as

20

' a sort of Hyperion.' 'One of the mighty ones of the earth,' Blakesley called him. The poetry which he wrote in those days reflected the topics which most interested him, natural science and politics. The statesmen whom he most admired were Canning, Peel and the Duke of Wellington. He professed himself ' wed to no party in the state,' and, loving Freedom, he distrusted the wisdom and sincerity of those who babbled its name in the ferment of Reform agitation.

In 1829 he was announced as the winner of the Chancellor's English Medal for his poem on the subject ' Timbuctoo.' In those days of young enthusiasm the competition for the Medal was keen, and the glory of winning it great. Whewell, Macaulay, Praed and Bulwer had gained the prize in recent years. Kinglake won it in the year after ' Timbuctoo.' Hallam and Monckton Milnes sent in poems to compete with Tennyson's.

Everybody remembers how Arthur Pendennis, of Boniface, spent his first summer vacation in composing a poem for the ' English Verse prize,' which was carried off by Jones—in historical fact by Venables—of Jesus. We know without reading them the tricks of such compositions. Their type may be gathered from Thackeray's burlesque of ' The Taking of Jerusalem '—the subject of Kinglake's successful poem in 1830. The author " bellows out with Tancred and Godfrey, ' On to the breach, ye soldiers of the Cross, Scale the red wall and swim the choking foss. Ye dauntless archers, twang your cross-bows well ; On, bill, and battle-axe and mangonel ! Ply battering-ram and hurtling catapult, Jerusalem is ours — *id Deus vult.*' After which comes a mellifluous description of the gardens of Sharon and the maids of

Salem, and a prophecy that roses shall deck the entire country of Syria, and a speedy reign of peace be established — all in undeniably decasyllabic lines and the queerest aping of sense and sentiment and poetry."

The examiners, if they expected anything of the conventional pattern travestied by Thackeray, must have been bothered by Tennyson's 'Timbuctoo.' It is breathless, pauseless, involved ; but it is undeniably original. The blank lines are not the echo of Milton, or of Keats, or of Wordsworth. They are concerted from all three, and yet they have something novel and sustained. As for the city of Timbuctoo—the luckless name occurs but once—it exists nowhere. It is Atlantis : it is Xanadu : unquestionably it is the New Jerusalem ' of burnish'd gold, or metal more ethereal,' and the translucent wave which winds through its argent streets gulfs itself in sands for fear of disclosing to the world the whereabouts of the city whose reflection it bore. Timbuctoo is a mystery of loveliness, doomed some day to render up its glory to keen Discovery, and then its miraged towers will ' darken, and shrink and shiver into huts, black specks amid a waste of dreary sand.' Seen in vision from Calpe it looks like a forecast of Lyonesse or of elfland with its faintly blowing horns, and the examiners must have perplexed themselves to find one known feature of African landscape. The truth of the matter is that Tennyson had no wish to compete, but did so at his father's request, and patched up an old poem, ' The Battle of Armageddon,' for the purpose.

Whatever the examiners may have thought of a performance so bizarre, younger men had no question of its high merit. Charles Wordsworth wrote from Oxford to his brother Christopher : " It is certainly a wonderful production, and if it had come out with Lord Byron's name, it would have been thought as fine as anything he ever wrote." At Oxford he says the author of such an exercise might have been rusticated and sent to a lunatic asylum; and Hallam thought that sober-minded people would think it absurd. But he adds: "The splendid imaginative power that pervades it all will be seen through all hindrances. I consider Tennyson as promising fair to be the greatest poet of our generation, perhaps of our century."

In 1830, Tennyson published his first volume, *Poems chiefly Lyrical*, containing ' Mariana' and ' The Arabian Nights.' Then followed a strange, Byronic episode in his life. Torrijos, a noble and patriotic Spaniard, living exiled in London, organised an expedition for the overthrow of King Ferdinand and the Inquisition. His cause was warmly taken up by several young Cambridge democrats—John Sterling of their number. A ship was procured in London to carry the adventurers to Gibraltar, and was on the eve of departure when it was seized by the Thames police, acting on instructions from the British Government, and Sterling only escaped arrest by dropping on board a passing wherry. By separate routes the conspirators made their way to Gibraltar, where they were joined by John Kemble, in the spring of 1830. The enterprise, lingering for some months, was brought to a head by the revolution in France. It ended in disastrous failure. Torrijos and his friends—including a retired British officer, named Boyd, but not Kemble—were captured and mercilessly shot down at Malaga. In the summer after Torrijos had quitted England, Tennyson and Hallam started for the Pyrenees with money to help the insurgents. They encountered various black-hearted revolutionists, who unfavourably impressed Tennyson, and returned to England without materially advancing matters.

In February 1831, Tennyson was summoned home by the news of his father's ill-health : he died in the following month.   Tennyson did not return to Cambridge or take a degree.

Arthur Hallam died in 1833. Sections of *In Memoriam* were written in the same year, but the completed work did not appear until 1850.   It is the sanctification of Cambridge, its crown and perpetual glory.   If at any time Cambridge had a gospel of its own to deliver to the world—a gospel which was not of party or of creed—it was in the young-eyed days of the ' Apostles.'   Milton and Wordsworth had their gospels, but Milton was a partisan and Wordsworth a solitary. Nor were *Lycidas* and *The Prelude* written under the immediate influences of Cambridge.   The flowers of *Lycidas* grew at Horton, and the breath of Cumbrian fells is in *The Prelude*.   The speculations of *In Memoriam* are the distillation of the fireside talk of the ' Apostles,' only matured by years and consideration.   And they made the stuff of the ideas and beliefs of thoughtful undergraduates of the next generation, who in turn passed them, with modification, to the present age. Perhaps there has never been a ' Cambridge mind,' for Cambridge does not think collectively.   If ever there was a distinctively Cambridge attitude of thought it was in Tennyson's young days, and it rested on the utmost latitude of interpretation of the common creed that man is shaped to divine ends.   The testimony of Bishop Westcott and of Henry Sidgwick illustrates the divergency of the acceptation of Tennyson's teaching by two men who, in different ways, were potent in their influence on Cambridge thought.

Westcott was above all things impressed by 'the splendid faith' of the poet and his sense that man's hope lies in the historic realisation of the Gospel. To the subtler mind of Sidgwick it seemed that the gospel which *In Memoriam* taught was that of humanity and not of revealed religion. In the 'sixties,' when thoughtful minds were struggling for freedom from the trammels of a historic religion, what impressed him was 'the ineffaceable and ineradicable conviction that humanity cannot acquiesce in a godless creed,' and 'the reverent docility to the lessons of science which belongs to the essence of our age.' It was, no doubt, the tyranny of traditional Theism at Oxford that compelled its poets—Shelley, Swinburne, and, in a less declared way, Arnold—to a negation of all religious systems : and their influence on Oxford was correspondingly small. The Cambridge poets— Coleridge, Wordsworth, Tennyson—gave to Cambridge and England a new gospel, 'which was from the beginning' and did not supersede the old, ' The kingdom of God is within you.'

Thackeray 'came up' to Trinity in a 'by-term,' February, 1829, four months after Alfred and Charles Tennyson. He left Cambridge without a degree in 1830. Apologists have suggested that the reason for his early withdrawal was that, going up in February instead of October, he had either to meet men who had three months' advantage of him at the May examination, or to wait for a whole year for the next examination. But Thackeray, who was a pollman, had no motive for distinguishing himself in May examinations, and could have taken his degree, after keeping the prescribed terms, without delay or difficulty. He left the University simply because he was not doing much good there, and, having independence of means as well as character, was minded to try his fortunes in wider and more congenial spheres.

" In the days of Thackeray," says Leslie Stephen, " there was not that kind of intellectual fermentation at Cambridge which was making Oxford the centre of a great religious movement." A singular thing for a Cambridge man to write, and more singular that Leslie Stephen should be the writer ; most singular when it is remembered that Tractarian views were unheard of in 1829, and that Newman dated the start of the Oxford Movement from Keble's sermon at Saint Mary's in July, 1833. Let Carlyle be heard on the other hand. Of Cambridge in 1824–1827 he says : " Of the two universities Cambridge is decidedly the more catholic (not Roman-catholic but Human-catholic) in its tendencies and habitudes, and, if we were reduced to choose from them, one would choose Cambridge as a place of culture for the young idea." One would suppose that fermentation was pretty active at Cambridge in 1829–1830, when Thackeray was contemporary with Tennyson and Darwin, and that it was likely to produce a demonic wine more potent than the Tractarian.

But of ' movements,' intellectual or religious, Thackeray knew nothing when he was at Trinity. He was not an ' Apostle,' but, though he knew little or nothing of Tennyson in those days, he was intimate with most of the Tennyson ' set,' and carried his affection for them throughout life. When, in his last days, he was asked which of his friends he had loved best, he answered, " Why, dear old Fitz (Fitzgerald), of course, and Brookfield." In 1850, Fitzgerald writes of a gathering of four Cambridge friends at Spedding's house, at which he was present with Thackeray and Venables. Venables had been at

Charterhouse with Thackeray, and had broken his nose in a historic fight there. Monckton Milnes, Sir Frederick Pollock and Charles Buller were other Trinity friends whose intimacy he cherished in later days.

We may well believe that Thackeray had no very definite aim in his brief undergraduate life. He was well provided with funds ; he had many tastes, and belonged to many circles. We do not accept his account of the experiences of Arthur Pendennis at ' Boniface ' as the abstract and true chronicle of his own at Trinity. Thackeray is at pains to mystify us about Pendennis and the ' University of Oxbridge.' Pendennis belongs, not to the great college of Saint George, whose undergraduates ' wear gowns of a peculiar cut, and give themselves no small airs of superiority over all other young men,' but to little Saint Boniface, which lies alongside of it. Yet ' the pretty fountain playing in the centre of the fair grass plots, the tall chapel windows and buttresses rising to the right ' on entering the court, ' the hall with its tapering lantern,' and ' the queer old tower at the corner of the quadrangle, by which the rooms of Mr. Buck, the tutor, were approached,' do not leave us in any doubt as to the college which was in the novelist's eye. The immensely great Crump, President of Saint Boniface in *The Book of Snobs*, is another studied ambiguity. Crump is certainly not Christopher Wordsworth, who was Master of Trinity when Thackeray was an undergraduate, nor his predecessor, Lort Mansel, who was Master in 1815. Nor are the features altogether those of Thackeray's tutor, the great Whewell, who became Master in 1841. Whewell did not earn his advancement, as Crump did, by inventing three new metres and editing an extremely improper Greek comedy. Yet, dates notwithstanding, there is no shadow of doubt that Crump was meant for Whewell. " When the allied monarchs came down and were made doctors of the University, a breakfast was given at Saint Boniface : on which occasion Crump allowed the Emperor Alexander to walk before him, but took the *pas* himself of the King of Prussia and Prince Blucher. He was going to put the Hetman Platoff to breakfast at a side-table with the under college tutors ; but he was induced to relent, and merely entertained that distinguished Cossack with a discourse on his own language, in which he showed that the Hetman knew nothing about it." Whewell's enormous self-conceit and donnishness, the theme of many undergraduate stories, come out plainly in the picture of Crump. "As for us undergraduates, we scarcely knew more about Crump than about the Grand Llama. A few favoured youths are asked occasionally to tea at the lodge ; but they do not speak unless first addressed by the Doctor ; and if they venture to sit down, Crump's follower, Mr. Toady, whispers, ' Gentlemen, will you have the kindness to get up ? The President is passing ' ; or, ' Gentlemen, the President prefers that undergraduates should not sit down ' ; or words to a similar effect." [1]

It is not easy to estimate the feelings with which Thackeray, in his writing days, looked back on Cambridge. Surely his heart went out to the old Greyfriars, the school to which he sent every one of the boys who became his heroes, and which he loved

---

[1] Whewell figures again as Dr. Sargent in *Lovel the Widower*. " He is rude ; he is ill-bred : he is bumptious beyond almost any man I ever knew : he is spoiled not a little by prosperity. But he is magnanimous : he can own that he has been in the wrong : and oh ! what a quantity of Greek he knows."

to revisit, just as his fathers, Rawdon Crawley and Thomas Newcome, did. But he had some reminiscences of schoolboy talk and ' theories of life ' learnt there which, he says, mammas would blush to know. For the education which either place of learning professed to impart he had no less contempt than Tennyson had for the stony bread of the classroom. No doubt it was deserved, but the small use which Thackeray made of his opportunities hardly qualified him to give an authoritative verdict.

Rather in his judgment of the finished product of the University we are to regard him as a critic who claims to be heard. And it must be confessed that it is an unfavourable one. Retrospect was always sombre to Thackeray, and the vanity of youth and the weariness of study are texts with him for constant comment. His University men make a procession which is always sad and mostly sordid. He can commend mirth in honest dunces, such as Foker, and, if he has a moral, it is that mirth is all that abides of the labour of days spent at the University. There is Hugby, the haberdasher's son, who never misses lecture or chapel, who walks in high-lows on the Trumpington Road, and by patient merit and sycophancy rises to the tutorship of his college ; and Tom Tusher, his obsequious predecessor in the days of William III. There are the scoundrels and blacklegs who belong to low tragedy—Deuceace, Dick Blewitt and Bloundell-Bloundell. There are the aristocratic roués, Rawdon Crawley, Cinqbars and Brummell Firmin : and there are the Spavins and Spicers and Jim Crawleys of the vulgar sporting sort. There are tufthunters such as Talbot Twysden and Tufton Hunt. All these types were known to Thackeray at Cambridge.

Melancholy claims the nobler characters. Henry Esmond by his proud reserve is condemned to solitude and is nicknamed Don Dismallo. ' Stunning ' Warrington, one of the hardest readers and hardest livers of his time at Oxbridge, is a derelict at twenty-five. The reverend Francis Bell, fellow of his college, and lover of Helen Pendennis, repeats the pitiful story of Warrington.

Of other aspects of Cambridge life Thackeray knew little. The athletic element which occupied so much of undergraduate activity when Alton Locke visited Cambridge makes little figure in his books. " Boat-racing had not risen in Pen's time to the *fureur* which, as we are given to understand, it has since attained in the University : and riding and tandem-driving were the fashions of the ingenuous youth." Yet Jim Crawley, by a strange anachronism, ' pulled stroke in the Boniface boat ' (at Oxford), about the year 1815. Warrington also ' pulled matches and won prizes ' at a later date : and he ' beat bargemen,' as Brandon Firmin and Tufton Hunt did on a certain occasion ' before Caius gate.' Religion is a subject too sacred for Thackeray to travesty : but Charles Honeyman, who is Mr. Batchelor's (*i.e.* Thackeray's) college acquaintance at ' Boniface,' is a type of the worldly seeker after ordination who survived in Kingsley's Cambridge story as the cousin of Alton Locke. But there is one class of undergraduate which Thackeray knew and did not reproduce. His Cambridge world is robust and vehement, whether in aimless study or animal enjoyment : but in the routine of its existence it never has time to think, or, if it thinks at all, it thinks in solitude, like Esmond. Of the sociable interchange of ideas, such as went on in the ' Apostles' ' circle, whose members he knew individually so well, there is no hint or suggestion in any line that he wrote about Cambridge.

In truth, Thackeray did not begin to 'find himself' until after Paris had taught him literature and art, and London had introduced him to life. His contributions to *The Snob* and *The Gownsman*, the two undergraduate periodicals of which so much has been made in his biographies, were as poor as his early *Punch* writings, and in them, and always in his later work, it is only the trivialities and superficialities of student life that he knows and deals with. "The whole place reeked with vulgarity," says the immaculate Pelham in Bulwer Lytton's novel, and, though Pelham's standard of what is gentlemanly deserved all the ridicule that Thackeray heaped on it, he was right in his estimate of the undergraduate manners that were most in evidence. Vice, in the naked form in which it walked in the age of Gray and Gunning, had been exchanged for the more irretrievable defect of vulgarity. If it seems incredible that the idealism of the 'Apostles' could have grown in an environment saturated with common thoughts and low ambitions, I would refer the reader to a little-known book, called *Alma Mater*, published in 1827 and descriptive of life in Trinity at about that date. The anonymous author was unquestionably a blackguard—it is said that he died in the hulks—but he was not devoid of ability, though he had neither humour nor imagination. 'Squalid' is the epithet to be applied to the thoughts and manners of the circle in which he moved. Fortunately it was not the only circle.

The Annus Mirabilis which introduced Alfred Tennyson to Trinity brought up Charles Darwin to

Christ's : but Darwin began his residence in the Lent term of that year, not in October. The study of Natural History, which in his youth claimed so much of the attention of Tennyson, did not seriously begin with Darwin until the later years of his residence, and it does not appear that the two men were ever brought in contact at Cambridge, or that Darwin was known to the ' Apostles' ' group.[1]

Darwin, in fact, spent his days at Christ's very much in ordinary undergraduate fashion, galloping across country, shooting in the fens and occupying his evenings with supper-parties and *vingt-et-un*. He had an easy-going tutor who was generally to be seen at Newmarket when there was a race-meeting, and the undergraduates condoned his neglect of them by following him thither. With such amusements Darwin combined the less ordinary recreations of beetle-hunting, music and art ; and food for these last was provided by the Fitzwilliam Museum collection of engravings and the anthems at King's. He attended lectures in an uninterested way, mastered the small requirements in classics and mathematics required for an ordinary degree, and was well content with the place, tenth in the poll, which rewarded him in January, 1832. He took his B.A. degree in the following June. During the three years which he spent at Cambridge he said that his time was completely wasted, as far as academical studies were concerned. The careful study of Paley's *Evidences* and *Moral Philosophy*, then prescribed among subjects for the ordinary degree course, was the only part of

---

[1] Darwin's rooms were in the southern range of the first court, on the first floor, right, of staircase G. His grandfather, the celebrated Erasmus, was of Saint John's and graduated, as first in the junior optimes, in 1754.

his enforced learning which was of the least use to him in the education of his mind.

The neglect of the study of Natural Science, as well as Medicine, in the first half of the eighteenth century, is almost inconceivable at the present time. The Regius Professorship of Physic had been founded in 1540 : but its endowment was only £40 *per annum*, and the post was practically a sinecure. For Natural Science, apart from Medicine, there was no University endowment until 1702, when the chair of Chemistry was established. Those of Anatomy, Botany, Geology, Experimental Philosophy and the Downing chair of Medicine were added before 1810. Then for half a century night descended on science study at Cambridge, so far as academic recognition affected it. No new professorship was created until 1866. Science formed no part of the course for the ordinary degree until the Special Examination in Natural Science was established in 1865. The Natural Science Tripos, tentatively started in 1851, was not made an avenue to the B.A. degree in Honours until 1861. The list in that year contained three names : the list of the First Part of that Tripos contained 194 in 1910. In 1865 the number of degrees conferred in Medicine was 6 : in 1910 those conferred in Medicine and Surgery were 117.

Concerning Medicine, Dyer remarked in 1814 : " Cambridge has never been considered as the proper place for the medical or anatomical student. The proper place is a great city like London or Edinburgh." Such teaching as was given was entirely theoretical : clinical lectures at Addenbrooke's Hospital were first introduced by Professor (Sir George) Paget in 1841. Equally Cambridge abrogated its concern in the new scientific learning which, outside its pale, was beginning to challenge the primacy of mathematics and classics. The classrooms of the few professors who gave science lectures were almost empty. It is told that the Downing Professor had a class of two, and it was held in the Professor's breakfast room in Downing. The Professor was usually in bed when 'the class' assembled and, arrayed in a dressing-gown, would put his head over the staircase banisters and beg his pupils to examine 'the specimens'—a venerable collection under glass cases—until he had completed his toilet and breakfast. Of the vast ranges of buildings, devoted to science, which occupy the site of the old Botanic Garden and that more recently acquired from Downing, no beginning had been made in Darwin's day : the earliest of them date from 1863. The professors were in many cases clergymen who held benefices at a distance from Cambridge and regarded their University offices as sinecures. In some cases they were little better informed than their classes. Adam Sedgwick knew practically no geology when he was appointed Professor in 1818.

To the enthusiasm of Sedgwick and Henslow is due the credit of creating at Cambridge an interest in scientific studies. Henslow, who was a fellow of Saint John's, took his degree, as sixteenth wrangler, in 1818. He succeeded E. D. Clarke as Professor of Mineralogy in 1822, and was transferred to the chair of Botany in 1825 : his predecessor, Martyn, had not lectured for many years. He held a country living while he was Professor, and attended to his parish duties not less actively than to his Cambridge work. Darwin, whose original intention in coming to Cambridge was to be ordained, was much drawn to the society of Henslow. " His kindness," he wrote, " was unbounded. He continually asked me to his house, and allowed me to accompany him in his walks. He talked on all subjects, including his deep sense of religion, and was entirely open. I owe more than I can express to this excellent man." To the Professor's field excursions Darwin owed the awakening of his interest in science. They walked together most days during the latter part of Darwin's stay at Cambridge, insomuch that Darwin got to be called ' the man that walks with Henslow.'

In the summer of 1831, after taking his degree, Darwin went on a geological tour in North Wales in company with Professor Sedgwick, and on returning home " found a letter from Henslow, informing me that Captain Fitzroy was willing to give up part of his cabin to any young man who would volunteer to go with him, without pay, as a naturalist to the voyage of the *Beagle*." The expedition started in December of that year, and Darwin remained with it until its return in September, 1836. He then resumed residence, for a time, at Cambridge, living in Fitzwilliam Street, and began to prepare his journals for publication. They were published in 1839. If Henslow was the inspirer of his first interest in scientific study it was another Cambridge man, Malthus, who, by the suggestions on the struggle for existence contained in his book *On Population*, directed Darwin's thoughts to the subject of the variation of species. His great work, *The Origin of Species*, was issued in 1859. It synchronised with the great development of the school of Natural Science at Cambridge : but it was not until after 1870 that the full significance of his theories came to be duly estimated. In the Calendar of that year his name is printed without the footnote that customarily distinguished any writer eminent in science or literature. Since then Cambridge has thought more of Darwinism than of Darwin, and the volume of his influence, extended by his immediate successors, Michael Foster, F. M. Balfour, G. J. Romanes and others, has extended over all the field of biological inquiry. The centenary of his birth brought to Cambridge, in 1909, hundreds of the chiefs of science from every region of the civilised world.

Darwin died in 1882, and was appropriately buried in Westminster Abbey, close to the grave of the greatest of his scientific predecessors at Cambridge, Isaac Newton.

EPILOGUE

IF what I have written in these pages has any claim to the character of History, it is the History of Episodes, new departures, not of Epochs. If epochs are 'halts,' there are no epochs in the history of Cambridge. With forward face, with steps accelerated or slow, the University has passed many milestones. It has never made fetishes of milestones or set up its abiding rest by them. The finger-posts point onwards.

Tennyson and Darwin are behind us. Elsewhere than in Cambridge the sound of their new gospel called for a halt and a retrospect. It was not so at Cambridge. There the doctrines of evolution and ordered progress were accepted with caution and assimilated only by degrees. They encountered no violent antagonism, and they were precipitated by no excess of enthusiasm. There is a letter of Kingsley's, written to A. P. Stanley at the height of the fever about *Essays and Reviews*, which characteristically describes the attitude of Cambridge to newly broached problems. "Cambridge lies in an attitude of magnificent repose, and shaking lazy ears stares at her elder sister, and asks what it is all about. . . . There is nothing, says Cambridge, in that book which we have not all of us been through already. Doubts, denials, destructions—we have faced them all, and are tired of them. But we have faced them in

THE MARKET PLACE

silence, hoping to find a positive solution." It is the positive solution, the construction of habitable mansions out of materials old as well as new that Cambridge keeps steadily in view, and beyond the voices that drowned the first exposition of Darwin's creed it has sought and obtained peace. In no region has the measured progress been more visible than in the Cambridge school of Theology. For the evidence of the acceptance of the Darwinian faith I would not turn only to its first and warm adherents, Maurice and Kingsley. The seal of its incorporation in the articles of the Christian religion was set by such modern Fathers as Westcott, Lightfoot and Benson.

By rights Kingsley and his following should have a place in any account of the influences which have moulded present Cambridge and dedicated it to national uses. No man more typically than Kingsley represented the Cambridge of mid-Victorian times alike in its practical energies and its intellectual limitations. It was his lot to occupy the chair of Modern History which once had been Gray's, and the conjunction of the two names serves to bring into relief the contrasted conditions of University life and teaching in 1768 and 1860. As Professor, Gray never lectured. The gentle moralist shrank from the rack of the tough world in which his lot was cast. To the undergraduates, whom he abhorred, he had no counsel to give, and they had no ears to hear. History was only Kingsley's text : he was not a qualified historian. But in the classroom he preached as no select preacher had done in three hundred years of sermons from the University pulpit. " Undergraduates," said one of his hearers, " are an affectionate race, and every one of us who wished to live as a man ought to live felt that the Professor of Modern History was a friend." It was the noble humanity with which he invested the teachings of History, and the practical lessons which he drew from it, which commanded the enthusiasm of his pupils. To him we should attribute, more than any whose names are more immediately associated with them, the experiments in what he called " Christian Socialism," of which Cambridge House in Camberwell and the college missions in many parts of London are present examples. To him too is due a share in the credit of extending the benefits of University education to populous centres where they had hitherto been unknown. Of these movements Kingsley was not, indeed, the originator. In directing the thoughts of the University to them Kingsley was the apostle of F. D. Maurice, who had begun the same work in London. But his personality, his energy, and his vivid sympathy with undergraduate interests, more than any contemporary influences, helped to re-create Cambridge. In *Alton Locke* he describes the undergraduates rather as he made them than as he found them : and he has idealised the portrait in his own fashion. But if it has any correspondence with reality we must think that a good many undergraduates had thoughts beyond the things of present Cambridge, and that those who had not were clean, honest and manly.

I have chosen to bring these chapters to an end with the episode of Darwin. The next, unwritten chapter is one of which we do not yet see the end. If it were written it would centre about no individuals. In the half-century which parts us from the publication of *The Origin of Species* there have been many new departures at Cambridge, and no time in its history has been illuminated by names more distinguished in science, in theology, and perhaps in letters. But no voice in recent years has spoken, or could speak, with the clear utterance and individual authority that was listened to half a century ago. Life pulses in the veins of the old University as actively as in the days of its first youth, and its pulsations reach through all grades and classes of its scholars as they have never done before. Sectional 'movements' are crowded in the general forward motion of the University, and they cease to have an individual impress because they spring from the universal activity. It is a fact, and a fact to be regretted, that at Cambridge, as beyond it, 'the individual withers, and the world is more and more.' But to the penalty is attached the unspeakable gain that the University is not parted, as it once was, from the common current of National and human feeling, and that to-day, perhaps better than in any of the centuries of its existence, it conforms to the ideal of the medieval Studium Generale, a world school for the enlargement of the bounds of human empire.

PARENTALIA

VALETE, MANES INCLUTORUM RHETORUM,
    VALETE, DOCTORES PROBI,
HISTORIA SI QUOS, VEL POETICUS STYLUS,
    FORUMVE FECIT NOBILES,
MEDICAE VEL ARTES, DOGMA VEL PLATONICUM
    DEDIT PERENNI GLORIAE.
SEDEM SEPULCRIS SERVET IMMOTUS CINIS:
    MEMORIA VIVAT NOMINUM,
DUM REMEAT ILLUD, JUDICIS DONO DEI,
    COMMUNE CUM DIS SECULUM.

                        AUSONIUS

INDEX

Printed by
MORRISON & GIBB LIMITED
Edinburgh

A SELECTION OF BOOKS PUBLISHED BY METHUEN AND CO. LTD., LONDON

36 ESSEX STREET

W.C.

CONTENTS

SEPTEMBER 1911

A SELECTION OF

MESSRS. METHUEN'S

PUBLICATIONS

In this Catalogue the order is according to authors. An asterisk denotes that the book is in the press.

Colonial Editions are published of all Messrs. METHUEN's Novels issued at a price above 2s. 6d., and similar editions are published of some works of General Literature. Colonial editions are only for circulation in the British Colonies and India.

All books marked net are not subject to discount, and cannot be bought at less than the published price. Books not marked net are subject to the discount which the bookseller allows.

Messrs. METHUEN's books are kept in stock by all good booksellers. If there is any difficulty in seeing copies, Messrs. Methuen will be very glad to have early information, and specimen copies of any books will be sent on receipt of the published price *plus* postage for net books, and of the published price for ordinary books.

This Catalogue contains only a selection of the more important books published by Messrs. Methuen. A complete and illustrated catalogue of their publications may be obtained on application.

Andrewes (Lancelot). PRECES PRI-VATAE. Translated and edited, with Notes, by F. E. BRIGHTMAN. *Cr. 8vo.* 6s.

Aristotle. THE ETHICS. Edited, with an Introduction and Notes, by JOHN BURNET. *Demy 8vo.* 10s. 6d. net.

Atkinson (C. T.). A HISTORY OF GER-MANY, from 1715-1815. Illustrated. *Demy 8vo.* 12s. 6d. net.

Atkinson (T. D.). ENGLISH ARCHI-TECTURE. Illustrated. *Fcap. 8vo.* 3s. 6d. net.

A GLOSSARY OF TERMS USED IN ENGLISH ARCHITECTURE. Illus-trated. *Second Edition. Fcap. 8vo.* 3s. 6d. net.

Bain (F. W.). A DIGIT OF THE MOON: A HINDOO LOVE STORY. *Eighth Edition. Fcap. 8vo.* 3s. 6d. net.

THE DESCENT OF THE SUN: A CYCLE OF BIRTH. *Fifth Edition. Fcap. 8vo.* 3s. 6d. net.

A HEIFER OF THE DAWN. *Sixth Edi-tion. Fcap. 8vo.* 2s. 6d. net.

IN THE GREAT GOD'S HAIR. *Fourth Edition. Fcap. 8vo.* 2s. 6d. net.

A DRAUGHT OF THE BLUE. *Fourth Edition. Fcap. 8vo.* 2s. 6d. net.

AN ESSENCE OF THE DUSK. *Second Edition. Fcap. 8vo.* 2s. 6d. net.

AN INCARNATION OF THE SNOW *Second Edition. Fcap. 8vo.* 3s. 6d. net.

A MINE OF FAULTS. *Second Edition. Fcap. 8vo.* 3s. 6d. net.

THE ASHES OF A GOD. *Fcap. 8vo.* 3s. 6d. net.

Balfour (Graham). THE LIFE OF ROBERT LOUIS STEVENSON. Illus-trated. *Fifth Edition in one Volume. Cr. 8vo. Buckram,* 6s.

Baring-Gould (S.). THE LIFE OF NAPOLEON BONAPARTE. Illustrated. *Second Edition. Royal 8vo.* 10s. 6d. net.

THE TRAGEDY OF THE CÆSARS: A STUDY OF THE CHARACTERS OF THE CÆSARS OF THE JULIAN AND CLAUDIAN HOUSES. Illustrated. *Seventh Edition. Royal 8vo.* 10s. 6d. net.

A BOOK OF FAIRY TALES. Illustrated. *Second Edition. Cr. 8vo.* 6s. Also *Medium 8vo.* 6d.

OLD ENGLISH FAIRY TALES. Illus-trated. *Third Edition. Cr. 8vo. Buck-ram.* 6s.

THE VICAR OF MORWENSTOW. With a Portrait. *Third Edition. Cr. 8vo.* 3s. 6d.

OLD COUNTRY LIFE. Illustrated. *Fifth Edition. Large Cr. 8vo.* 6s.

STRANGE SURVIVALS: SOME CHAPTERS IN THE HISTORY OF MAN. Illustrated. *Third Edition. Cr. 8vo.* 2s. 6d. net.

YORKSHIRE ODDITIES: INCIDENTS AND STRANGE EVENTS. *Fifth Edition. Cr. 8vo. 2s. 6d. net.*
A BOOK OF CORNWALL. Illustrated. *Second Edition. Cr. 8vo. 6s.*
A BOOK OF DARTMOOR. Illustrated. *Second Edition. Cr. 8vo. 6s.*
A BOOK OF DEVON. Illustrated. *Third Edition. Cr. 8vo. 6s.*
A BOOK OF NORTH WALES. Illustrated. *Cr. 8vo. 6s.*
A BOOK OF SOUTH WALES. Illustrated. *Cr. 8vo. 6s.*
A BOOK OF BRITTANY. Illustrated. *Second Edition. Cr. 8vo. 6s.*
A BOOK OF THE RHINE: From Cleve to Mainz. Illustrated. *Second Edition. Cr. 8vo. 6s.*
A BOOK OF THE RIVIERA. Illustrated. *Second Edition. Cr. 8vo. 6s.*
A BOOK OF THE PYRENEES. Illustrated. *Cr. 8vo. 6s.*

Baring-Gould (S.) and Sheppard (H. Fleetwood). A GARLAND OF COUNTRY SONG. English Folk Songs with their Traditional Melodies. *Demy 4to. 6s.*
SONGS OF THE WEST: Folk Songs of Devon and Cornwall. Collected from the Mouths of the People. New and Revised Edition, under the musical editorship of CECIL J. SHARP. *Large Imperial 8vo. 5s. net.*

Barker (E.). THE POLITICAL THOUGHT OF PLATO AND ARISTOTLE. *Demy 8vo. 10s. 6d. net.*

Bastable (C. F.). THE COMMERCE OF NATIONS. *Fifth Edition. Cr. 8vo. 2s. 6d.*

Batson (Mrs. Stephen). A CONCISE HANDBOOK OF GARDEN FLOWERS. *Fcap. 8vo. 3s. 6d.*

Beckett (Arthur). THE SPIRIT OF THE DOWNS: Impressions and Reminiscences of the Sussex Downs. Illustrated. *Second Edition. Demy 8vo. 10s. 6d. net.*

Beckford (Peter). THOUGHTS ON HUNTING. Edited by J. OTHO PAGET. Illustrated. *Second Edition. Demy 8vo. 6s.*

Belloc (H.). PARIS. Illustrated. *Second Edition, Revised. Cr. 8vo. 6s.*
HILLS AND THE SEA. *Third Edition. Fcap. 8vo. 5s.*
ON NOTHING AND KINDRED SUBJECTS. *Third Edition. Fcap. 8vo. 5s.*
ON EVERYTHING. *Second Edition. Fcap. 8vo. 5s.*
ON SOMETHING. *Second Edition. Fcap. 8vo. 5s.*
*FIRST AND LAST. *Fcap. 8vo. 5s.*
MARIE ANTOINETTE. Illustrated. *Third Edition. Demy 8vo. 15s. net.*
THE PYRENEES. Illustrated. *Second Edition. Demy 8vo. 7s. 6d. net.*

Bennett (W. H.). A PRIMER OF THE BIBLE. *Fifth Edition. Cr. 8vo. 2s. 6d.*

Bennett (W. H.) and Adeney (W. F.). A BIBLICAL INTRODUCTION. With a concise Bibliography. *Sixth Edition. Cr. 8vo. 7s. 6d.*

Benson (Archbishop). GOD'S BOARD. Communion Addresses. *Second Edition. Fcap. 8vo. 3s. 6d. net.*

Bensusan (Samuel L.). HOME LIFE IN SPAIN. Illustrated. *Second Edition. Demy 8vo. 10s. 6d. net.*

Betham-Edwards (Miss). HOME LIFE IN FRANCE. Illustrated. *Fifth Edition. Cr. 8vo. 6s.*

Bindley (T. Herbert). THE OECUMENICAL DOCUMENTS OF THE FAITH. With Introductions and Notes. *Second Edition. Cr. 8vo. 6s. net.*

Blake (William). ILLUSTRATIONS OF THE BOOK OF JOB. With a General Introduction by LAURENCE BINYON. Illustrated. *Quarto. 21s. net.*

Bloemfontein (Bishop of). ARA CŒLI: AN ESSAY IN MYSTICAL THEOLOGY. *Fourth Edition. Cr. 8vo. 3s. 6d. net.*
FAITH AND EXPERIENCE. *Cr. 8vo. 3s. 6d. net.*

Bowden (E. M.). THE IMITATION OF BUDDHA: Quotations from Buddhist Literature for each Day in the Year. *Sixth Edition. Cr. 16mo. 2s. 6d.*

Brabant (F. G.). RAMBLES IN SUSSEX. Illustrated. *Cr. 8vo. 6s.*

Bradley (A. G.). ROUND ABOUT WILTSHIRE. Illustrated. *Second Edition. Cr. 8vo. 6s.*
THE ROMANCE OF NORTHUMBERLAND. Illustrated. *Second Edition. Demy 8vo. 7s. 6d. net.*

Braid (James). ADVANCED GOLF. Illustrated. *Sixth Edition. Demy 8vo. 10s. 6d. net.*

Brailsford (H. N.). MACEDONIA: ITS RACES AND THEIR FUTURE. Illustrated. *Demy 8vo. 12s. 6d. net.*

Brodrick (Mary) and Morton (A. Anderson). A CONCISE DICTIONARY OF EGYPTIAN ARCHÆOLOGY. A Handbook for Students and Travellers. Illustrated. *Cr. 8vo. 3s. 6d.*

Browning (Robert). PARACELSUS. Edited with an Introduction, Notes, and Bibliography by MARGARET L. LEE and KATHARINE B. LOCOCK. *Fcap. 8vo. 3s. 6d. net.*

Buckton (A. M.). EAGER HEART: A Christmas Mystery-Play. *Ninth Edition.* *Cr. 8vo. 1s. net.*

Budge (E. A. Wallis). THE GODS OF THE EGYPTIANS. Illustrated. *Two Volumes. Royal 8vo. £3 3s. net.*

Bull (Paul). GOD AND OUR SOLDIERS. *Second Edition. Cr. 8vo. 6s.*

Burns (Robert). THE POEMS AND SONGS. Edited by ANDREW LANG and W. A. CRAIGIE. With Portrait. *Third Edition. Wide Demy 8vo. 6s.*

Busbey (Katherine G.). HOME LIFE IN AMERICA. Illustrated. *Second Edition. Demy 8vo. 10s. 6d. net.*

Butlin (F. M.). AMONG THE DANES. Illustrated. *Demy 8vo. 7s. 6d. net.*

Cain (Georges), WALKS IN PARIS. Translated by A. R. ALLINSON. Illustrated. *Demy 8vo. 7s. 6d. net.*

*Calman (W. T.). THE LIFE OF CRUSTACEA. Illustrated. *Cr. 8vo. 6s.*

Carlyle (Thomas). THE FRENCH REVOLUTION. Edited by C. R. L. FLETCHER. *Three Volumes. Cr. 8vo. 18s.*
THE LETTERS AND SPEECHES OF OLIVER CROMWELL. With an Introduction by C. H. FIRTH, and Notes and Appendices by S. C. LOMAS. *Three Volumes. Demy 8vo. 18s. net.*

Celano (Brother Thomas of). THE LIVES OF S. FRANCIS OF ASSISI. Translated by A. G. FERRERS HOWELL. Illustrated. *Cr. 8vo. 5s. net.*

Chambers (Mrs. Lambert). LAWN TENNIS FOR LADIES. Illustrated. *Cr. 8vo. 2s. 6d. net.*

Chesterfield (Lord). THE LETTERS OF THE EARL OF CHESTERFIELD TO HIS SON. Edited, with an Introduction by C. STRACHEY, and Notes by A. CALTHROP. *Two Volumes. Cr. 8vo. 12s.*

Chesterton (G.K.). CHARLES DICKENS. With two Portraits in Photogravure. *Seventh Edition. Cr. 8vo. 6s.*
ALL THINGS CONSIDERED. *Sixth Edition. Fcap. 8vo. 5s.*
TREMENDOUS TRIFLES. *Fourth Edition. Fcap. 8vo. 5s.*
ALARMS AND DISCURSIONS. *Second Edition. Fcap. 8vo. 5s.*
THE BALLAD OF THE WHITE HORSE. *Fcap. 8vo. 5s.*

Clausen (George). SIX LECTURES ON PAINTING. Illustrated. *Third Edition. Large Post 8vo. 3s. 6d. net.*
AIMS AND IDEALS IN ART. Eight Lectures delivered to the Students of the Royal Academy of Arts. Illustrated. *Second Edition. Large Post 8vo. 5s. net.*

Clutton-Brock (A.) SHELLEY: THE MAN AND THE POET. Illustrated. *Demy 8vo. 7s. 6d. net.*

Cobb (W.F.). THE BOOK OF PSALMS: with an Introduction and Notes. *Demy 8vo. 10s. 6d. net.*

Collingwood (W. G.). THE LIFE OF JOHN RUSKIN. With Portrait. *Sixth Edition. Cr. 8vo. 2s. 6d. net.*

Conrad (Joseph). THE MIRROR OF THE SEA: Memories and Impressions. *Third Edition. Cr. 8vo. 6s.*

Coolidge (W. A. B.). THE ALPS. Illustrated. *Demy 8vo. 7s. 6d. net.*

Coulton (G. G.). CHAUCER AND HIS ENGLAND. Illustrated. *Second Edition. Demy 8vo. 10s. 6d. net.*

Cowper (William). THE POEMS. Edited with an Introduction and Notes by J. C. BAILEY. Illustrated. *Demy 8vo. 10s. 6d. net.*

Crispe (T. E.). REMINISCENCES OF A K.C. With 2 Portraits. *Second Edition. Demy 8vo. 10s. 6d. net.*

Crowley (Ralph H.). THE HYGIENE OF SCHOOL LIFE. Illustrated. *Cr. 8vo. 3s. 6d. net.*

Dante Alighieri. LA COMMEDIA DI DANTE. The Italian Text edited by PAGET TOYNBEE. *Cr. 8vo. 6s.*

Davey (Richard). THE PAGEANT OF LONDON. Illustrated. *In Two Volumes. Demy 8vo. 15s. net.*

Davis (H. W. C.). ENGLAND UNDER THE NORMANS AND ANGEVINS: 1066-1272. Illustrated. *Second Edition. Demy 8vo. 10s. 6d. net.*

*Dawbarn (Charles.) FRANCE AND THE FRENCH. Illustrated. *Demy 8vo. 10s. 6d. net.*

Dearmer (Mabel). A CHILD'S LIFE OF CHRIST. Illustrated. *Large Cr. 8vo. 6s.*

Deffand (Madame Du). THE LETTERS OF MADAME DU DEFFAND TO HORACE WALPOLE. Edited, with Introduction, Notes, and Index, by Mrs. PAGET TOYNBEE. *In Three Volumes. Demy 8vo. £3 3s. net.*

Dickinson (G. L.). THE GREEK VIEW OF LIFE. *Seventh Edition. Crown 8vo. 2s. 6d. net.*

Ditchfield (P. H.). THE PARISH CLERK. Illustrated. *Third Edition. Demy 8vo. 7s. 6d. net.*
THE OLD-TIME PARSON. Illustrated. *Second Edition. Demy 8vo. 7s. 6d. net.*

Ditchfield (P. H.) and Roe (Fred). VANISHING ENGLAND. The Book by P. H. Ditchfield. Illustrated by FRED ROE. *Second Edition. Wide Demy 8vo.* 15s. *net.*

Douglas (Hugh A.). VENICE ON FOOT. With the Itinerary of the Grand Canal. Illustrated. *Second Edition. Fcap. 8vo.* 5s. *net.*
VENICE AND HER TREASURES. Illustrated. *Round corners. Fcap. 8vo.* 5s. *net.*

Dowden (J.). FURTHER STUDIES IN THE PRAYER BOOK. *Cr. 8vo.* 6s.

Driver (S. R.). SERMONS ON SUBJECTS CONNECTED WITH THE OLD TESTAMENT. *Cr. 8vo.* 6s.

Dumas (Alexandre). THE CRIMES OF THE BORGIAS AND OTHERS. With an Introduction by R. S. GARNETT. Illustrated. *Second Edition. Cr. 8vo.* 6s.
THE CRIMES OF URBAIN GRANDIER AND OTHERS. Illustrated. *Cr. 8vo.* 6s.
THE CRIMES OF THE MARQUISE DE BRINVILLIERS AND OTHERS. Illustrated. *Cr. 8vo.* 6s.
THE CRIMES OF ALI PACHA AND OTHERS. Illustrated. *Cr. 8vo.* 6s.
MY MEMOIRS. Translated by E. M. WALLER. With an Introduction by ANDREW LANG. With Frontispieces in Photogravure. In six Volumes. *Cr. 8vo.* 6s. *each volume.*
VOL. I. 1802–1821. VOL. IV. 1830–1831. VOL. II. 1822–1825. VOL. V. 1831–1832. VOL. III. 1826–1830. VOL. VI. 1832–1833.
MY PETS. Newly translated by A. R. ALLINSON. Illustrated. *Cr. 8vo.* 6s.

Duncan (F. M.). OUR INSECT FRIENDS AND FOES. Illustrated. *Cr. 8vo.* 6s.

Dunn-Pattison (R. P.). NAPOLEON'S MARSHALS. Illustrated. *Demy 8vo. Second Edition.* 12s. 6d. *net.*
THE BLACK PRINCE. Illustrated. *Second Edition. Demy 8vo.* 7s. 6d. *net.*

Durham (The Earl of). THE REPORT ON CANADA. With an Introductory Note. *Demy 8vo.* 4s. 6d. *net.*

Dutt (W. A.). THE NORFOLK BROADS. Illustrated. *Second Edition. Cr. 8vo.* 6s.
WILD LIFE IN EAST ANGLIA. Illustrated. *Second Edition. Demy 8vo.* 7s. 6d. *net.*

Edwardes (Tickner). THE LORE OF THE HONEY-BEE. Illustrated. *Third Edition. Cr. 8vo.* 6s.
LIFT-LUCK ON SOUTHERN ROADS. Illustrated. *Cr. 8vo.* 6s.
*NEIGHBOURHOOD: A YEAR'S LIFE IN AND ABOUT AN ENGLISH VILLAGE. Illustrated. *Cr. 8vo.* 6s.

Egerton (H. E.). A SHORT HISTORY OF BRITISH COLONIAL POLICY. *Third Edition. Demy 8vo.* 7s. 6d. *net.*

Exeter (Bishop of). REGNUM DEI. (The Bampton Lectures of 1901.) *A Cheaper Edition. Demy 8vo.* 7s. 6d. *net.*

Fairbrother (W. H.). THE PHILOSOPHY OF T. H. GREEN. *Second Edition. Cr. 8vo.* 3s. 6d.

Fea (Allan). THE FLIGHT OF THE KING. Illustrated. *Second and Revised Edition. Demy 8vo.* 7s. 6d. *net.*
SECRET CHAMBERS AND HIDING-PLACES. Illustrated. *Third and Revised Edition. Demy 8vo.* 7s. 6d. *net.*
JAMES II. AND HIS WIVES. Illustrated. *Demy 8vo.* 12s. 6d. *net.*

Firth (C. H.). CROMWELL'S ARMY: A History of the English Soldier during the Civil Wars, the Commonwealth, and the Protectorate. *Cr. 8vo.* 6s.

Fisher (H. A. L.). THE REPUBLICAN TRADITION IN EUROPE. *Cr. 8vo.* 6s. *net.*

FitzGerald (Edward). THE RUBAI'YAT OF OMAR KHAYYÁM. Printed from the Fifth and last Edition. With a Commentary by H. M. BATSON, and a Biographical Introduction by E. D. ROSS. *Cr. 8vo.* 6s.

Fletcher (J. S.). A BOOK OF YORKSHIRE. Illustrated. *Demy 8vo.* 7s. 6d. *net.*

Flux (A. W.). ECONOMIC PRINCIPLES *Demy 8vo.* 7s. 6d. *net.*

Fraser (J. F.). ROUND THE WORLD ON A WHEEL. Illustrated. *Fifth Edition. Cr. 8vo.* 6s.

Galton (Sir Francis). MEMORIES OF MY LIFE. Illustrated. *Third Edition. Demy 8vo.* 10s. 6d. *net.*

Gibbins (H. de B.). INDUSTRY IN ENGLAND: HISTORICAL OUTLINES. With 5 Maps. *Sixth Edition. Demy 8vo.* 10s. 6d.
THE INDUSTRIAL HISTORY OF ENGLAND. Illustrated. *Seventeenth Edition. Cr. 8vo.* 3s.
ENGLISH SOCIAL REFORMERS. *Second Edition. Cr. 8vo.* 2s. 6d.

Gibbon (Edward). THE MEMOIRS OF THE LIFE OF EDWARD GIBBON. Edited by G. BIRKBECK HILL. *Cr. 8vo.* 6s.
THE DECLINE AND FALL OF THE ROMAN EMPIRE. Edited, with Notes, Appendices, and Maps, by J. B. BURY. Illustrated. *In Seven Volumes. Demy 8vo. Each* 10s. 6d. *net.*

Gloag (M. R.) A BOOK OF ENGLISH GARDENS. Illustrated. *Demy 8vo.* 10s. 6d. net.

*Glover (J. M.). JIMMY GLOVER—HIS BOOK. *Demy 8vo.* 12s. 6d. net.

Glover (T. R.). THE CONFLICT OF RELIGIONS IN THE EARLY ROMAN EMPIRE. *Fourth Edition. Demy 8vo.* 7s. 6d. net.

Godfrey (Elizabeth). A BOOK OF RE-MEMBRANCE. Being Lyrical Selections for every day in the Year. Arranged by E. Godfrey. *Second Edition. Fcap. 8vo.* 2s. 6d. net.

Godley (A. D.). OXFORD IN THE EIGHTEENTH CENTURY. Illustrated. *Second Edition. Demy 8vo.* 7s. 6d. net.
LYRA FRIVOLA. *Fourth Edition. Fcap. 8vo.* 2s. 6d.
VERSES TO ORDER. *Second Edition. Fcap. 8vo.* 2s. 6d.
SECOND STRINGS. *Fcap. 8vo.* 2s. 6d.

Gordon (Lina Duff) (Mrs. Aubrey Water-field). HOME LIFE IN ITALY: Letters FROM THE APENNINES. Illustrated. *Second Edition. Demy 8vo.* 10s. 6d. net.

Gostling (Frances M.). THE BRETONS AT HOME. Illustrated. *Third Edition. Cr. 8vo.* 6s.
AUVERGNE AND ITS PEOPLE. Illustrated. *Demy 8vo.* 10s. 6d. net.

Grahame (Kenneth). THE WIND IN THE WILLOWS. Illustrated. *Fifth Edition. Cr. 8vo.* 6s.

*Grew (Edwin Sharpe). THE GROWTH OF A PLANET. Illustrated. *Cr. 8vo.* 6s.

Griffin (W. Hall) and Minchin (H. C.). THE LIFE OF ROBERT BROWNING. Illustrated. *Second Edition. Demy 8vo.* 12s. 6d. net.

Hale (J. R.). FAMOUS SEA FIGHTS: FROM SALAMIS TO TSU-SHIMA. Illustrated. *Cr. 8vo.* 6s. net.

Hall (Cyril). THE YOUNG CARPEN-TER. Illustrated. *Cr. 8vo.* 5s.

Hall (Hammond). THE YOUNG EN-GINEER; or MODERN ENGINES AND THEIR MODELS. Illustrated. *Second Edition. Cr. 8vo.* 5s.
THE YOUNG ELECTRICIAN. Illustrated. *Cr. 8vo.* 5s.

Hannay (D.). A SHORT HISTORY OF THE ROYAL NAVY. Vol. I., 1217-1688. Vol. II., 1689-1815. *Demy 8vo. Each* 7s. 6d. net.

Harper (Charles G.). THE AUTOCAR ROAD-BOOK. Four Volumes with Maps. *Cr. 8vo. Each* 7s. 6d. net.
Vol. I.—SOUTH OF THE THAMES.
Vol. II.—NORTH AND SOUTH WALES AND WEST MIDLANDS.

Hassall (Arthur). NAPOLEON. Illus-trated. *Demy 8vo.* 7s. 6d. net.

Headley (F. W.). DARWINISM AND MODERN SOCIALISM. *Second Edition. Cr. 8vo.* 5s. net.

Henderson (B. W.). THE LIFE AND PRINCIPATE OF THE EMPEROR NERO. Illustrated. *New and cheaper issue. Demy 8vo.* 7s. 6d. net.

Henderson (M. Sturge). GEORGE MEREDITH: NOVELIST, POET, REFORMER. Illustrated. *Second Edition. Cr. 8vo.* 6s.

Henderson (T. F.) and Watt (Francis). SCOTLAND OF TO-DAY. Illustrated. *Second Edition. Cr. 8vo.* 6s.

Henley (W. E.). ENGLISH LYRICS. CHAUCER TO POE. *Second Edition. Cr. 8vo.* 2s. 6d. net.

Hill (George Francis). ONE HUNDRED MASTERPIECES OF SCULPTURE. Illustrated. *Demy 8vo.* 10s. 6d. net.

Hind (C. Lewis). DAYS IN CORNWALL. Illustrated. *Third Edition. Cr. 8vo.* 6s.

Hobhouse (L. T.). THE THEORY OF KNOWLEDGE. *Demy 8vo.* 10s. 6d. net.

Hodgson (Mrs. W.). HOW TO IDENTIFY OLD CHINESE PORCELAIN. Illus-trated. *Second Edition. Post 8vo.* 6s.

Holdich (Sir T. H.). THE INDIAN BORDERLAND, 1880-1900. Illustrated. *Second Edition. Demy 8vo.* 10s. 6d. net.

Holdsworth (W. S.). A HISTORY OF ENGLISH LAW. *In Four Volumes. Vols. I., II., III. Demy 8vo. Each* 10s. 6d. net.

Holland (Clive). TYROL AND ITS PEOPLE. Illustrated. *Demy 8vo.* 10s. 6d. net.
*THE BELGIANS AT HOME. Illustrated. *Demy 8vo.* 10s. 6d. net.

Horsburgh (E. L. S.). LORENZO THE MAGNIFICENT; AND FLORENCE IN HER GOLDEN AGE. Illustrated. *Second Edition. Demy 8vo.* 15s. net.
WATERLOO: A NARRATIVE AND A CRIT-ICISM. With Plans. *Second Edition. Cr. 8vo.* 5s.
*THE LIFE OF SAVONAROLA. Illus-trated. *Fourth and Enlarged Edition. Cr. 8vo.* 5s. net.

Hosie (Alexander). MANCHURIA. Illus-trated. *Second Edition. Demy 8vo.* 7s. 6d. net.

Hudson (W. H.). A SHEPHERD'S LIFE: IMPRESSIONS OF THE SOUTH WILT-SHIRE DOWNS. Illustrated. *Third Edi-tion. Demy 8vo.* 7s. 6d. net.

*Hugon (Cécile). SOCIAL LIFE IN FRANCE IN THE XVII. CENTURY. Illustrated. *Demy 8vo.* 10s. 6d. net.

Humphreys (John H.). PROPORTIONAL REPRESENTATION. *Cr. 8vo.* 5s. net.

Hutchinson (Horace G.). THE NEW FOREST. Illustrated. *Fourth Edition. Cr. 8vo.* 6s.

Hutton (Edward). THE CITIES OF SPAIN. Illustrated. *Fourth Edition. Cr. 8vo.* 6s.
THE CITIES OF UMBRIA. Illustrated. *Fourth Edition. Cr. 8vo.* 6s.
FLORENCE AND THE CITIES OF NORTHERN TUSCANY WITH GENOA. Illustrated. *Second Edition. Cr. 8vo.* 6s.
SIENA AND SOUTHERN TUSCANY. Illustrated. *Second Edition. Cr. 8vo.* 6s.
*VENICE AND VENETIA. Illustrated. *Cr. 8vo.* 6s.
ROME. Illustrated. *Second Edition. Cr. 8vo.* 6s.
ENGLISH LOVE POEMS. Edited with an Introduction. *Fcap. 8vo.* 3s. 6d. net.
COUNTRY WALKS ABOUT FLORENCE. Illustrated. *Second Edition. Fcap. 8vo.* 5s. net.
IN UNKNOWN TUSCANY With Notes. by WILLIAM HEYWOOD. Illustrated. *Second Edition. Demy 8vo.* 7s. 6d. net.
*A BOOK OF THE WYE. Illustrated. *Demy 8vo.* 7s. 6d. net.

Ibsen (Henrik). BRAND. A Dramatic Poem, Translated by WILLIAM WILSON. *Fourth Edition. Cr. 8vo.* 3s. 6d.

Inge (W. R.). CHRISTIAN MYSTICISM. (The Bampton Lectures of 1899.) *Demy 8vo.* 12s. 6d. net.

Innes (A. D.). A HISTORY OF THE BRITISH IN INDIA. With Maps and Plans. *Cr. 8vo.* 6s.
ENGLAND UNDER THE TUDORS. With Maps. *Third Edition. Demy 8vo.* 10s. 6d. net.

Innes (Mary). SCHOOLS OF PAINTING. Illustrated. *Second Edition. Cr. 8vo.* 5s. net.

Jenks (E.). AN OUTLINE OF ENGLISH LOCAL GOVERNMENT. *Second Edition.* Revised by R. C. K. ENSOR, *Cr. 8vo.* 2s. 6d. net.

Jerningham (Charles Edward). THE MAXIMS OF MARMADUKE. *Second Edition. Cr. 8vo.* 5s.

*Jerrold (Walter). THE DANUBE. Illustrated. *Demy 8vo.* 10s. 6d. net.

Johnston (Sir H. H.). BRITISH CENTRAL AFRICA. Illustrated. *Third Edition. Cr. 4to.* 18s. net.
THE NEGRO IN THE NEW WORLD. Illustrated. *Demy 8vo.* 21s. net.

Julian (Lady) of Norwich. REVELATIONS OF DIVINE LOVE. Edited by GRACE WARRACK. *Fourth Edition. Cr. 8vo.* 3s. 6d.

Keats (John). THE POEMS. Edited with Introduction and Notes by E. de SÉLINCOURT. With a Frontispiece in Photogravure. *Third Edition. Demy 8vo.* 7s. 6d. net.

Keble (John). THE CHRISTIAN YEAR. With an Introduction and Notes by W. LOCK. Illustrated. *Third Edition. Fcap. 8vo.* 3s. 6d.

Kempis (Thomas à). THE IMITATION OF CHRIST. With an Introduction by DEAN FARRAR. Illustrated. *Third Edition. Fcap. 8vo.* 3s. 6d.; padded morocco, 5s.

Kipling (Rudyard). BARRACK-ROOM BALLADS. 100th Thousand. *Twenty-ninth Edition. Cr. 8vo.* 6s. Also *Fcap. 8vo, Leather.* 5s. net.
THE SEVEN SEAS. 84th Thousand. *Seventeenth Edition. Cr. 8vo.* 6s. Also *Fcap. 8vo, Leather.* 5s. net.
THE FIVE NATIONS. 70th Thousand. *Seventh Edition. Cr. 8vo.* 6s. Also *Fcap. 8vo, Leather.* 5s. net.
DEPARTMENTAL DITTIES. *Nineteenth Edition. Cr. 8vo.* 6s. Also *Fcap. 8vo, Leather.* 5s. net.

Knox (Winifred F.). THE COURT OF A SAINT. Illustrated. *Demy 8vo.* 10s. 6d. net.

*Lamb (Charles and Mary). THE WORKS. Edited with an Introduction and Notes by E. V. LUCAS. *A New and Revised Edition in Six Volumes. With Frontispiece. Fcap 8vo.* 5s. each. The volumes are :—
I. MISCELLANEOUS PROSE. II. ELIA AND THE LAST ESSAYS OF ELIA. III. BOOKS FOR CHILDREN. IV. PLAYS AND POEMS. V. and VI. LETTERS.

Lane-Poole (Stanley). A HISTORY OF EGYPT IN THE MIDDLE AGES. Illustrated. *Cr. 8vo.* 6s.

Lankester (Sir Ray). SCIENCE FROM AN EASY CHAIR. Illustrated. *Fifth Edition. Cr. 8vo.* 6s.

Le Braz (Anatole). THE LAND OF PARDONS. Translated by FRANCES M. GOSTLING. Illustrated. *Third Edition. Cr. 8vo.* 6s.

Lindsay (Mabel M.). ANNI DOMINI: A GOSPEL STUDY. With Maps. *Two Volumes. Super Royal 8vo.* 10s. *net.*

Lock (Walter). ST. PAUL, THE MASTER-BUILDER. *Third Edition Cr. 8vo.* 3s. 6d.
THE BIBLE AND CHRISTIAN LIFE. *Cr. 8vo.* 6s.

Lodge (Sir Oliver). THE SUBSTANCE OF FAITH, ALLIED WITH SCIENCE: A Catechism for Parents and Teachers. *Eleventh Edition. Cr. 8vo.* 2s. *net.*
MAN AND THE UNIVERSE: A STUDY OF THE INFLUENCE OF THE ADVANCE IN SCIENTIFIC KNOWLEDGE UPON OUR UNDERSTANDING OF CHRISTIANITY. *Ninth Edition. Demy 8vo.* 5s. *net.*
THE SURVIVAL OF MAN. A STUDY IN UNRECOGNISED HUMAN FACULTY. *Fifth Edition. Wide Crown 8vo.* 5s. *net.*
REASON AND BELIEF. *Fifth Edition. Cr. 8vo.* 3s. 6d. *net.*

Lorimer (George Horace). LETTERS FROM A SELF-MADE MERCHANT TO HIS SON. Illustrated. *Eighteenth Edition. Cr. 8vo.* 3s. 6d.
OLD GORGON GRAHAM. Illustrated. *Second Edition. Cr. 8vo.* 6s.

'Loyal Serviteur.' THE STORY OF BAYARD. Adapted by AMY G. ANDREWES. Illustrated. *Cr. 8vo.* 2s. 6d.

Lucas (E. V.). THE LIFE OF CHARLES LAMB. Illustrated. *Fifth Edition. Demy 8vo.* 7s. 6d. *net.*
A WANDERER IN HOLLAND. Illustrated. *Twelfth Edition. Cr. 8vo.* 6s.
Also Fcap. 8vo. 5s.
A WANDERER IN LONDON. Illustrated. *Eleventh Edition. Cr. 8vo.* 6s.
Also Fcap. 8vo. 5s.
A WANDERER IN PARIS. Illustrated. *Seventh Edition. Cr. 8vo.* 6s.
Also Fcap. 8vo. 5s.
THE OPEN ROAD: A Little Book for Wayfarers. *Eighteenth Edition. Fcap. 8vo.* 5s.; *India Paper,* 7s. 6d.
THE FRIENDLY TOWN: a Little Book for the Urbane. *Sixth Edition. Fcap. 8vo.* 5s.; *India Paper,* 7s. 6d.
FIRESIDE AND SUNSHINE. *Sixth Edition. Fcap. 8vo.* 5s.
CHARACTER AND COMEDY. *Sixth Edition. Fcap. 8vo.* 5s.
THE GENTLEST ART. A Choice of Letters by Entertaining Hands. *Sixth Edition. Fcap 8vo.* 5s.
THE SECOND POST. *Third Edition. Fcap. 8vo.* 5s.
A SWAN AND HER FRIENDS. Illustrated. *Demy 8vo.* 12s. 6d. *net.*
HER INFINITE VARIETY: A FEMININE PORTRAIT GALLERY. *Fifth Edition. Fcap. 8vo.* 5s.

GOOD COMPANY: A RALLY OF MEN. *Second Edition. Fcap. 8vo.* 5s.
ONE DAY AND ANOTHER. *Fourth Edition. Fcap. 8vo.* 5s.
*OLD LAMPS FOR NEW. *Fcap. 8vo.* 5s.
LISTENER'S LURE: AN OBLIQUE NARRATION. *Eighth Edition. Fcap. 8vo.* 5s.
OVER BEMERTON'S: AN EASY-GOING CHRONICLE. *Ninth Edition. Fcap. 8vo.* 5s.
*MR. INGLESIDE. *Fcap. 8vo.* 5s.
See also Lamb (Charles).

*Lydekker (R. and Others). REPTILES, AMPHIBIA, AND FISHES. Illustrated. *Demy 8vo.* 10s. 6d. *net,*

Lydekker (R.). THE OX. Illustrated. *Cr. 8vo.* 6s.

Macaulay (Lord). CRITICAL AND HISTORICAL ESSAYS. Edited by F. C. MONTAGUE. *Three Volumes. Cr. 8vo.* 18s.

McCabe (Joseph). THE DECAY OF THE CHURCH OF ROME. *Third Edition. Demy 8vo.* 7s. 6d. *net,*
*THE EMPRESSES OF ROME. Illustrated. *Demy 8vo.* 12s. 6d. *net.*

MacCarthy (Desmond) and Russell (Agatha). LADY JOHN RUSSELL: A MEMOIR. Illustrated. *Fourth Edition Demy 8vo.* 10s. 6d. *net.*

McCullagh (Francis). THE FALL OF ABD-UL-HAMID. Illustrated. *Demy 8vo.* 10s. 6d. *net.*

*MacDonagh (Michael). THE SPEAKER OF THE HOUSE. *Demy 8vo.* 10s. 6d. *net.*

McDougall (William). AN INTRODUCTION TO SOCIAL PSYCHOLOGY. *Fourth Edition. Cr. 8vo.* 5s. *net.*
*BODY AND MIND; A HISTORY AND A DEFENCE OF ANIMISM. *Demy 8vo.* 10s. 6d. *net.*

*'Mdlle. Mori' (Author of). ST. CATHERINE OF SIENA AND HER TIMES. Illustrated. *Second Edition. Demy 8vo.* 7s. 6d. *net.*

Maeterlinck (Maurice). THE BLUE BIRD: A FAIRY PLAY IN SIX ACTS. Translated by ALEXANDER TEIXEIRA DE MATTOS. *Twentieth Edition. Fcap. 8vo. Deckle Edges.* 3s. 6d. *net. Also Fcap. Paper covers,* 1s. *net.*
*THE BLUE BIRD: A FAIRY PLAY IN SIX ACTS. Translated by ALEXANDER TEIXEIRA DE MATTOS. Illustrated. *Cr. 4to.* 15s. *net.*
MARY MAGDALENE: A PLAY IN THREE ACTS. Translated by ALEXANDER TEIXEIRA DE MATTOS. *Third Edition. Fcap. 8vo. Deckle Edges.* 3s. 6d. *net.*

Mahaffy (J. P.). A HISTORY OF EGYPT UNDER THE PTOLEMAIC DYNASTY. Illustrated. *Cr. 8vo.* 6s.

Maitland (F. W.). ROMAN CANON LAW IN THE CHURCH OF ENGLAND. *Royal 8vo.* 7s. 6d.

Marett (R. R.). THE THRESHOLD OF RELIGION. *Cr. 8vo.* 3s. 6d. net.

Marriott (Charles). A SPANISH HOLIDAY. Illustrated. *Demy 8vo.* 7s. 6d. net.
•THE ROMANCE OF THE RHINE. Illustrated. *Demy 8vo.* 10s. 6d. net.

Marriott (J. A. R.). THE LIFE AND TIMES OF LUCIUS CARY, VISCOUNT FALKLAND. Illustrated. *Second Edition. Demy 8vo.* 7s. 6d. net.

Masefield (John). SEA LIFE IN NELSON'S TIME. Illustrated. *Cr. 8vo.* 3s. 6d. net.
A SAILOR'S GARLAND. Selected and Edited. *Second Edition. Cr. 8vo.* 3s. 6d. net.
AN ENGLISH PROSE MISCELLANY. Selected with an Introduction. *Cr. 8vo.* 6s.

Masterman (C. F. G.). TENNYSON AS A RELIGIOUS TEACHER. *Second Edition. Cr. 8vo.* 6s.
THE CONDITION OF ENGLAND. *Fourth Edition. Cr. 8vo.* 6s.

Medley (D. J.). ORIGINAL ILLUSTRATIONS OF ENGLISH CONSTITUTIONAL HISTORY. *Cr. 8vo.* 7s. 6d. net.

•**Meldrum (D. S.).** HOME LIFE IN HOLLAND. Illustrated. *Demy 8vo.* 10s. 6d. net.

Methuen (A. M. S.). ENGLAND'S RUIN: DISCUSSED IN FOURTEEN LETTERS TO A PROTECTIONIST. *Ninth Edition. Cr. 8vo.* 3d. net.

Meynell (Everard). COROT AND HIS FRIENDS. Illustrated. *Demy 8vo.* 10s. 6d. net.

Miles (Eustace). LIFE AFTER LIFE: OR, THE THEORY OF REINCARNATION. *Cr. 8vo.* 2s. 6d. net.
THE POWER OF CONCENTRATION: HOW TO ACQUIRE IT. *Third Edition. Cr. 8vo.* 3s. 6d. net.

Millais (J. G.). THE LIFE AND LETTERS OF SIR JOHN EVERETT MILLAIS. Illustrated. *New Edition. Demy 8vo.* 7s. 6d. net.

Milne (J. G.). A HISTORY OF EGYPT UNDER ROMAN RULE. Illustrated. *Cr. 8vo.* 6s.

Moffat (Mary M.). QUEEN LOUISA OF PRUSSIA. Illustrated. *Fourth Edition. Cr. 8vo.* 6s.
•MARIA THERESA. Illustrated. 10s. 6d. net.

Money (L. G. Chiozza). RICHES AND POVERTY, 1910. *Tenth and Revised Edition. Demy 8vo.* 5s. net.
MONEY'S FISCAL DICTIONARY, 1910. *Second Edition. Demy 8vo.* 5s. net.

Montague (C. E.). DRAMATIC VALUES. *Second Edition. Fcap. 8vo.* 5s.

Moorhouse (E. Hallam). NELSON'S LADY HAMILTON. Illustrated. *Third Edition. Demy 8vo.* 7s. 6d. net.

Morgan (J. H.), THE HOUSE OF LORDS AND THE CONSTITUTION. With an Introduction by the LORD CHANCELLOR. *Cr. 8vo.* 1s. net.

Nevill (Lady Dorothy). UNDER FIVE REIGNS. Edited by her son. Illustrated. *Fifth Edition. Demy 8vo.* 15s. net.

Norway (A. H.). NAPLES. PAST AND PRESENT. Illustrated. *Third Edition. Cr. 8vo.* 6s.

Oman (C. W. C.), A HISTORY OF THE ART OF WAR IN THE MIDDLE AGES. Illustrated. *Demy 8vo.* 10s. 6d. net.
ENGLAND BEFORE THE NORMAN CONQUEST. With Maps. *Second Edition. Demy 8vo.* 10s. 6d. net.

Oxford (M. N.), A HANDBOOK OF NURSING. *Fifth Edition. Cr. 8vo.* 3s. 6d.

Pakes (W. C. C.). THE SCIENCE OF HYGIENE. Illustrated. *Demy 8vo.* 15s.

Parker (Eric). THE BOOK OF THE ZOO; BY DAY AND NIGHT. Illustrated. *Second Edition. Cr. 8vo.* 6s.

•**Pears (Sir Edwin).** TURKEY AND ITS PEOPLE. *Demy 8vo.* 12s. 6d. net.

Petrie (W. M. Flinders). A HISTORY OF EGYPT. Illustrated. *In Six Volumes. Cr. 8vo.* 6s. each.
VOL. I. FROM THE IST TO THE XVITH DYNASTY. *Sixth Edition.*
VOL. II. THE XVIITH AND XVIIITH DYNASTIES. *Fourth Edition.*
VOL. III. XIXTH TO XXXTH DYNASTIES.
VOL. IV. EGYPT UNDER THE PTOLEMAIC DYNASTY. J. P. MAHAFFY.
VOL. V. EGYPT UNDER ROMAN RULE. J. G. MILNE.
VOL. VI. EGYPT IN THE MIDDLE AGES. STANLEY LANE-POOLE.
RELIGION AND CONSCIENCE IN ANCIENT EGYPT. Illustrated *Cr. 8vo.* 2s. 6d.
SYRIA AND EGYPT, FROM THE TELL EL AMARNA LETTERS. *Cr. 8vo.* 2s. 6d.

EGYPTIAN TALES. Translated from the Papyri. First Series, ivth to xiith Dynasty. Illustrated. *Second Edition. Cr. 8vo.* 3s. 6d.

EGYPTIAN TALES. Translated from the Papyri. Second Series, xviiith to xixth Dynasty. Illustrated. *Cr. 8vo.* 3s. 6d.

EGYPTIAN DECORATIVE ART. Illustrated. *Cr. 8vo.* 3s. 6d.

Phelps (Ruth S.). SKIES ITALIAN: A LITTLE BREVIARY FOR TRAVELLERS IN ITALY. *Fcap. 8vo.* 5s. net.

Podmore (Frank). MODERN SPIRITUALISM. *Two Volumes. Demy 8vo.* 21s. net.

MESMERISM AND CHRISTIAN SCIENCE: A Short History of Mental Healing. *Second Edition. Demy 8vo.* 10s. 6d. net.

Pollard (Alfred W.). SHAKESPEARE FOLIOS AND QUARTOS. A Study in the Bibliography of Shakespeare's Plays, 1594–1685. Illustrated. *Folio.* 21s. net.

*Porter (G. R.) THE PROGRESS OF THE NATION. A New Edition. Edited by F. W. HIRST. *Demy 8vo.* 21s. net.

Powell (Arthur E.). FOOD AND HEALTH. *Cr. 8vo.* 3s. 6d. net.

Power (J. O'Connor). THE MAKING OF AN ORATOR. *Cr. 8vo.* 6s.

*Price (Eleanor C.). CARDINAL DE RICHELIEU. Illustrated. *Demy 8vo.* 10s. 6d. net.

Price (L. L.). A SHORT HISTORY OF POLITICAL ECONOMY IN ENGLAND FROM ADAM SMITH TO ARNOLD TOYNBEE. *Seventh Edition. Cr. 8vo.* 2s. 6d.

Pycraft (W. P.). A HISTORY OF BIRDS. Illustrated. *Demy 8vo.* 10s. 6d. net.

*Rappoport (Angelo S.). HOME LIFE IN RUSSIA. Illustrated. *Demy 8vo.* 10s. 6d. net.

Rawlings (Gertrude B.). COINS AND HOW TO KNOW THEM. Illustrated. *Third Edition. Cr. 8vo.* 6s.

Read (C. Stanford). FADS AND FEEDING. *Cr. 8vo.* 2s. 6d. net.

*Regan (C. Tate). THE FRESHWATER FISHES OF THE BRITISH ISLES. Illustrated. *Cr. 8vo.* 6s.

Reid (Archdall). THE LAWS OF HEREDITY. *Second Edition. Demy 8vo.* 21s. net.

Robertson (C. Grant). SELECT STATUTES, CASES, AND DOCUMENTS, 1660–1894. *Demy 8vo.* 10s. 6d. net.

ENGLAND UNDER THE HANOVERIANS. Illustrated. *Demy 8vo.* 10s. 6d. net.

Roe (Fred). OLD OAK FURNITURE. Illustrated. *Second Edition. Demy 8vo.* 10s. 6d. net.

Royde-Smith (N. G.). THE PILLOW BOOK: A GARNER OF MANY MOODS. Collected. *Second Edition. Cr. 8vo.* 4s. 6d. net.

POETS OF OUR DAY. Selected, with an Introduction. *Fcap. 8vo.* 5s.

Russell (W. Clark). THE LIFE OF ADMIRAL LORD COLLINGWOOD. Illustrated. *Fourth Edition. Cr. 8vo.* 6s.

*Ryan (P. F. W.). STUART LIFE AND MANNERS: A SOCIAL HISTORY. Illustrated. *Demy 8vo.* 10s. 6d. net.

St. Francis of Assisi. THE LITTLE FLOWERS OF THE GLORIOUS MESSER, AND OF HIS FRIARS. Done into English, with Notes by WILLIAM HEYWOOD. Illustrated. *Demy 8vo.* 5s. net.

'Saki' (H. H. Munro). REGINALD. *Second Edition. Fcap. 8vo.* 2s. 6d. net.

REGINALD IN RUSSIA. *Fcap. 8vo.* 2s. 6d. net.

Sandeman (G. A. C.). METTERNICH. Illustrated. *Demy 8vo.* 10s. 6d. net.

Selous (Edmund). TOMMY SMITH'S ANIMALS. Illustrated. *Eleventh Edition. Fcap. 8vo.* 2s. 6d.

TOMMY SMITH'S OTHER ANIMALS. Illustrated. *Fifth Edition. Fcap. 8vo.* 2s. 6d.

JACK'S INSECTS. Illustrated. *Cr. 8vo.* 6s.

Shakespeare (William).

THE FOUR FOLIOS, 1623; 1632; 1664; 1685. Each £4 4s. net, or a complete set, £12 12s. net.

THE POEMS OF WILLIAM SHAKESPEARE. With an Introduction and Notes by GEORGE WYNDHAM. *Demy 8vo. Buckram.* 10s. 6d.

Sharp (A.). VICTORIAN POETS. *Cr. 8vo.* 2s. 6d.

Sidgwick (Mrs. Alfred). HOME LIFE IN GERMANY. Illustrated. *Second Edition. Demy 8vo.* 10s. 6d. net.

Sladen (Douglas). SICILY: The New Winter Resort. Illustrated. *Second Edition. Cr. 8vo.* 5s. net.

Smith (Adam). THE WEALTH OF NATIONS. Edited by EDWIN CANNAN. *Two Volumes. Demy 8vo.* 21s. net.

*Smith (G. Herbert). GEMS AND PRECIOUS STONES. Illustrated. *Cr. 8vo.* 6s.

Snell (F. J.). A BOOK OF EXMOOR. Illustrated. *Cr. 8vo.* 6s.

'Stancliffe.' GOLF DO'S AND DONT'S. *Third Edition. Fcap 8vo. 1s. net.*

Stevenson (R.L.). THE LETTERS OF ROBERT LOUIS STEVENSON. Edited by Sir SIDNEY COLVIN. *A New and Enlarged Edition in 4 volumes. Second Edition. Fcap. 8vo. Leather, each 5s. net.*
VAILIMA LETTERS. With an Etched Portrait by WILLIAM STRANG. *Eighth Edition. Cr. 8vo. Buckram. 6s.*
THE LIFE OF R. L. STEVENSON. *See* BALFOUR (G.).

Stevenson (M. I.). FROM SARANAC TO THE MARQUESAS AND BEYOND. Being Letters written by Mrs. M. I. STEVENSON during 1887-88. *Cr. 8vo. 6s. net.*
LETTERS FROM SAMOA, 1891-95. Edited and arranged by M. C. BALFOUR. Illustrated. *Second Edition. Cr. 8vo. 6s. net.*

Storr (Vernon F.). DEVELOPMENT AND DIVINE PURPOSE. *Cr. 8vo. 5s. net.*

Streatfeild (R. A.). MODERN MUSIC AND MUSICIANS. Illustrated. *Second Edition. Demy 8vo. 7s. 6d. net.*

Swanton (E. W.). FUNGI AND HOW TO KNOW THEM. Illustrated. *Cr. 8vo. 6s. net.*

Sykes (Ella C.). PERSIA AND ITS PEOPLE. Illustrated. *Demy 8vo. 10s. 6d. net.*

Symes (J. E.). THE FRENCH REVOLUTION. *Second Edition. Cr. 8vo. 2s. 6d.*

Tabor (Margaret E.). THE SAINTS IN ART. Illustrated. *Fcap. 8vo. 3s. 6d. net.*

Taylor (A. E.). THE ELEMENTS OF METAPHYSICS. *Second Edition. Demy 8vo. 10s. 6d. net.*

Thibaudeau (A. C.). BONAPARTE AND THE CONSULATE. Translated and Edited by G. K. FORTESCUE. Illustrated. *Demy 8vo. 10s. 6d. net.*

*Thomas (Edward). MAURICE MAETERLINCK. Illustrated. *Cr. 8vo. 5s. net.*

Thompson (Francis). S E L E C T E D POEMS OF FRANCIS THOMPSON. With a Biographical Note by WILFRID MEYNELL. With a Portrait in Photogravure. *Seventh Edition. Fcap. 8vo. 5s. net.*

Tileston (Mary W.). DAILY STRENGTH FOR DAILY NEEDS. *Eighteenth Edition. Medium 16mo. 2s. 6d. net. Lambskin 3s. 6d. net.* Also an edition in superior binding, 6s.
*THE STRONGHOLD OF HOPE. *Medium 16mo. 2s. 6d. net.*

Toynbee (Paget). DANTE ALIGHIERI : HIS LIFE AND WORKS. With 16 Illustrations. *Fourth and Enlarged Edition. Cr. 8vo. 5s. net.*

Trench (Herbert). DEIRDRE WEDDED, AND OTHER POEMS. *Second and Revised Edition. Large Post 8vo. 6s.*
NEW POEMS. *Second Edition. Large Post 8vo. 6s.*
APOLLO AND THE SEAMAN. *Large Post 8vo. Paper, 1s. 6d. net ; cloth, 2s. 6d. net.*

Trevelyan (G. M.). ENGLAND UNDER THE STUARTS. With Maps and Plans. *Fourth Edition. Demy 8vo. 10s. 6d. net.*

Triggs (Inigo H.). TOWN PLANNING : PAST, PRESENT, AND POSSIBLE. Illustrated. *Second Edition. Wide Royal 8vo. 15s. net.*

Underhill (Evelyn). MYSTICISM. A Study in the Nature and Development of Man's Spiritual Consciousness. *Second Edition. Demy 8vo. 15s. net.*

Vaughan (Herbert M.). THE NAPLES RIVIERA. Illustrated. *Second Edition. Cr. 8vo. 6s.*
*FLORENCE AND HER TREASURES. Illustrated. *Fcap. 8vo. 5s. net.*

Vernon (Hon. W. Warren). READINGS ON THE INFERNO OF DANTE. With an Introduction by the REV. DR. MOORE. *Two Volumes. Second Edition. Cr. 8vo. 15s. net.*
READINGS ON THE PURGATORIO OF DANTE. With an Introduction by the late DEAN CHURCH. *Two Volumes. Third Edition. Cr. 8vo. 15s. net.*
READINGS ON THE PARADISO OF DANTE. With an Introduction by the BISHOP OF RIPON. *Two Volumes. Second Edition. Cr. 8vo. 15s. net.*

Waddell (Col. L. A.). LHASA AND ITS MYSTERIES. With a Record of the Expedition of 1903-1904. Illustrated. *Third and Cheaper Edition. Medium 8vo. 7s. 6d. net.*

Wagner (Richard). RICHARD WAGNER'S MUSIC DRAMAS : Interpretations, embodying Wagner's own explanations. By ALICE LEIGHTON CLEATHER and BASIL CRUMP. *Fcap. 8vo. 2s. 6d. each.*
THE RING OF THE NIBELUNG. *Fourth Edition.*
TRISTAN AND ISOLDE.

Waterhouse (Elizabeth). WITH THE SIMPLE-HEARTED : Little Homilies to Women in Country Places. *Third Edition. Small Pott 8vo. 2s. net.*
THE HOUSE BY THE CHERRY TREE. A Second Series of Little Homilies to Women in Country Places. *Small Pott 8vo. 2s. net.*
COMPANIONS OF THE WAY. Being Selections for Morning and Evening Reading. Chosen and arranged by ELIZABETH WATERHOUSE. *Large Cr. 8vo. 5s. net.*
THOUGHTS OF A TERTIARY. *Small Pott 8vo. 1s. net.*

Waters (W. G.). ITALIAN SCULPTORS AND SMITHS. Illustrated. *Cr. 8vo. 7s. 6d. net.*

*Watt (Francis). EDINBURGH AND THE LOTHIANS. Illustrated. *Cr. 8vo. 7s. 6d. net.*

Weigall (Arthur E. P.). A GUIDE TO THE ANTIQUITIES OF UPPER EGYPT: From Abydos to the Sudan Frontier. Illustrated. *Cr. 8vo. 7s. 6d. net.*

Welch (Catharine). THE LITTLE DAUPHIN. Illustrated. *Cr. 8vo. 6s.*

Wells (J.). OXFORD AND OXFORD LIFE. *Third Edition. Cr. 8vo. 3s. 6d.* A SHORT HISTORY OF ROME. *Tenth Edition.* With 3 Maps. *Cr. 8vo. 3s. 6d.*

Westell (W. Percival). THE YOUNG NATURALIST. Illustrated. *Cr. 8vo. 6s.* *THE YOUNG ORNITHOLOGIST. Illustrated. *Cr. 8vo. 5s.*

Westell (W. Percival), and Cooper (C. S.). THE YOUNG BOTANIST. Illustrated. *Cr. 8vo. 3s. 6d. net.*

White (George F.). A CENTURY OF SPAIN AND PORTUGAL, 1788-1898. *Demy 8vo. 12s. 6d. net.*

Wilde (Oscar). DE PROFUNDIS. *Twelfth Edition. Cr. 8vo. 5s. net.* THE WORKS OF OSCAR WILDE. *In Twelve Volumes. Fcap. 8vo. 5s. net each volume.*

I. LORD ARTHUR SAVILE'S CRIME AND THE PORTRAIT OF MR. W. H. II. THE DUCHESS OF PADUA. III. POEMS. IV. LADY WINDERMERE'S FAN. V. A WOMAN OF NO IMPORTANCE. VI. AN IDEAL HUSBAND. VII. THE IMPORTANCE OF BEING EARNEST. VIII. A HOUSE OF POMEGRANATES. IX. INTENTIONS. X. DE PROFUNDIS AND PRISON LETTERS. XI. ESSAYS. XII. SALOMÉ, A FLORENTINE TRAGEDY, and LA SAINTE COURTISANE.

Williams (H. Noel). THE WOMEN BONAPARTES. The Mother and three Sisters of Napoleon. Illustrated. *In Two Volumes. Demy 8vo. 24s. net.*

A ROSE OF SAVOY: MARIE ADÉLAÏDE OF SAVOY, DUCHESSE DE BOURGOGNE, MOTHER OF LOUIS XV. Illustrated. *Second Edition. Demy 8vo. 15s. net.*

THE FASCINATING DUC DE RICHELIEU: LOUIS FRANÇOIS ARMAND DU PLESSIS (1696-1788). Illustrated. *Demy 8vo. 15s. net.*

*A PRINCESS OF ADVENTURE: MARIE CAROLINE, DUCHESSE DE BERRY (1798-1870). Illustrated. *Demy 8vo. 15s. net.*

Wood (Sir Evelyn). FROM MIDSHIPMAN TO FIELD-MARSHAL. Illustrated. *Fifth and Cheaper Edition. Demy 8vo. 7s. 6d. net.*

THE REVOLT IN HINDUSTAN. 1857-59. Illustrated. *Second Edition. Cr. 8vo. 6s.*

Wood (W. Birkbeck), and Edmonds (Lieut.-Col. J. E.). A HISTORY OF THE CIVIL WAR IN THE UNITED STATES (1861-5). With an Introduction by H. SPENSER WILKINSON. With 24 Maps and Plans. *Third Edition. Demy 8vo. 12s. 6d. net.*

Wordsworth (W.). THE POEMS. With an Introduction and Notes by NOWELL C. SMITH. *In Three Volumes. Demy 8vo. 15s. net.*

Wyllie (M. A.). NORWAY AND ITS FJORDS. Illustrated. *Second Edition. Cr. 8vo. 6s.*

Yeats (W. B.). A BOOK OF IRISH VERSE. *Third Edition. Cr. 8vo. 3s. 6d.*

PART II.—A SELECTION OF SERIES.

Ancient Cities.

General Editor, B. C. A. WINDLE.

Cr. 8vo. 4s. 6d. net each volume.

With Illustrations by E. H. NEW, and other Artists.

BRISTOL. Alfred Harvey.
CANTERBURY. J. C. Cox.
CHESTER. B. C. A. Windle.
DUBLIN. S. A. O. Fitzpatrick.

EDINBURGH. M. G. Williamson.
LINCOLN. E. Mansel Sympson.
SHREWSBURY. T. Auden.
WELLS and GLASTONBURY. T. S. Holmes.

The Antiquary's Books.

General Editor, J. CHARLES COX.

Demy 8vo. 7s. 6d. net each volume.

With Numerous Illustrations.

ARCHÆOLOGY AND FALSE ANTIQUITIES.
R. Munro.

BELLS OF ENGLAND, THE. Canon J. J. Raven.
Second Edition.

BRASSES OF ENGLAND, THE. Herbert W.
Macklin. *Second Edition.*

CELTIC ART IN PAGAN AND CHRISTIAN
TIMES. J. Romilly Allen.

CASTLES AND WALLED TOWNS OF ENGLAND.
A. Harvey.

DOMESDAY INQUEST, THE. Adolphus Ballard.

ENGLISH CHURCH FURNITURE. J. C. Cox
and A. Harvey. *Second Edition.*

ENGLISH COSTUME. From Prehistoric Times
to the End of the Eighteenth Century.
George Clinch.

ENGLISH MONASTIC LIFE. The Right Rev.
Abbot Gasquet. *Fourth Edition.*

ENGLISH SEALS. J. Harvey Bloom.

FOLK-LORE AS AN HISTORICAL SCIENCE.
Sir G. L. Gomme.

GILDS AND COMPANIES OF LONDON, THE.
George Unwin.

MANOR AND MANORIAL RECORDS, THE.
Nathaniel J. Hone.

MEDIÆVAL HOSPITALS OF ENGLAND, THE.
Rotha Mary Clay.

OLD ENGLISH INSTRUMENTS OF MUSIC.
F. W. Galpin. *Second Edition.*

OLD ENGLISH LIBRARIES. James Hutt.

OLD SERVICE BOOKS OF THE ENGLISH
CHURCH. Christopher Wordsworth and
Henry Littlehales. *Second Edition.*

PARISH LIFE IN MEDIÆVAL ENGLAND.
The Right Rev. Abbot Gasquet. *Third
Edition.*

PARISH REGISTERS OF ENGLAND, THE.
J. C. Cox.

REMAINS OF THE PREHISTORIC AGE IN
ENGLAND. B. C. A. Windle. *Second
Edition.*

*ROMAN ERA IN BRITAIN, THE. J. Ward.

*ROMAN-BRITISH BUILDINGS AND EARTH-
WORKS. J. Ward.

ROYAL FORESTS OF ENGLAND, THE. J. C.
Cox.

SHRINES OF BRITISH SAINTS. J. C. Wall.

The Arden Shakespeare.

Demy 8vo. 2s. 6d. net each volume.

An edition of Shakespeare in single Plays ; each edited with a full Introduction,
Textual Notes, and a Commentary at the foot of the page.

ALL'S WELL THAT ENDS WELL.

ANTONY AND CLEOPATRA.

CYMBELINE.

COMEDY OF ERRORS, THE.

HAMLET. *Second Edition.*

JULIUS CAESAR.

KING HENRY IV. PT. I.

KING HENRY V.

KING HENRY VI. PT. I.

KING HENRY VI. PT. II.

KING HENRY VI. PT. III.

KING LEAR.

KING RICHARD III.

LIFE AND DEATH OF KING JOHN, THE.

LOVE'S LABOUR'S LOST.

MACBETH.

MEASURE FOR MEASURE.

MERCHANT OF VENICE, THE.

MERRY WIVES OF WINDSOR, THE.

MIDSUMMER NIGHT'S DREAM, A.

OTHELLO.

PERICLES.

ROMEO AND JULIET.

TAMING OF THE SHREW, THE.

TEMPEST, THE.

TIMON OF ATHENS.

TITUS ANDRONICUS.

TROILUS AND CRESSIDA.

TWO GENTLEMEN OF VERONA, THE.

TWELFTH NIGHT.

VENUS AND ADONIS.

Classics of Art.

Edited by Dr. J. H. W. LAING.

With numerous Illustrations. Wide Royal 8vo.

THE ART OF THE GREEKS. H. B. Walters. 12s. 6d. net.

THE ART OF THE ROMANS. H. B. Walters. 15s. net.

CHARDIN. H. E. A. Furst. 12s. 6d. net.

DONATELLO. Maud Cruttwell. 15s. net.

FLORENTINE SCULPTORS OF THE RENAISSANCE. Wilhelm Bode. Translated by Jessie Haynes. 12s. 6d. net.

GEORGE ROMNEY. Arthur B. Chamberlain. 12s. 6d. net.

GHIRLANDAIO. Gerald S. Davies. *Second Edition.* 10s. 6d.

MICHELANGELO. Gerald S. Davies. 12s. 6d. net.

RUBENS. Edward Dillon. 25s. net.

RAPHAEL. A. P. Oppé. 12s. 6d. net.

*REMBRANDT'S ETCHINGS. A. M. Hind.

TITIAN. Charles Ricketts. 12s. 6d. net.

TINTORETTO. Evelyn March Phillipps. 15s. net.

TURNER'S SKETCHES AND DRAWINGS. A. J. FINBERG. 12s. 6d. net. *Second Edition.*

VELAZQUEZ. A. de Beruete. 10s. 6d. net.

The Complete Series.

Fully Illustrated. Demy 8vo.

THE COMPLETE BILLIARD PLAYER. Charles Roberts. 10s. 6d. net.

THE COMPLETE COOK. Lilian Whitling. 7s. 6d. net.

THE COMPLETE CRICKETER. Albert E. Knight. 7s. 6d. net. *Second Edition.*

THE COMPLETE FOXHUNTER. Charles Richardson. 12s. 6d. net. *Second Edition.*

THE COMPLETE GOLFER. Harry Vardon. 10s. 6d. net. *Eleventh Edition.*

THE COMPLETE HOCKEY-PLAYER. Eustace E. White. 5s. net. *Second Edition.*

THE COMPLETE LAWN TENNIS PLAYER. A. Wallis Myers. 10s. 6d. net. *Second Edition.*

THE COMPLETE MOTORIST. Filson Young. 12s. 6d. net. *New Edition (Seventh).*

THE COMPLETE MOUNTAINEER. G. D. Abraham. 15s. net. *Second Edition.*

THE COMPLETE OARSMAN. R. C. Lehmann. 10s. 6d. net.

THE COMPLETE PHOTOGRAPHER. R. Child Bayley. 10s. 6d. net. *Fourth Edition.*

THE COMPLETE RUGBY FOOTBALLER, ON THE NEW ZEALAND SYSTEM. D. Gallaher and W. J. Stead. 10s. 6d. net. *Second Edition.*

THE COMPLETE SHOT. G. T. Teasdale Buckell. 12s. 6d. net. *Third Edition.*

The Connoisseur's Library.

With numerous Illustrations. Wide Royal 8vo. 25s. net each volume.

ENGLISH FURNITURE. F. S. Robinson.

ENGLISH COLOURED BOOKS. Martin Hardie.

*ETCHINGS. F. Wedmore.

EUROPEAN ENAMELS. Henry H. Cunynghame.

GLASS. Edward Dillon.

GOLDSMITHS' AND SILVERSMITHS' WORK. Nelson Dawson. *Second Edition.*

ILLUMINATED MANUSCRIPTS. J. A. Herbert.

IVORIES. Alfred Maskell.

JEWELLERY. H. Clifford Smith. *Second Edition.*

MEZZOTINTS. Cyril Davenport.

MINIATURES. Dudley Heath.

PORCELAIN. Edward Dillon.

SEALS. Walter de Gray Birch.

*WOOD SCULPTURE. Alfred Maskell.

Handbooks of English Church History.

Edited by J. H. BURN. *Crown 8vo. 2s. 6d. net each volume.*

THE FOUNDATIONS OF THE ENGLISH CHURCH. J. H. Maude.

THE SAXON CHURCH AND THE NORMAN CONQUEST. C. T. Cruttwell.

THE MEDIÆVAL CHURCH AND THE PAPACY. A. C. Jennings.

THE REFORMATION PERIOD. Henry Gee.

THE STRUGGLE WITH PURITANISM. Bruce Blaxland.

THE CHURCH OF ENGLAND IN THE EIGHTEENTH CENTURY. Alfred Plummer.

Handbooks of Theology.

THE DOCTRINE OF THE INCARNATION. R. L. Ottley. *Fifth Edition, Revised.* Demy 8vo. 12s. 6d.

A HISTORY OF EARLY CHRISTIAN DOCTRINE. J. F. Bethune-Baker. *Demy 8vo.* 10s. 6d.

AN INTRODUCTION TO THE HISTORY OF RELIGION. F. B. Jevons. *Fifth Edition.* Demy 8vo. 10s. 6d.

AN INTRODUCTION TO THE HISTORY OF THE CREEDS. A. E. Burn. *Demy 8vo.* 10s. 6d.

THE PHILOSOPHY OF RELIGION IN ENGLAND AND AMERICA. Alfred Caldecott. *Demy 8vo.* 10s. 6d.

THE XXXIX. ARTICLES OF THE CHURCH OF ENGLAND. Edited by E. C. S. Gibson, *Seventh Edition. Demy 8vo.* 12s. 6d.

The Illustrated Pocket Library of Plain and Coloured Books.

Fcap. 8vo. 3s. 6d. net each volume.

WITH COLOURED ILLUSTRATIONS.

OLD COLOURED BOOKS. George Paston. 2s. net.

THE LIFE AND DEATH OF JOHN MYTTON, ESQ. Nimrod. *Fifth Edition.*

THE LIFE OF A SPORTSMAN. Nimrod.

HANDLEY CROSS. R. S. Surtees. *Third Edition.*

MR. SPONGE'S SPORTING TOUR. R. S. Surtees.

JORROCKS'S JAUNTS AND JOLLITIES. R. S. Surtees. *Third Edition.*

ASK MAMMA. R. S. Surtees.

THE ANALYSIS OF THE HUNTING FIELD. R. S. Surtees.

THE TOUR OF DR. SYNTAX IN SEARCH OF THE PICTURESQUE. William Combe.

THE TOUR OF DR. SYNTAX IN SEARCH OF CONSOLATION. William Combe.

THE THIRD TOUR OF DR. SYNTAX IN SEARCH OF A WIFE. William Combe.

THE HISTORY OF JOHNNY QUAE GENUS. the Author of 'The Three Tours.'

THE ENGLISH DANCE OF DEATH, from the Designs of T. Rowlandson, with Metrical Illustrations by the Author of 'Doctor Syntax.' *Two Volumes.*

THE DANCE OF LIFE: A Poem. The Author of 'Dr. Syntax.'

LIFE IN LONDON. Pierce Egan.

REAL LIFE IN LONDON. An Amateur (Pierce Egan). *Two Volumes.*

THE LIFE OF AN ACTOR. Pierce Egan.

THE VICAR OF WAKEFIELD. Oliver Goldsmith.

THE MILITARY ADVENTURES OF JOHNNY NEWCOMBE. An Officer.

THE NATIONAL SPORTS OF GREAT BRITAIN. With Descriptions and 50 Coloured Plates by Henry Alken.

THE ADVENTURES OF A POST CAPTAIN. A Naval Officer.

GAMONIA. Lawrence Rawstorne.

AN ACADEMY FOR GROWN HORSEMEN. Geoffrey Gambado.

REAL LIFE IN IRELAND. A Real Paddy.

THE ADVENTURES OF JOHNNY NEWCOMBE IN THE NAVY. Alfred Burton.

THE OLD ENGLISH SQUIRE. John Careless.

THE ENGLISH SPY. Bernard Blackmantle. *Two Volumes. 7s. net.*

WITH PLAIN ILLUSTRATIONS.

THE GRAVE: A Poem. Robert Blair.

ILLUSTRATIONS OF THE BOOK OF JOB. Invented and engraved by William Blake.

WINDSOR CASTLE. W. Harrison Ainsworth.

THE TOWER OF LONDON. W. Harrison Ainsworth.

FRANK FAIRLEGH. F. E. Smedley.

HANDY ANDY. Samuel Lover.

THE COMPLEAT ANGLER. Izaak Walton and Charles Cotton.

THE PICKWICK PAPERS. Charles Dickens.

Leaders of Religion.

Edited by H. C. BEECHING. *With Portraits.*

Crown 8vo. 2s. net each volume.

CARDINAL NEWMAN. R. H. Hutton.

JOHN WESLEY. J. H. Overton.

BISHOP WILBERFORCE. G. W. Daniell.

CARDINAL MANNING. A. W. Hutton.

CHARLES SIMEON. H. C. G. Moule.

JOHN KNOX. F. MacCunn. *Second Edition.*

JOHN HOWE. R. F. Horton.

THOMAS KEN. F. A. Clarke.

GEORGE FOX, THE QUAKER. T. Hodgkin. *Third Edition.*

JOHN KEBLE. Walter Lock.

THOMAS CHALMERS. Mrs. Oliphant. *Second Edition.*

LANCELOT ANDREWES. R. L. Ottley. *Second Edition.*

AUGUSTINE OF CANTERBURY. E. L. Cutts.

WILLIAM LAUD. W. H. Hutton. *Third Ed.*

JOHN DONNE. Augustus Jessop.

THOMAS CRANMER. A. J. Mason.

BISHOP LATIMER. R. M. Carlyle and A. J. Carlyle.

BISHOP BUTLER. W. A. Spooner.

The Library of Devotion.

With Introductions and (where necessary) Notes.

Small Pott 8vo, cloth, 2s. ; leather, 2s. 6d. net each volume.

THE CONFESSIONS OF ST. AUGUSTINE. *Seventh Edition.*

THE IMITATION OF CHRIST. *Sixth Edition.*

THE CHRISTIAN YEAR. *Fourth Edition.*

LYRA INNOCENTIUM. *Second Edition.*

THE TEMPLE. *Second Edition.*

A BOOK OF DEVOTIONS. *Second Edition.*

A SERIOUS CALL TO A DEVOUT AND HOLY LIFE. *Fourth Edition.*

A GUIDE TO ETERNITY.

THE INNER WAY. *Second Edition.*

ON THE LOVE OF GOD.

THE PSALMS OF DAVID.

LYRA APOSTOLICA.

THE SONG OF SONGS.

THE THOUGHTS OF PASCAL. *Second Edition.*

A MANUAL OF CONSOLATION FROM THE SAINTS AND FATHERS.

DEVOTIONS FROM THE APOCRYPHA.

THE SPIRITUAL COMBAT.

THE DEVOTIONS OF ST. ANSELM.

BISHOP WILSON'S SACRA PRIVATA.

GRACE ABOUNDING TO THE CHIEF OF SINNERS.

LYRA SACRA : A Book of Sacred Verse. *Second Edition.*

A DAY BOOK FROM THE SAINTS AND FATHERS.

A LITTLE BOOK OF HEAVENLY WISDOM. A Selection from the English Mystics.

LIGHT, LIFE, and LOVE. A Selection from the German Mystics.

AN INTRODUCTION TO THE DEVOUT LIFE.

THE LITTLE FLOWERS OF THE GLORIOUS MESSER ST. FRANCIS AND OF HIS FRIARS.

DEATH AND IMMORTALITY.

THE SPIRITUAL GUIDE. *Second Edition.*

DEVOTIONS FOR EVERY DAY IN THE WEEK AND THE GREAT FESTIVALS.

PRECES PRIVATÆ.

HORÆ MYSTICÆ : A Day Book from the Writings of Mystics of Many Nations.

Little Books on Art.

With many Illustrations. Demy 16mo. 2s. 6d. net each volume.

Each volume consists of about 200 pages, and contains from 30 to 40 Illustrations, including a Frontispiece in Photogravure.

ALBRECHT DÜRER. J. Allen.

ARTS OF JAPAN, THE. E. Dillon. *Second Edition.*

BOOKPLATES. E. Almack.

BOTTICELLI. Mary L. Bonnor.

BURNE-JONES. F. de Lisle.

CHRISTIAN SYMBOLISM. Mrs. H. Jenner.

CHRIST IN ART. Mrs. H. Jenner.

CLAUDE. E. Dillon.

CONSTABLE. H. W. Tompkins. *Second Edition.*

COROT. A. Pollard and E. Birnstingl.

ENAMELS. Mrs. N. Dawson.

FREDERIC LEIGHTON. A. Corkran.

GEORGE ROMNEY. G. Paston.

GREEK ART. H. B. Walters. *Fourth Edition.*

GREUZE AND BOUCHER. E. F. Pollard.

HOLBEIN. Mrs. G. Fortescue.

ILLUMINATED MANUSCRIPTS. J. W. Bradley.

JEWELLERY. C. Davenport.

JOHN HOPPNER. H. P. K. Skipton.

SIR JOSHUA REYNOLDS. J. Sime. *Second Edition.*

MILLET. N. Peacock.

MINIATURES. C. Davenport.

OUR LADY IN ART. Mrs. H. Jenner.

RAPHAEL. A. R. Dryhurst.

REMBRANDT. Mrs. E. A. Sharp.

TURNER. F. Tyrrell-Gill.

VANDYCK. M. G. Smallwood.

VELASQUEZ. W. Wilberforce and A. R. Gilbert.

WATTS. R. E. D. Sketchley.

The Little Galleries.

Demy 16mo. 2s. 6d. net each volume.

Each volume contains 20 plates in Photogravure, together with a short outline of the life and work of the master to whom the book is devoted.

A LITTLE GALLERY OF REYNOLDS.

A LITTLE GALLERY OF ROMNEY.

A LITTLE GALLERY OF HOPPNER.

A LITTLE GALLERY OF MILLAIS.

A LITTLE GALLERY OF ENGLISH POETS.

The Little Guides.

With many Illustrations by E. H. NEW and other artists, and from photographs.

Small Pott 8vo, cloth, 2s. 6d. net; leather, 3s. 6d. net, each volume.

The main features of these Guides are (1) a handy and charming form; (2) illustrations from photographs and by well-known artists; (3) good plans and maps; (4) an adequate but compact presentation of everything that is interesting in the natural features, history, archæology, and architecture of the town or district treated.

CAMBRIDGE AND ITS COLLEGES. A. H. Thompson. *Third Edition, Revised.*

CHANNEL ISLANDS, THE. E. E. Bicknell.

ENGLISH LAKES, THE. F. G. Brabant.

ISLE OF WIGHT, THE. G. Clinch.

MALVERN COUNTRY, THE. B. C. A. Windle.

NORTH WALES. A. T. Story.

OXFORD AND ITS COLLEGES. J. Wells. *Ninth Edition.*

SHAKESPEARE'S COUNTRY. B. C. A. Windle. *Third Edition.*

ST. PAUL'S CATHEDRAL. G. Clinch.

WESTMINSTER ABBEY. G. E. Troutbeck. *Second Edition.*

BERKSHIRE. F. G. Brabant.

BUCKINGHAMSHIRE. E. S. Roscoe.

CHESHIRE. W. M. Gallichan.

THE LITTLE GUIDES—*continued.*

CORNWALL. A. L. Salmon
DERBYSHIRE. J. C. Cox.
DEVON. S. Baring-Gould. *Second Edition.*
DORSET. F. R. Heath. *Second Edition.*
ESSEX. J. C. Cox.
HAMPSHIRE. J. C. Cox.
HERTFORDSHIRE. H. W. Tompkins.
KENT. G. Clinch.
KERRY. C. P. Crane.
MIDDLESEX. J. B. Firth.
MONMOUTHSHIRE. G. W. Wade and J. H. Wade.
NORFOLK. W. A. Dutt. *Second Edition, Revised.*
NORTHAMPTONSHIRE. W. Dry. *Second Ed.*
NORTHUMBERLAND. J. E. Morris.
NOTTINGHAMSHIRE. L. Guilford.
OXFORDSHIRE. F. G. Brabant.

SOMERSET. G. W. and J. H. Wade.
STAFFORDSHIRE. C. E. Masefield.
SUFFOLK. W. A. Dutt.
SURREY. J. C. Cox.
SUSSEX. F. G. Brabant. *Third Edition.*
WILTSHIRE. F. R. Heath.
YORKSHIRE, THE EAST RIDING. J. E. Morris.
YORKSHIRE, THE NORTH RIDING. J. E. Morris.
YORKSHIRE, THE WEST RIDING. J. E. Morris. *Cloth, 3s. 6d. net; leather, 4s. 6d. net.*

———

BRITTANY. S. Baring-Gould.
NORMANDY. C. Scudamore.
ROME. C. G. Ellaby.
SICILY. F. H. Jackson.

The Little Library.

With Introductions, Notes, and Photogravure Frontispieces.

Small Pott 8vo. Each Volume, cloth, 1s. 6d. net.

Anon. A LITTLE BOOK OF ENGLISH LYRICS. *Second Edition.*

Austen (Jane). PRIDE AND PREJUDICE. *Two Volumes.*
NORTHANGER ABBEY.

Bacon (Francis). THE ESSAYS OF LORD BACON.

Barham (R. H.). THE INGOLDSBY LEGENDS. *Two Volumes.*

Barnet (Annie). A LITTLE BOOK OF ENGLISH PROSE.

Beckford (William). THE HISTORY OF THE CALIPH VATHEK.

Blake (William). SELECTIONS FROM THE WORKS OF WILLIAM BLAKE.

Borrow (George). LAVENGRO. *Two Volumes.*
THE ROMANY RYE.

Browning (Robert). SELECTIONS FROM THE EARLY POEMS OF ROBERT BROWNING.

Canning (George). SELECTIONS FROM THE ANTI-JACOBIN : with GEORGE CANNING's additional Poems.

Cowley (Abraham). THE ESSAYS OF ABRAHAM COWLEY.

Crabbe (George). SELECTIONS FROM THE POEMS OF GEORGE CRABBE.

Craik (Mrs.). JOHN HALIFAX, GENTLEMAN. *Two Volumes.*

Crashaw (Richard). THE ENGLISH POEMS OF RICHARD CRASHAW.

Dante Alighieri. THE INFERNO OF DANTE. Translated by H. F. CARY.
THE PURGATORIO OF DANTE. Translated by H. F. CARY.
THE PARADISO OF DANTE. Translated by H. F. CARY.

Darley (George). SELECTIONS FROM THE POEMS OF GEORGE DARLEY.

Deane (A. C.). A LITTLE BOOK OF LIGHT VERSE.

Dickens(Charles). CHRISTMAS BOOKS. *Two Volumes.*

Ferrier (Susan). MARRIAGE. *Two Volumes.*
THE INHERITANCE. *Two Volumes.*

Gaskell (Mrs.). CRANFORD. *Second Ed.*

Hawthorne (Nathaniel). THE SCARLET LETTER.

Henderson (T. F.). A LITTLE BOOK OF SCOTTISH VERSE.

Keats (John). POEMS.

Kinglake (A. W.). EOTHEN. *Second Edition.*

THE LITTLE LIBRARY—*continued.*

Lamb (Charles). ELIA, AND THE LAST ESSAYS OF ELIA.

Locker (F.). LONDON LYRICS.

Longfellow (H. W.). SELECTIONS FROM THE POEMS OF H. W. LONGFELLOW.

Marvell (Andrew). THE POEMS OF ANDREW MARVELL.

Milton (John). THE MINOR POEMS OF JOHN MILTON.

Moir (D. M.). MANSIE WAUCH.

Nichols (J. B. B.). A LITTLE BOOK OF ENGLISH SONNETS.

Rochefoucauld (La). THE MAXIMS OF LA ROCHEFOUCAULD.

Smith (Horace and James). REJECTED ADDRESSES.

Sterne (Laurence). A SENTIMENTAL JOURNEY.

Tennyson (Alfred, Lord). THE EARLY POEMS OF ALFRED, LORD TENNYSON.
IN MEMORIAM.
THE PRINCESS.
MAUD.

Thackeray (W. M.). VANITY FAIR. *Three Volumes.*
PENDENNIS. *Three Volumes.*
ESMOND.
CHRISTMAS BOOKS.

Vaughan (Henry). THE POEMS OF HENRY VAUGHAN.

Walton (Izaak). THE COMPLEAT ANGLER.

Waterhouse (Elizabeth). A LITTLE BOOK OF LIFE AND DEATH. *Thirteenth Edition.*

Wordsworth (W.). SELECTIONS FROM THE POEMS OF WILLIAM WORDSWORTH.

Wordsworth (W.) and Coleridge (S. T.). LYRICAL BALLADS. *Second Edition.*

The Little Quarto Shakespeare.

Edited by W. J. CRAIG. With Introductions and Notes.

Pott 16mo. In 40 Volumes. Leather, price 1s. net each volume.
Mahogany Revolving Book Case. 10s. net.

Miniature Library.

EUPHRANOR : A Dialogue on Youth. Edward FitzGerald. *Demy 32mo. Leather, 2s. net.*

THE LIFE OF EDWARD, LORD HERBERT OF CHERBURY. Written by himself. *Demy 32mo. Leather, 2s. net.*

POLONIUS : or Wise Saws and Modern Instances. Edward FitzGerald. *Demy 32mo. Leather, 2s. net.*

THE RUBÁIYÁT OF OMAR KHAYYÁM. Edward FitzGerald. *Fourth Edition. Leather, 1s. net.*

The New Library of Medicine.

Edited by C. W. SALEEBY. *Demy 8vo.*

CARE OF THE BODY, THE. F. Cavanagh. *Second Edition. 7s. 6d. net.*

CHILDREN OF THE NATION, THE. The Right Hon. Sir John Gorst. *Second Edition. 7s. 6d. net.*

CONTROL OF A SCOURGE, THE ; or, How Cancer is Curable. Chas. P. Childe. *7s. 6d. net.*

DISEASES OF OCCUPATION. Sir Thomas Oliver. *10s. 6d. net. Second Edition.*

DRINK PROBLEM, THE, in its Medico-Sociological Aspects. Edited by T. N. Kelynack. *7s. 6d. net.*

DRUGS AND THE DRUG HABIT. H. Sainsbury.

FUNCTIONAL NERVE DISEASES. A. T. Schofield. *7s. 6d. net.*

HYGIENE OF MIND, THE. T. S. Clouston. *Fifth Edition. 7s. 6d. net.*

INFANT MORTALITY. Sir George Newman *7s. 6d. net.*

PREVENTION OF TUBERCULOSIS (CONSUMPTION), THE. Arthur Newsholme. *10s. 6d. net. Second Edition.*

AIR AND HEALTH. Ronald C. Macfie. *7s. 6d. net. Second Edition.*

The New Library of Music.

Edited by ERNEST NEWMAN.   *Illustrated.   Demy 8vo.   7s. 6d. net.*

BRAHMS.   J. A. Fuller-Maitland.   *Second Edition.*

HANDEL.   R. A. Streatfeild.   *Second Edition.*

HUGO WOLF.   Ernest Newman.

Oxford Biographies.

Illustrated.   Fcap. 8vo.   Each volume, cloth, 2s. 6d. net; leather, 3s. 6d. net.

DANTE ALIGHIERI.   Paget Toynbee.   *Third Edition.*

GIROLAMO SAVONAROLA.   E. L. S. Horsburgh.   *Fourth Edition.*

JOHN HOWARD.   E. C. S. Gibson.

ALFRED TENNYSON.   A. C. Benson.   *Second Edition.*

SIR WALTER RALEIGH.   I. A. Taylor.

ERASMUS.   E. F. H. Capey.

THE YOUNG PRETENDER.   C. S. Terry

ROBERT BURNS.   T. F. Henderson.

CHATHAM.   A. S. M'Dowall.

FRANCIS OF ASSISI.   Anna M. Stoddart

CANNING.   W. Alison Phillips.

BEACONSFIELD.   Walter Sichel.

JOHANN WOLFGANG GOETHE.   H. G. Atkins.

FRANÇOIS FÉNELON.   Viscount St. Cyres.

Romantic History.

Edited by MARTIN HUME.   *Illustrated.   Demy 8vo.*

A series of attractive volumes in which the periods and personalities selected are such as afford romantic human interest, in addition to their historical importance.

THE FIRST GOVERNESS OF THE NETHER-LANDS, MARGARET OF AUSTRIA.   Eleanor E. Tremayne.   10s. 6d. net.

TWO ENGLISH QUEENS AND PHILIP.   Martin Hume.   15s. net.

THE NINE DAYS' QUEEN.   Richard Davey. With a Preface by Martin Hume.   *Second Edition.*   10s. 6d. net.

The States of Italy.

Edited by E. ARMSTRONG and R. LANGTON DOUGLAS.

Illustrated.   Demy 8vo.

A HISTORY OF MILAN UNDER THE SFORZA. Cecilia M. Ady.   10s. 6d. net.

A HISTORY OF PERUGIA.   W. Heywood.   12s. 6d. net.

A HISTORY OF VERONA.   A. M. Allen.   12s. 6d. net.

The Westminster Commentaries.
General Editor, WALTER LOCK.

THE ACTS OF THE APOSTLES. Edited by R. B. Rackham. *Demy 8vo. Fifth Edition.* 10s. 6d.

THE FIRST EPISTLE OF PAUL THE APOSTLE TO THE CORINTHIANS. Edited by H. L. Goudge. *Third Edition. Demy 8vo.* 6s.

THE BOOK OF EXODUS. Edited by A. H. M'Neile. With a Map and 3 Plans. *Demy 8vo.* 10s. 6d.

THE BOOK OF EZEKIEL. Edited by H. A. Redpath. *Demy 8vo.* 10s. 6d.

THE BOOK OF GENESIS. Edited with Introduction and Notes by S. R. Driver. *Eighth Edition. Demy 8vo.* 10s. 6d.

THE BOOK OF THE PROPHET ISAIAH. Edited by G. W. Wade. *Demy 8vo.* 10s. 6d.

ADDITIONS AND CORRECTIONS IN THE SEVENTH EDITION OF THE BOOK OF GENESIS. S. R. Driver. *Demy 8vo.* 1s.

THE BOOK OF JOB. Edited by E. C. S. Gibson. *Second Edition. Demy 8vo.* 6s.

THE EPISTLE OF ST. JAMES. Edited with Introduction and Notes by R. J. Knowling. *Second Edition. Demy 8vo.* 6s.

Methuen's Shilling Library.
Fcap. 8vo.

DE PROFUNDIS. Oscar Wilde.

THE LORE OF THE HONEY-BEE. Tickner Edwardes.

LETTERS FROM A SELF-MADE MERCHANT TO HIS SON. George Horace Lorimer.

*SELECTED POEMS. Oscar Wilde.

*THE LIFE OF ROBERT LOUIS STEVENSON. Graham Balfour.

*THE LIFE OF JOHN RUSKIN. W. G. Collingwood.

*THE CONDITION OF ENGLAND. G. F. G. Masterman.

PART III.—A SELECTION OF WORKS OF FICTION

Albanesi (E. Maria). SUSANNAH AND ONE OTHER. *Fourth Edition. Cr. 8vo.* 6s.
LOVE AND LOUISA. *Second Edition. Cr. 8vo.* 6s.
THE BROWN EYES OF MARY. *Third Edition. Cr. 8vo.* 6s.
I KNOW A MAIDEN. *Third Edition. Cr. 8vo.* 6s.
THE INVINCIBLE AMELIA; OR, THE POLITE ADVENTURESS. *Third Edition. Cr. 8vo.* 3s. 6d.
THE GLAD HEART. *Fifth Edition. Cr. 8vo.* 6s.

Bagot (Richard). A ROMAN MYSTERY. *Third Edition. Cr. 8vo.* 6s.
THE PASSPORT. *Fourth Edition. Cr. 8vo.* 6s.
ANTHONY CUTHBERT. *Fourth Edition. Cr. 8vo.* 6s.
LOVE'S PROXY. *Cr. 8vo.* 6s.
DONNA DIANA. *Second Edition. Cr. 8vo.* 6s.
CASTING OF NETS. *Twelfth Edition. Cr. 8vo.* 6s.
THE HOUSE OF SERRAVALLE. *Third Edition. Cr. 8vo.* 6s.

Bailey (H. C.). STORM AND TREASURE. *Third Edition. Cr. 8vo.* 6s.
*THE LONELY QUEEN. *Second Edition. Cr. 8vo.* 6s.

Baring-Gould (S.). IN THE ROAR OF THE SEA. *Eighth Edition. Cr. 8vo.* 6s.
MARGERY OF QUETHER. *Second Edition. Cr. 8vo.* 6s.
THE QUEEN OF LOVE. *Fifth Edition. Cr. 8vo.* 6s.
JACQUETTA. *Third Edition. Cr. 8vo.* 6s.
KITTY ALONE. *Fifth Edition. Cr. 8vo.* 6s.
NOÉMI. Illustrated. *Fourth Edition. Cr. 8vo.* 6s.
THE BROOM-SQUIRE. Illustrated. *Fifth Edition. Cr. 8vo.* 6s.
DARTMOOR IDYLLS. *Cr. 8vo.* 6s.
GUAVAS THE TINNER. Illustrated. *Second Edition. Cr. 8vo.* 6s.
BLADYS OF THE STEWPONEY. Illustrated. *Second Edition. Cr. 8vo.* 6s.
PABO THE PRIEST. *Cr. 8vo.* 6s.
WINEFRED. Illustrated. *Second Edition. Cr. 8vo.* 6s.
ROYAL GEORGIE. Illustrated. *Cr. 8vo.* 6s.

CHRIS OF ALL SORTS. *Cr. 8vo. 6s.*
IN DEWISLAND. *Second Edition. Cr. 8vo. 6s.*
THE FROBISHERS. *Cr. 8vo. 6s.*
MRS. CURGENVEN OF CURGENVEN. *Fifth Edition. Cr. 8vo. 6s.*

Barr (Robert). IN THE MIDST OF ALARMS. *Third Edition. Cr. 8vo. 6s.*
THE COUNTESS TEKLA. *Fifth Edition. Cr. 8vo. 6s.*
THE MUTABLE MANY. *Third Edition. Cr. 8vo. 6s.*

Begbie (Harold). THE CURIOUS AND DIVERTING ADVENTURES OF SIR JOHN SPARROW, BART. ; OR, THE PROGRESS OF AN OPEN MIND. *Second Edition. Cr. 8vo. 6s.*

Belloc (H.). EMMANUEL BURDEN, MERCHANT. Illustrated. *Second Edition. Cr. 8vo. 6s.*
A CHANGE IN THE CABINET. *Third Edition. Cr. 8vo. 6s.*

Bennett (Arnold). CLAYHANGER. *Seventh Edition. Cr. 8vo. 6s.*
THE CARD. *Fifth Edition. Cr. 8vo. 6s.*
*HILDA LESSWAYS. *Cr. 8vo. 6s.*

Benson (E. F.). DODO: A DETAIL OF THE DAY. *Sixteenth Edition. Cr. 8vo. 6s.*

Birmingham (George A.). THE BAD TIMES. *Second Edition. Cr. 8vo. 6s.*
SPANISH GOLD. *Sixth Edition. Cr. 8vo. 6s.*
THE SEARCH PARTY. *Fifth Edition. Cr. 8vo. 6s.*
*LALAGE'S LOVERS. *Cr. 8vo. 6s.*
*THE ADVENTURES OF DR. WHITTY. *Cr. 8vo. 6s.*

Bowen (Marjorie). I WILL MAINTAIN. *Sixth Edition. Cr. 8vo. 6s.*
DEFENDER OF THE FAITH. *Fourth Edition. Cr. 8vo. 6s.*

Castle (Agnes and Egerton). FLOWER O' THE ORANGE, and Other Tales. *Third Edition. Cr. 8vo. 6s.*

Clifford (Mrs. W. K.). THE GETTING WELL OF DOROTHY. Illustrated. *Second Edition. Cr. 8vo. 3s. 6d.*

Conrad (Joseph). THE SECRET AGENT: A Simple Tale. *Fourth Ed. Cr. 8vo. 6s.*
A SET OF SIX. *Fourth Edition. Cr. 8vo. 6s.*
UNDER WESTERN EYES. *Cr. 8vo. 6s.*

Corelli (Marie). A ROMANCE OF TWO WORLDS. *Thirtieth Ed. Cr. 8vo. 6s.*
VENDETTA. *Twenty-eighth Edition. Cr. 8vo. 6s.*
THELMA : A NORWEGIAN PRINCESS. *Forty-first Edition. Cr. 8vo. 6s.*
▲RDATH : THE STORY OF A DEAD SELF. *Twentieth Edition. Cr. 8vo. 6s.*

THE SOUL OF LILITH. *Seventeenth Edition. Cr. 8vo. 6s.*
WORMWOOD : A DRAMA OF PARIS. *Eighteenth Edition. Cr. 8vo. 6s.*
BARABBAS : A DREAM OF THE WORLD'S TRAGEDY. *Forty-fifth Edition. Cr. 8vo. 6s.*
THE SORROWS OF SATAN. *Fifty-sixth Edition. Cr. 8vo. 6s.*
THE MASTER CHRISTIAN. *Thirteenth Edition. 179th Thousand. Cr. 8vo. 6s.*
TEMPORAL POWER : A STUDY IN SUPREMACY. *Second Edition. 150th Thousand. Cr. 8vo. 6s.*
GOD'S GOOD MAN : A SIMPLE LOVE STORY. *Fifteenth Edition. 154th Thousand. Cr. 8vo. 6s.*
HOLY ORDERS: THE TRAGEDY OF A QUIET LIFE. *Second Edition. 120th Thousand. Crown 8vo. 6s.*
THE MIGHTY ATOM. *Twenty-ninth Edition. Cr. 8vo. 6s.*
BOY: a Sketch. *Twelfth Edition. Cr. 8vo. 6s.*
CAMEOS. *Fourteenth Edition. Cr. 8vo. 6s.*
THE LIFE EVERLASTING. *Second Ed. Cr. 8vo. 6s.*

Crockett (S. R.). LOCHINVAR. Illustrated. *Third Edition. Cr. 8vo. 6s.*
THE STANDARD BEARER. *Second Edition. Cr. 8vo. 6s.*

Croker (B. M.). THE OLD CANTONMENT. *Second Edition. Cr. 8vo. 6s.*
JOHANNA. *Second Edition. Cr. 8vo. 6s.*
THE HAPPY VALLEY. *Fourth Edition. Cr. 8vo. 6s.*
A NINE DAYS' WONDER. *Fourth Edition. Cr. 8vo. 6s.*
PEGGY OF THE BARTONS. *Seventh Edition. Cr. 8vo. 6s.*
ANGEL. *Fifth Edition. Cr. 8vo. 6s.*
KATHERINE THE ARROGANT. *Sixth Edition. Cr. 8vo. 6s.*
BABES IN THE WOOD. *Fourth Edition. Cr. 8vo. 6s.*

Doyle (A. Conan). ROUND THE RED LAMP. *Twelfth Edition. Cr. 8vo. 6s.*

Duncan (Sara Jeannette) (Mrs. Everard Cotes). A VOYAGE OF CONSOLATION. Illustrated. *Third Edition. Cr. 8vo. 6s.*
COUSIN CINDERELLA. *Second Edition. Cr. 8vo. 6s.*
THE BURNT OFFERING. *Second Edition. Cr. 8vo. 6s.*

Fenn (G. Manville). SYD BELTON : THE BOY WHO WOULD NOT GO TO SEA. Illustrated. *Second Ed. Cr. 8vo. 3s. 6d.*

Findlater (J. H.). THE GREEN GRAVES OF BALGOWRIE. *Fifth Edition. Cr. 8vo. 6s.*
THE LADDER TO THE STARS. *Second Edition. Cr. 8vo. 6s.*

Findlater (Mary). A NARROW WAY.
Third Edition. Cr. 8vo. 6s.
OVER THE HILLS. *Second Edition. Cr.
8vo. 6s.*
THE ROSE OF JOY. *Third Edition.
Cr. 8vo. 6s.*
A BLIND BIRD'S NEST. Illustrated.
Second Edition. Cr. 8vo. 6s.

Fry (B. and C. B.). A MOTHER'S SON.
Fifth Edition. Cr. 8vo. 6s.

*Gibbon (Perceval). MARGARET
HARDING. *Cr. 8vo. 6s.*

Gissing (George). THE CROWN OF
LIFE. *Cr. 8vo. 6s.*

Harraden (Beatrice). IN VARYING
MOODS. *Fourteenth Edition. Cr. 8vo. 6s.*
THE SCHOLAR'S DAUGHTER. *Fourth
Edition. Cr. 8vo. 6s.*
HILDA STRAFFORD and THE REMIT-
TANCE MAN. *Twelfth Ed. Cr. 8vo. 6s.*
INTERPLAY. *Fifth Edition. Cr. 8vo. 6s.*

Hichens (Robert). THE PROPHET OF
BERKELEY SQUARE. *Second Edition.
Cr. 8vo. 6s.*
TONGUES OF CONSCIENCE. *Third
Edition. Cr. 8vo. 6s.*
FELIX. *Seventh Edition. Cr. 8vo. 6s.*
THE WOMAN WITH THE FAN. *Eighth
Edition. Cr. 8vo. 6s.*
BYEWAYS. *Cr. 8vo. 6s.*
THE GARDEN OF ALLAH. *Twentieth
Edition. Cr. 8vo. 6s.*
THE BLACK SPANIEL. *Cr. 8vo. 6s.*
THE CALL OF THE BLOOD. *Seventh
Edition. Cr. 8vo. 6s.*
BARBARY SHEEP. *Second Edition. Cr.
8vo. 6s.*
THE DWELLER ON THE THRES-
HOLD. *Cr. 8vo. 6s.*

Hope (Anthony). THE GOD IN THE
CAR. *Eleventh Edition. Cr. 8vo. 6s.*
A CHANGE OF AIR. *Sixth Edition. Cr.
8vo. 6s.*
A MAN OF MARK. *Seventh Ed. Cr. 8vo. 6s.*
THE CHRONICLES OF COUNT AN-
TONIO. *Sixth Edition. Cr. 8vo. 6s.*
PHROSO. Illustrated. *Eighth Edition.
Cr. 8vo. 6s.*
SIMON DALE. Illustrated. *Eighth Edition.
Cr. 8vo. 6s.*
THE KING'S MIRROR. *Fifth Edition.
Cr. 8vo. 6s.*
QUISANTE. *Fourth Edition. Cr. 8vo. 6s.*
THE DOLLY DIALOGUES. *Cr. 8vo. 6s.*
A SERVANT OF THE PUBLIC. Illus-
trated. *Fourth Edition. Cr. 8vo. 6s.*
TALES OF TWO PEOPLE. *Third Edi-
tion. Cr. 8vo. 6s.*
THE GREAT MISS DRIVER. *Fourth
Edition. Cr. 8vo. 6s.*
*MRS. MAXON PROTESTS. *Cr. 8vo. 6s.*

Hutten (Baroness von). THE HALO.
Fifth Edition. Cr. 8vo. 6s.

Hyne (C. J. Cutcliffe). MR. HOR-
ROCKS, PURSER. *Fifth Edition. Cr.
8vo. 6s.*

'Inner Shrine' (Author of the). THE
WILD OLIVE. *Third Edition. Cr. 8vo.
6s.*

Jacobs (W. W.). MANY CARGOES.
Thirty-second Edition. Cr. 8vo. 3s. 6d.
SEA URCHINS. *Sixteenth Edition. Cr.
8vo. 3s. 6d.*
A MASTER OF CRAFT. Illustrated.
Ninth Edition. Cr. 8vo. 3s. 6d.
LIGHT FREIGHTS. Illustrated. *Eighth
Edition. Cr. 8vo. 3s. 6d.*
THE SKIPPER'S WOOING. *Tenth Ed.
Cr. 8vo. 3s. 6d.*
AT SUNWICH PORT. Illustrated. *Tenth
Edition. Cr. 8vo. 3s. 6d.*
DIALSTONE LANE. Illustrated. *Eighth
Edition. Cr. 8vo. 3s. 6d.*
ODD CRAFT. Illustrated. *Fourth Edition.
Cr. 8vo. 3s. 6d.*
THE LADY OF THE BARGE. Illustrated.
Eighth Edition. Cr. 8vo. 3s. 6d.
SALTHAVEN. Illustrated. *Third Edition.
Cr. 8vo. 3s. 6d.*
SAILORS' KNOTS. Illustrated. *Fifth
Edition. Cr. 8vo. 3s. 6d.*
SHORT CRUISES. *Third Edition. Cr.
8vo. 3s. 6d.*

James (Henry). THE GOLDEN BOWL.
Third Edition. Cr. 8vo. 6s.
THE FINER GRAIN. *Third Edition.
Cr. 8vo. 6s.*

Le Queux (William). THE HUNCHBACK
OF WESTMINSTER. *Third Edition.
Cr. 8vo. 6s.*
THE CLOSED BOOK. *Third Edition.
Cr. 8vo. 6s.*
THE VALLEY OF THE SHADOW.
Illustrated. *Third Edition. Cr. 8vo. 6s.*
BEHIND THE THRONE. *Third Edition.
Cr. 8vo. 6s.*
THE CROOKED WAY. *Second Edition.
Cr. 8vo. 6s.*

London (Jack). WHITE FANG. *Eighth
Edition. Cr. 8vo. 6s.*

Lucas (E. V.). LISTENER'S LURE : AN
OBLIQUE NARRATION. *Eighth Edition.
Fcap. 8vo. 5s.*
OVER BEMERTON'S : AN EASY-GOING
CHRONICLE. *Ninth Edition. Fcap 8vo. 5s.*
MR. INGLESIDE. *Eighth Edition. Cr.
8vo. 6s.*

Lyall (Edna). DERRICK VAUGHAN,
NOVELIST. *44th Thousand. Cr. 8vo.
3s. 6d.*

Macnaughtan (S.). THE FORTUNE OF
CHRISTINA M'NAB. *Fifth Edition.
Cr. 8vo. 6s.*
*PETER AND JANE. *Cr. 8vo. 6s.*

Malet (Lucas). COLONEL ENDERBY'S WIFE. *Fifth Edition. Cr. 8vo. 6s.*
A COUNSEL OF PERFECTION. *Second Edition. Cr. 8vo. 6s.*
THE WAGES OF SIN. *Sixteenth Edition. Cr. 8vo. 6s.*
THE CARISSIMA. *Fifth Ed. Cr. 8vo. 6s.*
THE GATELESS BARRIER. *Fifth Edition. Cr. 8vo. 6s.*
THE HISTORY OF SIR RICHARD CALMADY. *Seventh Edition. Cr. 8vo. 6s.*

Mann (Mrs. M. E.). THE PARISH NURSE. *Fourth Edition. Cr. 8vo. 6s.*
A SHEAF OF CORN. *Second Edition. Cr. 8vo. 6s.*
THE HEART-SMITER. *Second Edition. Cr. 8vo. 6s.*
AVENGING CHILDREN. *Second Edition. Cr. 8vo. 6s.*
ASTRAY IN ARCADY. *Second Edition. Cr. 8vo. 6s.*
THERE WAS A WIDOW. *Cr. 8vo. 6s.*

Marsh (Richard). THE COWARD BEHIND THE CURTAIN. *Cr. 8vo. 6s.*
THE SURPRISING HUSBAND. *Second Edition. Cr. 8vo. 6s.*
A ROYAL INDISCRETION. *Second Edition. Cr. 8vo. 6s.*
LIVE MEN'S SHOES. *Second Edition. Cr. 8vo. 6s.*

Marshall (Archibald). MANY JUNES. *Second Edition. Cr. 8vo. 6s.*
THE SQUIRE'S DAUGHTER. *Third Edition. Cr. 8vo. 6s.*
THE ELDEST SON. *Third Edition. Cr. 8vo. 6s.*

Mason (A. E. W.). CLEMENTINA. Illustrated. *Seventh Edition. Cr. 8vo. 2s. net.*

Maxwell (W. B.). VIVIEN. *Tenth Edition. Cr. 8vo. 6s.*
THE RAGGED MESSENGER. *Third Edition. Cr. 8vo. 6s.*
FABULOUS FANCIES. *Cr. 8vo. 6s.*
THE GUARDED FLAME. *Seventh Edition. Cr. 8vo. 6s.*
ODD LENGTHS. *Second Ed. Cr. 8vo. 6s.*
HILL RISE. *Fourth Edition. Cr. 8vo. 6s.*
THE COUNTESS OF MAYBURY: BETWEEN YOU AND I. *Fourth Edition Cr. 8vo. 6s.*
THE REST CURE. *Fourth Edition. Cr. 8vo. 6s.*

Meade (L. T.). DRIFT. *Second Edition. Cr. 8vo. 6s.*
RESURGAM. *Second Edition. Cr. 8vo. 6s.*
VICTORY. *Cr. 8vo. 6s.*
A GIRL OF THE PEOPLE. Illustrated. *Fourth Edition. Cr. 8vo. 3s. 6d.*
HEPSY GIPSY. Illustrated. *Cr. 8vo. 2s. 6d.*
THE HONOURABLE MISS; A STORY OF AN OLD-FASHIONED TOWN. Illustrated. *Second Edition. Cr. 8vo. 3s. 6d.*

Mitford (Bertram). THE SIGN OF THE SPIDER. Illustrated. *Seventh Edition. Cr. 8vo. 3s. 6d.*

Molesworth (Mrs.). THE RED GRANGE. Illustrated. *Second Edition. Cr. 8vo. 3s. 6d.*

Montague (C. E.). A HIND LET LOOSE. *Third Edition. Cr. 8vo. 6s.*

Morrison (Arthur). TALES OF MEAN STREETS. *Seventh Edition. Cr. 8vo. 6s.*
A CHILD OF THE JAGO. *Sixth Edition. Cr. 8vo. 6s.*
THE HOLE IN THE WALL. *Fourth Edition. Cr. 8vo. 6s.*
DIVERS VANITIES. *Cr. 8vo. 6s.*

Nesbit (E.), (Mrs. H. Bland). THE RED HOUSE. Illustrated. *Fifth Edition. Cr. 8vo. 6s.*
*DORMANT. *Cr. 8vo. 6s.*

Ollivant (Alfred). OWD BOB, THE GREY DOG OF KENMUIR. With a Frontispiece. *Eleventh Ed. Cr. 8vo. 6s.*
*THE TAMING OF JOHN BLUNT. *Cr. 8vo. 6s.*

Onions (Oliver). GOOD BOY SELDOM ; A ROMANCE OF ADVERTISEMENT. *Cr. 8vo. 6s.*

Oppenheim (E. Phillips). MASTER OF MEN. *Fourth Edition. Cr. 8vo. 6s.*
THE MISSING DELORA. Illustrated. *Fourth Edition. Cr. 8vo. 6s.*

*Orczy (Baroness).** FIRE IN STUBBLE. *Cr. 8vo. 6s.*

Oxenham (John). A WEAVER OF WEBS. Illustrated. *Fifth Ed. Cr. 8vo. 6s.*
THE GATE OF THE DESERT. *Seventh Edition. Cr. 8vo. 2s. net.*
PROFIT AND LOSS. *Fourth Edition. Cr. 8vo. 6s.*
THE LONG ROAD. *Fourth Edition. Cr. 8vo. 6s.*
THE SONG OF HYACINTH, AND OTHER STORIES. *Second Edition. Cr. 8vo. 6s.*
MY LADY OF SHADOWS. *Fourth Edition. Cr. 8vo. 6s.*
LAURISTONS. *Fourth Edition. Cr. 8vo. 6s.*
THE COIL OF CARNE. *Fifth Edition. Cr. 8vo. 6s.*

Pain (Barry). THE EXILES OF FALOO. *Second Edition. Crown 8vo. 6s.*

Parker (Gilbert). PIERRE AND HIS PEOPLE. *Seventh Edition. Cr. 8vo. 6s.*
MRS. FALCHION. *Fifth Edition. Cr. 8vo. 6s.*
THE TRANSLATION OF A SAVAGE. *Fourth Edition. Cr. 8vo. 6s.*
THE TRAIL OF THE SWORD. Illustrated. *Tenth Edition. Cr. 8vo. 6s.*

WHEN VALMOND CAME TO PONTIAC:
The Story of a Lost Napoleon. *Sixth
Edition. Cr. 8vo. 6s.*
AN ADVENTURER OF THE NORTH.
The Last Adventures of ' Pretty Pierre.'
Fifth Edition. Cr. 8vo. 6s.
THE SEATS OF THE MIGHTY. Illus-
trated. *Seventeenth Edition. Cr. 8vo. 6s.*
THE BATTLE OF THE STRONG: a
Romance of Two Kingdoms. Illustrated.
Seventh Edition. Cr. 8vo. 6s.
THE POMP OF THE LAVILETTES.
Third Edition. Cr. 8vo. 3s. 6d.
NORTHERN LIGHTS. *Fourth Edition
Cr. 8vo. 6s.*

Pasture (Mrs. Henry de la). THE
TYRANT. *Fourth Edition. Cr. 8vo. 6s.*

Pemberton (Max). THE FOOTSTEPS
OF A THRONE. Illustrated. *Fourth
Edition. Cr. 8vo. 6s.*
I CROWN THEE KING. Illustrated. *Cr.
8vo. 6s.*
LOVE THE HARVESTER: A STORY OF
THE SHIRES. Illustrated. *Third Edition.
Cr. 8vo. 3s. 6d.*
THE MYSTERY OF THE GREEN
HEART. *Third Edition. Cr. 8vo. 6s.*

Perrin (Alice). THE CHARM. *Fifth
Edition. Cr. 8vo. 6s.*

Phillpotts (Eden). LYING PROPHETS.
Third Edition. Cr. 8vo. 6s.
CHILDREN OF THE MIST. *Fifth Edi-
tion. Cr. 8vo. 6s.*
THE HUMAN BOY. With a Frontispiece.
Seventh Edition. Cr. 8vo. 6s.
SONS OF THE MORNING. *Second
Edition. Cr. 8vo. 6s.*
THE RIVER. *Fourth Edition. Cr. 8vo. 6s.*
THE AMERICAN PRISONER. *Fourth
Edition. Cr. 8vo. 6s.*
THE SECRET WOMAN. *Fourth Edition.
Cr. 8vo. 6s.*
KNOCK AT A VENTURE. *Third Edition.
Cr. 8vo. 6s.*
THE PORTREEVE. *Fourth Edition. Cr.
8vo. 6s.*
THE POACHER'S WIFE. *Second Edition.
Cr. 8vo. 6s.*
THE STRIKING HOURS. *Second Edition.
Cr. 8vo. 6s.*
DEMETER'S DAUGHTER. *Third
Edition. Cr. 8vo. 6s.*

Pickthall (Marmaduke). SAÏD THE
FISHERMAN. *Eighth Edition. Cr. 8vo.
6s.*

'Q' (A. T. Quiller Couch). THE WHITE
WOLF. *Second Edition. Cr. 8vo. 6s.*
THE MAYOR OF TROY. *Fourth Edition.
Cr. 8vo. 6s.*
MERRY-GARDEN AND OTHER STORIES.
Cr. 8vo. 6s.
MAJOR VIGOUREUX. *Third Edition.
Cr. 8vo. 6s.*

Ridge (W. Pett). ERB. *Second Edition.
Cr. 8vo. 6s.*
A SON OF THE STATE. *Third Edition
Cr. 8vo. 3s. 6d.*
A BREAKER OF LAWS. *Cr. 8vo. 3s. 6d.*
MRS. GALER'S BUSINESS. Illustrated
Second Edition. Cr. 8vo. 6s.
THE WICKHAMSES. *Fourth Edition
Cr. 8vo. 6s.*
NAME OF GARLAND. *Third Edition
Cr. 8vo. 6s.*
SPLENDID BROTHER. *Fourth Edition
Cr. 8vo. 6s.*
NINE TO SIX-THIRTY. *Third Edition.
Cr. 8vo. 6s.*
*THANKS TO SANDERSON. *Cr. 8vo. 6s.*

Robins (Elizabeth). THE CONVERT.
Third Edition. Cr. 8vo. 6s.

Russell (W. Clark). MY DANISH
SWEETHEART. Illustrated. *Fifth
Edition. Cr. 8vo. 6s.*
HIS ISLAND PRINCESS. Illustrated.
Second Edition. Cr. 8vo. 6s.
ABANDONED. *Second Edition. Cr. 8vo. 6s.*
MASTER ROCKAFELLAR'S VOYAGE
Illustrated. *Fourth Edition. Cr. 8vo. 3s. 6d.*

Sidgwick (Mrs. Alfred). THE KINS-
MAN. Illustrated. *Third Edition. Cr.
8vo. 6s.*
THE SEVERINS. *Sixth Edition. Cr.
8vo. 6s.*
THE LANTERN-BEARERS. *Third Ed.
Cr. 8vo. 6s.*
*ANTHEA'S GUEST. *Cr. 8vo. 6s.*

*Somerville (E. Œ.) and Ross (Martin).
DAN RUSSEL THE FOX. Illustrated.
Cr. 8vo. 6s.

Thurston (E. Temple). MIRAGE. *Fourth
Edition. Cr. 8vo. 6s.*

Watson (H. B. Marriott). TWISTED
EGLANTINE. Illustrated. *Third Edi-
tion. Cr. 8vo. 6s.*
THE HIGH TOBY. *Third Edition. Cr.
8vo. 6s.*
A MIDSUMMER DAY'S DREAM. *Third
Edition. Cr. 8vo. 6s.*
THE CASTLE BY THE SEA. *Third
Edition. Cr. 8vo. 6s.*
THE PRIVATEERS. Illustrated. *Second
Edition. Cr. 8vo. 6s.*
A POPPY SHOW: BEING DIVERS AND
DIVERSE TALES. *Cr. 8vo. 6s.*
THE FLOWER OF THE HEART. *Third
Edition. Cr. 8vo. 6s.*
ALISE OF ASTRA. *Third Edition. Cr.
8vo. 6s.*

Webling (Peggy). THE STORY OF
VIRGINIA PERFECT. *Third Edition.
Cr. 8vo. 6s.*
THE SPIRIT OF MIRTH. *Fifth Edition
Cr. 8vo. 6s.*

Wells (H. G.). THE SEA LADY. *Cr.
8vo. 6s.*

Weyman (Stanley). UNDER THE RED ROBE. Illustrated. *Twenty-third Edition. Cr. 8vo. 6s.*

Whitby (Beatrice). THE RESULT OF AN ACCIDENT. *Second Edition. Cr. 8vo. 6s.*
ROSAMUND. *Second Edition. Cr. 8vo. 6s.*

Williamson (C. N. and A. M.). THE LIGHTNING CONDUCTOR: The Strange Adventures of a Motor Car. Illustrated. *Seventeenth Edition. Cr. 8vo. 6s.* Also *Cr. 8vo. 1s. net.*
THE PRINCESS PASSES : A Romance of a Motor. Illustrated. *Ninth Edition. Cr. 8vo. 6s.*
MY FRIEND THE CHAUFFEUR. Illustrated. *Tenth Edition. Cr. 8vo. 6s.*
LADY BETTY ACROSS THE WATER. *Eleventh Edition. Cr. 8vo. 6s.*

THE CAR OF DESTINY AND ITS ERRAND IN SPAIN. Illustrated. *Fifth Edition. Cr. 8vo. 6s.*
THE BOTOR CHAPERON. Illustrated. *Sixth Edition. Cr. 8vo. 6s.*
SCARLET RUNNER. Illustrated. *Third Edition. Cr. 8vo. 6s.*
SET IN SILVER. Illustrated. *Third Edition. Cr. 8vo. 6s.*
LORD LOVELAND DISCOVERS AMERICA. *Second Edition. Cr. 8vo. 6s.*
THE GOLDEN SILENCE. *Sixth Edition. Cr. 8vo. 6s.*
*A NEW NOVEL. *Cr. 8vo. 6s.*

Wyllarde (Dolf). THE PATHWAY OF THE PIONEER (Nous Autres). *Fourth Edition. Cr. 8vo. 6s.*
*THE UNOFFICIAL HONEYMOON *Cr. 8vo. 6s.*

Methuen's Two-Shilling Novels.

Cr. 8vo. 2s. net.

THE GATE OF THE DESERT. John Oxenham.
THE SEVERINS. Mrs. Alfred Sidgwick.
CLEMENTINA. A. E. W. Mason.

THE PRINCESS VIRGINIA. C. N. and A. M Williamson.
COLONEL ENDERBY'S WIFE. Lucas Malet

Books for Boys and Girls.

Illustrated. Crown 8vo. 3s. 6d.

CROSS AND DAGGER. The Crusade of the Children, 1212. W. Scott Durrant.
THE GETTING WELL OF DOROTHY. Mrs. W. K. Clifford.
ONLY A GUARD-ROOM DOG. Edith E. Cuthell.
MASTER ROCKAFELLAR'S VOYAGE. W. Clark Russell.
SYD BELTON : The Boy who would not go to Sea. G. Manville Fenn.

THE RED GRANGE. Mrs. Molesworth.
A GIRL OF THE PEOPLE. L. T. Meade.
HEPSY GIPSY. L. T. Meade. 2s. 6d.
THE HONOURABLE MISS. L. T. Meade.
THERE WAS ONCE A PRINCE. Mrs. M. E. Mann.
WHEN ARNOLD COMES HOME. Mrs. M. E. Mann.

Methuen's Shilling Novels.

JANE. Marie Corelli.
UNDER THE RED ROBE. Stanley J. Weyman.
LADY BETTY ACROSS THE WATER. C. N. & A. M. Williamson.

MIRAGE. E. Temple Thurston.
VIRGINIA PERFECT. Peggy Webling.
SPANISH GOLD. G. A. Birmingham.
*BARBARY SHEEP. Robert Hichens.

The Novels of Alexandre Dumas.

Medium 8vo. Price 6d. Double Volumes, 1s.

ACTÉ.
THE ADVENTURES OF CAPTAIN PAMPHILE.
AMAURY.
THE BIRD OF FATE.
THE BLACK TULIP.
THE CASTLE OF EPPSTEIN.
CATHERINE BLUM.
CÉCILE.
THE CHÂTELET.
THE CHEVALIER D'HARMENTAL. (Double volume.)
CHICOT THE JESTER.
CHICOT REDIVIVUS.
THE COMTE DE MONTGOMMERY.
CONSCIENCE.
THE CONVICT'S SON.
THE CORSICAN BROTHERS; and OTHO THE ARCHER.
CROP-EARED JACQUOT.
DOM GORENFLOT.
THE DUC D'ANJOU.
THE FATAL COMBAT.
THE FENCING MASTER.
FERNANDE.
GABRIEL LAMBERT.
GEORGES.
THE GREAT MASSACRE.
HENRI DE NAVARRE.
HÉLÈNE DE CHAVERNY.
THE HOROSCOPE.

LEONE-LEONA.
LOUISE DE LA VALLIÈRE. (Double volume.)
THE MAN IN THE IRON MASK. (Double volume.)
MAÎTRE ADAM.
THE MOUTH OF HELL.
NANON. (Double volume.)
OLYMPIA.
PAULINE; PASCAL BRUNO; and BONTEKOE.
PÈRE LA RUINE.
THE PORTE SAINT-ANTOINE.
THE PRINCE OF THIEVES.
THE REMINISCENCES OF ANTONY.
ST. QUENTIN.
ROBIN HOOD.
SAMUEL GELB.
THE SNOWBALL AND THE SULTANETTA.
SYLVANDIRE.
THE TAKING OF CALAIS.
TALES OF THE SUPERNATURAL.
TALES OF STRANGE ADVENTURE.
TALES OF TERROR.
THE THREE MUSKETEERS. (Double volume.)
TOURNEY OF THE RUE ST. ANTOINE.
THE TRAGEDY OF NANTES.
TWENTY YEARS AFTER. (Double volume.)
THE WILD-DUCK SHOOTER.
THE WOLF-LEADER.

Methuen's Sixpenny Books.

Medium 8vo.

Albanesi (E. Maria). LOVE AND LOUISA.
I KNOW A MAIDEN.
THE BLUNDER OF AN INNOCENT.
PETER A PARASITE.

Anstey (F.). A BAYARD OF BENGAL.

Austen (J.). PRIDE AND PREJUDICE.

Bagot (Richard). A ROMAN MYSTERY.
CASTING OF NETS.
DONNA DIANA.

Balfour (Andrew). BY STROKE OF SWORD.

Baring-Gould (S.). FURZE BLOOM.
CHEAP JACK ZITA.
KITTY ALONE.
URITH.
THE BROOM SQUIRE.
IN THE ROAR OF THE SEA.
NOÉMI.
A BOOK OF FAIRY TALES. Illustrated.
LITTLE TU'PENNY.
WINEFRED.
THE FROBISHERS.
THE QUEEN OF LOVE.
ARMINELL.
BLADYS OF THE STEWPONEY.
CHRIS OF ALL SORTS.

Barr (Robert). JENNIE BAXTER.
IN THE MIDST OF ALARMS.
THE COUNTESS TEKLA.
THE MUTABLE MANY.

Benson (E. F.). DODO.
THE VINTAGE.

Brontë (Charlotte). SHIRLEY.

Brownell (C. L.). THE HEART OF JAPAN.

Burton (J. Bloundelle). ACROSS THE SALT SEAS.

Caffyn (Mrs.). ANNE MAULEVERER.

Capes (Bernard) THE LAKE OF WINE.
THE GREAT SKENE MYSTERY.

Clifford (Mrs. W. K.). A FLASH OF SUMMER.
MRS. KEITH'S CRIME.

Corbett (Julian). A BUSINESS IN GREAT WATERS.

Croker (Mrs. B. M.). ANGEL.
A STATE SECRET.
PEGGY OF THE BARTONS.
JOHANNA.

Dante (Alighieri). THE DIVINE COMEDY (Cary).

Doyle (A. Conan). ROUND THE RED LAMP.

Duncan (Sara Jeannette). THOSE DELIGHTFUL AMERICANS.

Eliot (George). THE MILL ON THE FLOSS.

Findlater (Jane H.). THE GREEN GRAVES OF BALGOWRIE.

Gallon (Tom). RICKERBY'S FOLLY.

Gaskell (Mrs.). CRANFORD.
MARY BARTON.
NORTH AND SOUTH.

Gerard (Dorothea). HOLY MATRIMONY.
THE CONQUEST OF LONDON.
MADE OF MONEY.

Gissing (G.). THE TOWN TRAVELLER.
THE CROWN OF LIFE.

Glanville (Ernest). THE INCA'S TREASURE.
THE KLOOF BRIDE.

Gleig (Charles). BUNTER'S CRUISE.

Grimm (The Brothers). GRIMM'S FAIRY TALES.

Hope (Anthony). A MAN OF MARK.
A CHANGE OF AIR.
THE CHRONICLES OF COUNT ANTONIO.
PHROSO.
THE DOLLY DIALOGUES.

Hornung (E. W.). DEAD MEN TELL NO TALES.

Hyne (C. J. C.). PRINCE RUPERT THE BUCCANEER.

Ingraham (J. H.). THE THRONE OF DAVID.

Le Queux (W.). THE HUNCHBACK OF WESTMINSTER.
THE CROOKED WAY.
*THE VALLEY OF THE SHADOW.

Levett-Yeats (S. K.). THE TRAITOR'S WAY.
ORRAIN.

Linton (E. Lynn). THE TRUE HISTORY OF JOSHUA DAVIDSON.

Lyall (Edna). DERRICK VAUGHAN.

Malet (Lucas). THE CARISSIMA.
A COUNSEL OF PERFECTION.

Mann (Mrs. M. E.). MRS. PETER HOWARD.
A LOST ESTATE.
THE CEDAR STAR.
ONE ANOTHER'S BURDENS.
THE PATTEN EXPERIMENT.
A WINTER'S TALE.

Marchmont (A. W.). MISER HOADLEY'S SECRET.
A MOMENT'S ERROR.

Marryat (Captain). PETER SIMPLE.
JACOB FAITHFUL.

March (Richard). A METAMORPHOSIS.
THE TWICKENHAM PEERAGE.
THE GODDESS.
THE JOSS.

Mason (A. E. W.). CLEMENTINA.

Mathers (Helen). HONEY.
GRIFF OF GRIFFITHSCOURT.
SAM'S SWEETHEART.
THE FERRYMAN.

Meade (Mrs. L. T.). DRIFT.

Miller (Esther). LIVING LIES.

Mitford (Bertram). THE SIGN OF THE SPIDER.

Montresor (F. F.). THE ALIEN.

Morrison (Arthur). THE HOLE IN THE WALL.

Nesbit (E.). THE RED HOUSE.

Norris (W. E.). HIS GRACE.
GILES INGILBY.
THE CREDIT OF THE COUNTY.
LORD LEONARD THE LUCKLESS.
MATTHEW AUSTEN.
CLARISSA FURIOSA.

Oliphant (Mrs.). THE LADY'S WALK
SIR ROBERT'S FORTUNE.
THE PRODIGALS.
THE TWO MARYS.

Oppenheim (E. P.). MASTER OF MEN.

Parker (Gilbert). THE POMP OF THE LAVILETTES.
WHEN VALMOND CAME TO PONTIAC.
THE TRAIL OF THE SWORD.

Pemberton (Max). THE FOOTSTEPS OF A THRONE.
I CROWN THEE KING.

Phillpotts (Eden). THE HUMAN BOY.
CHILDREN OF THE MIST.
THE POACHER'S WIFE.
THE RIVER.

'Q' (A. T. Quiller Couch). THE WHITE WOLF.

Ridge (W. Pett). A SON OF THE STATE.
LOST PROPERTY.
GEORGE and THE GENERAL.
A BREAKER OF LAWS.
ERB.

Russell (W. Clark). ABANDONED.
A MARRIAGE AT SEA.
MY DANISH SWEETHEART.
HIS ISLAND PRINCESS.

Sergeant (Adeline). THE MASTER OF BEECHWOOD.
BALBARA'S MONEY.
THE YELLOW DIAMOND.
THE LOVE THAT OVERCAME.

Sidgwick (Mrs. Alfred). THE KINSMAN.

Surtees (R. S.). HANDLEY CROSS.
MR. SPONGE'S SPORTING TOUR.
ASK MAMMA.

Walford (Mrs. L. B.). MR. SMITH.
COUSINS.
THE BABY'S GRANDMOTHER.
TROUBLESOME DAUGHTERS.

Wallace (General Lew). BEN-HUR.
THE FAIR GOD.

Watson (H. B. Marriott). THE ADVENTURERS.
CAPTAIN FORTUNE.

Weekes (A. B.). PRISONERS OF WAR.

Wells (H. G.). THE SEA LADY.

Whitby (Beatrice). THE RESULT OF AN ACCIDENT.

White (Percy). A PASSIONATE PILGRIM.

Williamson (Mrs. C. N.). PAPA.

Books for Travellers.

Crown 8vo. 6s. each.

Each volume contains a number of Illustrations in Colour.

A WANDERER IN PARIS. E. V. Lucas.

A WANDERER IN HOLLAND. E. V. Lucas.

A WANDERER IN LONDON. E. V. Lucas

THE NORFOLK BROADS. W. A. Dutt.

THE NEW FOREST. Horace G. Hutchinson.

NAPLES. Arthur H. Norway.

THE CITIES OF UMBRIA. Edward Hutton.

THE CITIES OF SPAIN. Edward Hutton.

FLORENCE AND THE CITIES OF NORTHERN TUSCANY, WITH GENOA. Edward Hutton.

ROME. Edward Hutton.

VENICE AND VENETIA. Edward Hutton.

THE BRETONS AT HOME. F. M. Gostling.

THE LAND OF PARDONS (Brittany). Anatole Le Braz.

A BOOK OF THE RHINE. S. Baring-Gould.

THE NAPLES RIVIERA. H. M. Vaughan.

DAYS IN CORNWALL. C. Lewis Hind.

THROUGH EAST ANGLIA IN A MOTOR CAR. J. E. Vincent.

THE SKIRTS OF THE GREAT CITY. Mrs. A. G. Bell.

ROUND ABOUT WILTSHIRE. A. G. Bradley.

SCOTLAND OF TO-DAY. T. F. Henderson and Francis Watt.

NORWAY AND ITS FJORDS. M. A. Wyllie

Some Books on Art.

ART AND LIFE. T. Sturge Moore. Illustrated. *Cr. 8vo. 5s. net.*

AIMS AND IDEALS IN ART. George Clausen. Illustrated. *Second Edition. Large Post 8vo. 5s. net.*

SIX LECTURES ON PAINTING. George Clausen. Illustrated. *Third Edition. Large Post 8vo. 3s. 6d. net.*

FRANCESCO GUARDI, 1712–1793. G. A. Simonson. Illustrated. *Imperial 4to. £2 2s. net.*

ILLUSTRATIONS OF THE BOOK OF JOB. William Blake. *Quarto. £1 1s. net.*

JOHN LUCAS, PORTRAIT PAINTER, 1828–1874. Arthur Lucas. Illustrated. *Imperial 4to. £3 3s. net.*

ONE HUNDRED MASTERPIECES OF PAINTING. With an Introduction by R. C. Witt. Illustrated. *Second Edition. Demy 8vo. 10s. 6d. net.*

ONE HUNDRED MASTERPIECES OF SCULPTURE. With an Introduction by G. F. Hill. Illustrated. *Demy 8vo. 10s. 6d. net.*

A ROMNEY FOLIO. With an Essay by A. B. Chamberlain. *Imperial Folio. £15 15s. net.*

THE SAINTS IN ART. Margaret E. Tabor. Illustrated. *Fcap. 8vo. 3s. 6d. net.*

SCHOOLS OF PAINTING. Mary Innes. Illustrated. *Cr. 8vo. 5s. net.*

THE POST IMPRESSIONISTS. C. Lewis Hind Illustrated. *Royal 8vo. 7s. 6d. net.*

CELTIC ART IN PAGAN AND CHRISTIAN TIMES. J. R. Allen. Illustrated. *Demy 8vo. 7s. 6d. net.*

"CLASSICS OF ART." See page 14.

"THE CONNOISSEUR'S LIBRARY." See page 14.

"LITTLE BOOKS ON ART." See page 17.

"THE LITTLE GALLERIES." See page 17.

Some Books on Italy.

A HISTORY OF MILAN UNDER THE SFORZA. Cecilia M. Ady. Illustrated. *Demy 8vo.* 10s. 6d. net.

A HISTORY OF VERONA. A. M. Allen. Illustrated. *Demy 8vo.* 12s. 6d. net.

A HISTORY OF PERUGIA. William Heywood. Illustrated. *Demy 8vo.* 12s. 6d. net.

THE LAKES OF NORTHERN ITALY. Richard Bagot. Illustrated. *Fcap. 8vo.* 5s. net.

WOMAN IN ITALY. W. Boulting. Illustrated. *Demy 8vo.* 10s. 6d. net.

OLD ETRURIA AND MODERN TUSCANY. Mary L. Cameron. Illustrated. *Second Edition. Cr. 8vo.* 6s. net.

FLORENCE AND THE CITIES OF NORTHERN TUSCANY, WITH GENOA. Edward Hutton. Illustrated. *Second Edition. Cr. 8vo.* 6s.

SIENA AND SOUTHERN TUSCANY. Edward Hutton. Illustrated. *Second Edition. Cr. 8vo.* 6s.

IN UNKNOWN TUSCANY. Edward Hutton. Illustrated. *Second Edition. Demy 8vo.* 7s. 6d. net.

VENICE AND VENETIA. Edward Hutton. Illustrated. *Cr. 8vo.* 6s.

VENICE ON FOOT. H. A. Douglas. Illustrated. *Fcap. 8vo.* 5s. net.

VENICE AND HER TREASURES. H. A. Douglas. Illustrated. *Fcap. 8vo.* 5s. net.

FLORENCE: Her History and Art to the Fall of the Republic. F. A. Hyett. *Demy 8vo.* 7s. 6d. net.

FLORENCE AND HER TREASURES. H. M. Vaughan. Illustrated. *Fcap. 8vo.* 5s. net.

COUNTRY WALKS ABOUT FLORENCE. Edward Hutton. Illustrated. *Fcap. 8vo.* 5s. net.

NAPLES: Past and Present. A. H. Norway. Illustrated. *Third Edition. Cr. 8vo.* 6s.

THE NAPLES RIVIERA. H. M. Vaughan. Illustrated. *Second Edition. Cr. 8vo.* 6s.

SICILY: The New Winter Resort. Douglas Sladen. Illustrated. *Second Edition. Cr. 8vo.* 5s. net.

SICILY. F. H. Jackson. Illustrated. *Small Pott 8vo. Cloth,* 2s. 6d. net; *leather,* 3s. 6d. net.

ROME. Edward Hutton. Illustrated. *Second Edition. Cr. 8vo.* 6s.

A ROMAN PILGRIMAGE. R. E. Roberts. Illustrated. *Demy 8vo.* 10s. 6d. net.

ROME. C. G. Ellaby. Illustrated. *Small Pott 8vo. Cloth,* 2s. 6d. net; *leather,* 3s. 6d. net.

THE CITIES OF UMBRIA. Edward Hutton. Illustrated. *Fourth Edition. Cr. 8vo.* 6s.

THE LIVES OF S. FRANCIS OF ASSISI. Brother Thomas of Celano. *Cr. 8vo.* 5s. net.

LORENZO THE MAGNIFICENT. E. L. S. Horsburgh. Illustrated. *Second Edition. Demy 8vo.* 15s. net.

GIROLAMO SAVONAROLA. E. L. S. Horsburgh. Illustrated. *Cr. 8vo.* 5s. net.

ST. CATHERINE OF SIENA AND HER TIMES. By the Author of " Mdlle Mori." Illustrated *Second Edition. Demy 8vo.* 7s. 6d. net.

DANTE AND HIS ITALY. Lonsdale Ragg Illustrated. *Demy 8vo.* 12s. 6d. net.

DANTE ALIGHIERI: His Life and Works Paget Toynbee. Illustrated. *Cr. 8vo.* 5s. net.

THE MEDICI POPES. H. M. Vaughan Illustrated. *Demy 8vo.* 15s. net.

SHELLEY AND HIS FRIENDS IN ITALY. Helen R. Angeli. Illustrated. *Demy 8vo.* 10s. 6d. net.

HOME LIFE IN ITALY. Lina Duff Gordon. Illustrated. *Second Edition. Demy 8vo.* 10s. 6d. net.

SKIES ITALIAN: A Little Breviary for Travellers in Italy. Ruth S. Phelps. *Fcap. 8vo.* 5s. net.

PRINTED BY

WILLIAM CLOWES AND SONS, LIMITED,

LONDON AND BECCLES.